A FORTUNATE SOLDIER

Other titles from Brassey's

BAYNES
Soldiers of Scotland

DIETZ
Garrison: Ten British Military Towns

JACKSON
The Alternative Third World War: 1985–2035

JOLLY
Military Man, Family Man: Crown Property?

KARPOV
The Commander

LIDDLE
Gallipoli 1915: Pens, Pencils and Cameras at War

LIDDLE
Home Fires and Foreign Fields: British Social
and Military Experience in the First World War

O'BALLANCE
The Gulf War

A FORTUNATE SOLDIER

Ken Perkins

With a Foreword by
Field Marshal The Lord Bramall

BRASSEY'S DEFENCE PUBLISHERS
(A member of Maxwell Pergamon Publishing Corporation plc)
LONDON · OXFORD · WASHINGTON · NEW YORK
BEIJING · FRANKFURT · SÃO PAULO
SYDNEY · TOKYO · TORONTO

U.K. (Editorial)	Brassey's Defence Publishers Ltd., 24 Gray's Inn Road, London WC1X 8HR
(Orders)	Brassey's Defence Publishers Ltd., Headington Hill Hall, Oxford OX3 0BW, England
U.S.A. (Editorial)	Pergamon-Brassey's International Defense Publishers, Inc., 8000 Westpark Drive, Fourth Floor, McLean, Virginia 22102, U.S.A.
(Orders)	Pergamon Press, Inc., Maxwell House, Fairview Park, Elmsford, New York 10523, U.S.A.
PEOPLE'S REPUBLIC OF CHINA	Pergamon Press, Room 4037, Qianmen Hotel, Beijing, People's Republic of China
FEDERAL REPUBLIC OF GERMANY	Pergamon Press GmbH, Hammerweg 6, D-6242 Kronberg, Federal Republic of Germany
BRAZIL	Pergamon Editora Ltda, Rua Eça de Queiros, 346, CEP 04011, Paraiso, São Paulo, Brazil
AUSTRALIA	Pergamon-Brassey's Defence Publishers Pty Ltd., P.O. Box 544, Potts Point, N.S.W. 2011, Australia
JAPAN	Pergamon Press, 5th Floor, Matsuoka Central Building, 1–7–1 Nishishinjuku, Shinjuku-ku, Tokyo 160, Japan
CANADA	Pergamon Press Canada Ltd., Suite No. 271, 253 College Street, Toronto, Ontario, Canada M5T 1R5

Copyright © 1988 Brassey's Defence Publishers Ltd.

First edition 1988

Library of Congress Cataloging in Publication Data
Perkins, K. (Ken)
A fortunate soldier.
1. Perkins, K. (Ken) 2. Generals—Great Britain—
Biography. 3. Great Britain. Army—Biography.
4. Great Britain—History, Military—20th century.
I. Title.
DA69.3P47A3   1988   355'.0092'4   [B]   88–4310

British Library Cataloguing in Publication Data
Perkins, Ken
A fortunate soldier.
1. Great Britain. Army. Perkins, Ken
I. Title
355.3'31

ISBN 0-08-034762-2

Printed in Great Britain by A. Wheaton & Co. Ltd., Exeter

FOR ALEXANDER

Contents

List of Photographs and Maps

Photographs

1. My first uniform 1931.
2. My Mother and Father.
3. With my Grandfather 1929.
4. 2nd Lieutenant Home Guard. Seaford 1944. Author in shirt sleeves.
5. 2nd Lieutenant. Egypt 1946.
6. Army pilots in Korea 1952.
   Left to Right: Captain Tees (Canada), Author, Captain Deacon (Australia), Captain Joyce (United Kingdom). (*Photo. Flight*)
7. Auster under fire, Korean War. (*From an original painting by the Author*)
8. Quetta 1958. Author and Yazdani second and third from left.
9. Malaya 1954. Briefing Captain Stuart Whitehead for a sortie.
10. Military wedding 1957. With Captain John Hoare.
11. Malaya 1955. The Sultan of Selangor presents the Distinguished Conduct Medal.
12. Malaya 1954. Jane's christening—with Anne and Maureen.
13. Nicola. Aged 5.
14. Colchester 1968. With Garry Wilson.
15. Caribbean 1972. With Major General Glyn Gilbert. (*Photo. Soldier*)
16. Muscat 1975. The Sultan with his Council of Ministers.
    Extreme left: Qais Zawai. On the Sultan's immediate left: Sayid Faher. Author right (in beret). (*Photo. Mohammad Mustapha*)
17. Dhofar 1975. Sharing a joke with Sultan Qaboos. (*Photo. Mohammad Mustapha*)
18. Muscat 1975. Left to Right: Jim Treadwell (H.M. Ambassador), the Author, Roy Mason (Secretary of State for Defence), John Mayne (Private Secretary.

Maps

Foreword

by

FIELD MARSHAL THE LORD BRAMALL

GCB, OBE, MC, JP

I AM delighted to write this foreword, because to my mind, Major General Perkins' account of his most interesting and colourful military career so typifies the great variety and breadth of activity which the British Army and the British Armed Forces have been experiencing since the end of the Second World War. It also illustrates so clearly why, even with the changing face of international conflict and, to some extent, Britain's role in the world, the Profession of Arms still provides such an absorbing and rewarding career for an adventurous and able young man.

Of course, Ken Perkins being a soldier through and through, has always contrived to be where action abounded, whether it be in Korea, where the British Army was engaged in its, to date, last Conventional War, (other than for a few rather unusual weeks in the Falklands), or the jungles of Malaya or in Dhofar where there was taking place a Counter Revolutionary War par excellence.

And indeed, this is truly a Soldier's story. For it follows the career of a young man who, without any privilege or social advantages to speed him on his way, but entirely by dint of his own merits and talents became an Army flyer and did his duty with conspicuous success and gallantry all over the world, commanded one of the most prestigious units in the British Army—The Royal Horse Artillery, and rose, well before he was fifty, to the rank of Major General, in which capacity he commanded and completed successfully a real campaign against a real live enemy in the volatile and very harsh conditions of the Oman.

It is a story which could well act as an inspiration to many an ambitious and adventurous young man, who should be proud to emulate his example.

Later in his service, when I had taken over as the Professional Head of the British Army, I worked closely with him, as he makes mention. Indeed, together we were instrumental in ensuring that Military Assistance, for which he was responsible, had a major part to play in our Foreign and Strategic Policy as a whole, in that for a very small outlay it was able significantly to help friends help themselves in areas of critical strategic importance, where maintaining the correct balance was so vital to us. This often preempted trouble and avoided having to react with much more risky and often counter productive intervention when things had gone wrong. Whitehall was perhaps, rather slow in appreciating the full potential and cost effectiveness of Military Assistance, but gradually came to accept the essential part it had to play in our strategy; and Ken Perkins with his clear thinking and imaginative approach played a major role in bringing this about.

So altogether I find this a fascinating book, by someone who has seen a lot of proper soldiering and, at the same time, has increasingly been at the centre of our political/military strategy at an interesting time in international relations. During this period, he has met and done business with many international figures, in addition to our Prime Minister, all of whom have held the centre of the world stage at particular times and places. This, in itself, makes for compelling reading.

I am glad Ken Perkins had declared himself 'a fortunate soldier'. Certainly, the British Army has been fortunate to have included him and others like him amongst their number over these last thirty-five years. I wish him well in his retirement, which I suspect will be more of a springboard to develop his many talents (including being a most accomplished artist); and I commend warmly this book, written with modesty but quiet satisfaction as to what has been achieved from such modest beginnings, to all those who value the adventurous life and who take a real interest in Britain's place in the world.

September 1987   EDWIN BRAMALL
                                                              FM

Acknowledgements

MY first thanks go to the many friends and colleagues whose companionship and co-operation made my military career so enjoyable. Not all can be mentioned individually and having let the narrative suggest where names should appear, I hasten to disclaim any invidious intent. I am deeply grateful to my wife for recognising I had a story which others might care to read and to my publisher for his faith in my ability adequately to record it. The fact that it is appearing in printed form is due to Mrs Ivy Fisher, whom I thank for patiently transcribing my tapes and deciphering my scribbled redrafting.

For permission to reproduce excerpts from articles of mine they had published, I thank the editors of The British Army Review, the Journal of the Royal Artillery and the Journal of the Royal United Services Institute.

The Old House, Chieveley
July 1987   KEN PERKINS

Chapter 1

Quick March

THIRTY young newly commissioned officers marched shoulder to shoulder, ten abreast in three ranks across the parade ground. They moved quickly, their heels striking the asphalt in time with the martial music. Their brass buttons and polished Sam Browne belts reflected the noonday sun, contrasting with the dull battle dress of the several hundred cadets standing rigidly to attention in the background. An order was heard above the music and thirty heads turned sharply to the right as they passed the silver haired general standing at the salute on the white painted dais, on either side of which were seated the proud parents and admiring friends. It was the culmination of almost two years' rigorous training in which not a few of the starters had failed to reach the finishing post. A few more paces, a turn to the right and the young men would march off to another life. They were now officers. They had made it! The young man in charge gathered his breath so that his voice would overcome the music: 'Left turn'. We all knew that we should have been turning to the right but having been taught that orders were orders twenty nine did as they were instructed. The extreme left hand man, who had recognised early in life that mistaken orders are best disregarded, turned to the right and the impeccably drilled squad disintegrated into a melee of khaki figures. Thus, on the 10th August 1946, began an unconventional military career.

At the time it did not seem a propitious moment to be setting out as a professional soldier, for the Second World War had just ended with a nuclear bang which promised to outlaw military conflict for ever. The great majority of civilisation no doubt welcomed this but Second Lieutenant Perkins thought differently. From a fairly early age he had been attracted to soldiering and as he marched off that parade ground in 1946 he was concerned that, in the new era of peace, his military talents would remain undeveloped. Most of the others involved in that August day mêlée were in uniform for only two or three years and looked upon me as someone unfortunately destined to spend a lifetime playing soldiers. No one would have prophesied that the three decades which were to follow would be as interesting and varied as any in British military history, providing situations which demanded initiative and offering opportunities to match those of any previous era. None of those passing out with me in 1946 thought that one day they would consider me to have been among the more fortunate of their number but if never exactly a soldier of fortune I was certainly to become a fortunate soldier.

At the start I was lucky with my parents. My father was a gardener all his working days and most of his retired ones too. He was the most uncomplicated and least materialistic man I have ever known. Each Thursday evening he placed his unopened pay packet on the mantelpiece and asked for nothing back. My mother purchased all his clothes and necessities. She bought him a bottle of Bulmers cider once a week and a packet of Gold Flake cigarettes at longer intervals, the sum total of his personal luxuries other than at Christmas. It was only much later, as he approached retirement and the house had been paid for, that he began to carry a few coins in his pocket.

I do not know how my father would have coped had any responsibility for managing family affairs been thrust upon him. Perhaps it was lucky he was not put to the test for my mother took charge of all financial and domestic matters. Through her efforts we were able to achieve a great deal more than my father's meagre wage would have permitted. For many years she made all her own clothes and many of mine. She took full advantage of our living by the sea and accommodated lodgers during the summer season, somehow managing in a three bedroomed house to provide full board in sufficient style for our guests to return year after year. My father's armchair could be converted into a bed and when the visitors numbered more than two I slept in the living room. Through such measures my parents bought their own house, afforded adequate medical care before the days of national health and were always well dressed.

I was their only child, born on 15 August 1926 in my grandfather's house at Newhaven. He was one of the then aristocrats of the working class, an engine driver, and something of an Edwardian toff when taking his Sunday morning walk, sporting his gold half-hunter and ebony walking stick. Of his three children, my mother was grandfather's favourite and I know he helped us out at particularly hard times. I spent many hours in and around his house and he too had some influence over my early development.

My parents had settled in Seaford to be close to my grandparents and when I arrived were renting an isolated house called Woodlands Cottage on the outskirts of the small seaside town. A dirt track left the main road and, after about a hundred yards between bramble hedges, ended at a semi-detached and somewhat dilapidated dwelling. Our half provided two up and two down including the kitchen. There was no bathroom but jugs and basins in each bedroom. There was one cold tap in the house and water was heated on the hob or, when larger quantities were required, in a wood-fired copper just outside the back door. Bath nights were a ritual centred on a galvanised tub in front of the fire. From this distance it seems very austere but we thought it comfortable enough at the time, contrasting favourably with the squalor of our neighbour. He was one of the local dustmen with whose children I spent a good deal of my time, often playing with the pickings of his job, which provided us with an endless supply of props for our imaginative games. My mother tolerated these companions as there were no others at hand but she disapproved of the grime next door and I was forbidden to enter their house, and they were not welcome in mine. Thus, on rainy days I was much on my own and I remember many hours spent manoeuvring an army of lead soldiers across the linoleum and around the furniture as they assaulted a wooden toy fortress, the incumbents of which sallied forth in response. I had already decided that attack was the best form of defence.

It was from this house my mother walked me to and from my first school when I was a little under five. A mile there in the morning and back again in the afternoon; two miles for me but four for mother, at least until I could go alone. It was a private school, a convent, for my father had decided that lack of money should not prevent me enjoying opportunities denied to him. Prolonged private education was quite beyond the family means but he calculated that three years of it would help me progress to further education when I joined the state system. It must have been a struggle for my parents and I can see now why it was that we so seldom had family outings and why I have only one recollection of the cinema of this time, Garbo in Queen Christina.

Although I was then unaware of it, my father's ambitions were settled vicariously upon me from the start and, leaving nothing to chance, he set about his contribution to my education: homework based on a considerable collection of books. Although his own education had ended at the age of fourteen at a village school in the Cotswolds, his horizons had been widened by friendship with a schoolmaster during the First World War following which he had become well read and acquired some knowledge of mathematics and science. However, he had little imagination when it came to teaching and assumed I would learn from reading as he had done. I profited considerably from his text books on mathematics and English but did not get far when introduced later to Shakespeare and the Classics. With no accompanying text and in the absence of any commentary, these seemed at best boring and at worst incomprehensible, with the result that I never subsequently overcame the aversion so early acquired. Dad did better with Tennyson and I thought The Charge of the Light Brigade a jolly good read. Perhaps it was because with toy soldiers Tennyson's Five Hundred came alive in Woodlands Cottage.

At the age of eight I joined an elementary school, a grey flint building with the appearance of an early Victorian chapel. It was ruled by a headmaster who seemed to live for nothing else, Dad Phillips as he was known with both fear and affection to pupils and parents alike. Dad Phillips taught the class preparing for the scholarship and was renowned for his success rate. Securing a scholarship, with the consequent elevation to secondary education, was vital to anyone with ambition as the elementary system extended only to the age of fourteen, when a boy would leave school and start work with no recognisable qualification of any sort. Indeed, many parents, more concerned with the earning power of their sons than with higher education, were quite content that school should so abruptly end. In my case, from well before I ascended the granite steps into my new school, I was constantly aware that the scholarship had to be passed although, surprisingly, I do not recall worrying about it.

Life was now quite different. We had moved some months earlier into the newly built house in which my parents were to spend the rest of their lives. By present day standards it was spartan, but luxurious in comparison to our previous environment. School, however, was distinctly less comfortable as I immediately discovered on joining the first class. Here, under instruction from a spinster known with little affection as Spazzy, we recited our lessons in unison, she meanwhile pacing the length of the classroom to ensure that we were speaking with a single voice. Anyone heard faltering would be required to stay behind when lessons had finished. A sharp rap on the knuckles with the edge of a ruler was the punishment for intoning 'God save the King, fish and chips', the standard ploy for concealing a gap in memory or knowledge. More serious misdemeanours were dealt with in front of the class by strokes of a ruler on the palm of a hand, unless Dad Phillips was in attendance when the miscreant would receive a mighty swipe with the headmaster's cane. His aim was none too precise and as each desk accommodated two boys it was advisable to avoid sitting beside habitual offenders. But it was in the playground and on the way to and from home that the new school was most alarming. As one who had arrived from a private school and came top of the class I was fair game for various bullies who enhanced their reputation at my expense, and although in the army I became a regimental boxer of some repute, in the first class at school it was no contest every time. After a while I learned to look after myself but it had been a disagreeable experience, with the result that when I moved to the secondary school at the age of twelve I was in an unfortunately aggressive frame of mine.

Lewes County Secondary School for Boys drew its pupils from the elementary schools in the urban and rural districts within a radius of some twenty miles of Lewes and, with an annual intake of a little under sixty, accommodated about three hundred. On opening in 1930 it had heralded a new concept in education, at least in East Sussex: a grammar school provided by the local authority. How significant a development this was may not now be generally recognised but snatches from speeches at the opening ceremony give some idea of attitudes then prevalent. According to the press (as quoted in *A First Chapter in the History of a Grammar School* by Mr J. Bradshaw), the Right Honourable the Viscount Gage '.......supposed that most of those present were in favour of secondary education... There were men holding high positions in the country and leaders of trades unions who, through no fault of their own, had very little opportunity for education. If they were to be given executive powers they should have the same opportunity for education as were given to people who used to hold those high positions (Applause). He was not afraid of being governed by any particular class because he did not believe that ability was confined to any particular class. He would feel less apprehension if he felt that everyone had an opportunity of learning something from the point of view of being able to take up any of the professions'. No doubt the spoken word conveyed the message a good deal more articulately than the local reporter who clearly had not had the benefit of secondary schooling but, even allowing for this, it makes strange reading. The new headmaster, on responding, struck a more modern note when he said, 'The real test of any school is the type of boy it turns out'.

This was the school I joined in September 1938. The two storey modern building was spacious and well appointed. It was surrounded by eight acres of playing fields and possessed a swimming pool, built largely by self-help. Of the thirty pupils who were accepted each year as scholarship pupils, almost all were educated free; only one or two parents, who were thought well enough off, were asked to contribute a little. A further thirty or so full fee paying pupils were admitted from the brightest of those who had not quite made the scholarship grade and whose parents were in a position to pay. Thus, the school housed a beneficial mixture of boys from various walks of life while, having so few vacancies in comparison to its catchment area, simultaneously achieved high academic standards.

I found I could hold my own academically and, equally important to me, physically. I was clearly not a Latin scholar but I quickly settled in the top third of the form, and did well at games. Had my father been less ambitious for me I might have become a good all rounder early on and got through without much difficulty. As it was, he expressed considerable dissatisfaction and seemed to think that I had not worked sufficiently hard when, at the end of the first term, I came eleventh in the class. I can see now that his disappointment arose from his failure to recognise the considerable shift in standards from my previous school, while my similar lack of perception left me without an adequate explanation. Neither of us understood the current educational scene; he was self taught and I was too young.

An aggressive frame of mind, born of my experience at the previous school, came to the fore and as I sought to make a mark by one means or another, I turned to trouble making and sport. Within a year I was at the bottom of the form, had won a competition organized by me in the lower half of the school to see who could acquire most strokes of the headmaster's cane in one term, and had become the schoolboy quarter-mile champion of East Sussex. I had also boxed in an exhibition bout in the school fete, my opponent being one Mike Barrett, now an international promoter of some renown in the world of boxing. Eventually I became so undisciplined that my father was summoned to school.

My rehabilitation was due entirely to the headmaster, Mr Bradshaw. The significance of this early watershed became apparent to me only later when I was at university, since when it has coloured my attitude to young people who find themselves on the wrong side of authority. The headmaster would not have been unreasonable had he expelled me but instead, with tolerance and understanding, he induced a realistic attitude in my father and a responsible reaction from me. We discussed the military career on which I was determined and plotted a sensible course of study so that by my sixteenth birthday I was again in the top half of the form and playing for the school rugby first XV. I was also a member of the Seaford Home Guard, soldiering in my spare time in the part time defence force which had been raised when invasion was imminent—for the Second World War had engulfed us all three years since.

The Home Guard was well established in the south east of England when I joined in 1941. Situated in Seaford was B Company of the 16th Battalion in which I enrolled at the age of fifteen by falsely advancing my age. Moving through the ranks of lance corporal and corporal I found myself a second lieutenant at the impressionable age of seventeen and placed in charge of a platoon of fifty NCOs and men, many of whom had seen service in the First World War. While the age span of my small command and the appearance of some of it resembled Mr Mainwaring's platoon in the television comedy Dad's Army, its duties, to protect key points immediately across the water from occupied France, were discharged with considerably more competence.

The South East units were well equipped with small arms but our heavier weapons were somewhat Heath Robinson in design, having been conceived, produced and pressed into service in great haste, leaving the users considerable latitude in the manner of their employment. One such weapon was a favourite of mine, the Blacker Bombard, a squat cannonlike device mounted on what appeared to be a horizontal cruciform of drain pipes. It heaved a twenty pound bomb up to one hundred yards with precision and a smaller bomb something over a quarter of a mile with much less accuracy. The Bombard in my platoon was sited to cover the overland approaches to a coastal battery of naval guns emplaced in the gardens of several large requisitioned houses on Seaford promenade. One of these was owned by a member of my platoon who was forever sneaking away to assess the increasing damage being done to his property by the Royal Artillery then in occupation. He was highly indignant that the front elevation had been spoiled by an extension to house a large range finder and, to placate him, the rest of us suggested useful purposes to which this concrete addition might be put when he again was allowed to take up residence. It was a wonderful picture window we said. He took our advice and the house still boasts a prominent sun lounge, the concrete now so weathered by the annual gales that no one would suspect its military origin. The Blacker Bombard almost got me to sea when the Royal Navy adopted it for the gun boats which sallied forth at night from Newhaven to attack shipping along the French coast. I provided instruction and then offered to sail as a gunner. The naval officer thanked me for the tuition but unfortunately declined my further services. Perhaps it was as well, for soon after, while I was sitting school certificate, the boats returned from the night's sortie shot to pieces and the decks red with blood.

My first brush with some of the more unpleasant aspects of war was with my Home Guard colleagues when looking for casualties after an air raid. I was fortunate to be bolstered by the company of one or two who had seen such carnage in the trenches that, forty years later, they could remain outwardly unmoved when handling mutilated bodies or pieces of flesh recognisable as human only by the associated fragments of cloth. Looking back I have always thought how unfortunate it was that this team spirit died with the end of the war. My platoon included a road sweeper, a bank manager and what might be called landed gentry. There were First World War privates and officers, now with roles reversed. Yet backgrounds barely intruded and when, as a youthful platoon commander, I tried to remove all vestiges of class on parade, my efforts were unsuccessful only because the habits of a lifetime are difficult to break. 'I will not have,' I had said, 'Private Tindall being called Mr Tindall while Private Healey is simply called Healey. It has to be Private Tindall and Private Healey.' I should have recognised that Healey could not have cared less, he had always been just Healey and was happy thus to remain. Such naivety no doubt amused my older subordinates who remained ever willing to help me. 'Now you are an officer you must not whistle,' advised Lance Corporal Browne who, as Lieutenant Browne, had won a Military Cross for bravery in Flanders. I am afraid his advice had no effect and my whistle annoys even to this day.

The need to improvise and the nature of my responsibilities undoubtedly helped shape me for the future. But it was weekends spent training with the Canadian Army which most influenced my subsequent military attitudes. This was a wartime army stationed in a foreign land and training for D-Day. It was noisy, boisterous and seemed a little careless of authority. Above all it was adventurous and unconstrained by preconceived doctrine. Some of it had seen action in the amphibious raid on Dieppe in 1942. A Canadian who had fought through the streets there showed me how to throw a grenade 'so that no son-of-a-bitch can throw it back.' He let the lever go and the four second fuse began to fizz before he threw the grenade and not, as properly and safely taught, on leaving his hand. This is how I have thrown a grenade ever since, much to the consternation of people around me. We used explosives liberally and there were occasional mishaps. One Sunday I organised a demonstration in which the chimney of a derelict factory was demolished to form a road block. As I pressed the plunger from behind the safety of a wall, Corporal Parry, at one time an international tennis star but now approaching seventy, stepped forward to view the spectacle and was whacked in the shin by a piece of flying debris. In pain as we applied first aid, he grabbed the offending missile. 'Fancy having lead pipe in a brick chimney,' he winced. Through 1943 we exercised with live ammunition in circumstances which would now be considered downright dangerous. It was training such as I did not meet again until years later when in command of a foreign army. It was exhilarating and if there were serious casualties I did not see them. I was already recognising that in the military world, fortune favours the bold.

The war profoundly affected all who lived through it, although individual reaction varied considerably. For me it was an entirely beneficial experience. Food rationing, and the absence of what we would now consider essential commodities, may have worried my mother but never left me hungry. Air raids were an undoubted hazard where we lived but they worried me considerably less than they would now and it was with great reluctance I exchanged the comfort of my bed for the alleged security of the Anderson shelter, one of the small corrugated steel constructions provided for each household and dug into the garden by the occupants. I suppose the quality of life in the classroom suffered from the influx of evacuees from London, for we were hosts to Tooting Bec school with at least as many pupils as us, but the standard of teaching remained high in spite of over-crowding and makeshift facilities. For schoolboys, these difficulties and others added to the fun, like the good looking young lady recently down from Cambridge to replace a master who had left for the forces. She found it hard going in front of thirty adolescents just discovering sex and there was something of a riot when a pair of knickers fell around her shapely ankles as she scribbled across the blackboard. Outside the classroom there could be no doubt that the quality of life was ever improving. The shortage of unskilled labour caused by conscription enabled me to earn what seemed princely sums during holidays working variously as a milk roundsman, postman and farm hand. During long summers on the land we toiled from dawn to dusk bringing in the harvest from every acre which could be cultivated, a job which gave me my first bank balance, bought me my first suit and introduced me to the girl I was later to marry.

The majority of people today, to whom the war is history rather than a distant experience, may wonder how the country faced its greatest ordeal with so few qualms. Although the population would undoubtedly have felt more apprehensive if the debacle in the Low Countries had been seen nightly in the parlours of Southern England, it is unlikely that the reaction to such television reporting would have proved so catastrophic as it might now. Public attitudes were based on a long established social structure which the war swept away for ever but which meanwhile obviated bickering, buttressed authority and sustained morale when the going was rough. Ultimate victory was taken for granted, even when Britain stood alone in 1940 after the fall of France. British stoicism played its part but the major factor was the leadership of Winston Churchill and I remember vividly my father striking the arm of his chair and exclaiming, 'Thank God, at last!', on hearing that Churchill had become Prime Minister. Like many of the generation who grew up in the time of his wartime premiership, I subsequently came to regard him as the Colossus of the Twentieth Century, and still do. I have devoured all his books and simply say to those who question whether history should be written by the man who made it, that the unvarnished truth is both very rare and very dull.

In February 1944, aged seventeen and a half, I enlisted at the recruiting office in Brighton on a Saturday morning off from school. On Mr Bradshaw's advice I was applying to undergo a university course before joining a basic training depot. He thought such an entry would in the circumstances provide me with the best start to a regular career, besides effecting an introduction to a university should I ever decide to return. I was interviewed by an irascible staff sergeant with First War ribbons who had little time for universities. Privately, I had some sympathy for his views as I was anxious to get into uniform and away to the war, but I followed the advice I had received and applied for the Royal Artillery and a university short course. I swore allegiance to His Majesty King George the Sixth, was attested and transferred to the reserve to await the selection process. This I underwent over three days at a War Office Selection Board at Redhill after which followed an interminable wait for the result. Meanwhile Mr Bradshaw arranged that I should see out my days at school as the laboratory assistant, for which I received a small wage. He had always been alive to my parents' struggle in keeping me at school and this latest subvention was in addition to an educational grant he had earlier obtained on my behalf. The educational grant was four shillings and sixpence and the wage, I seem to remember, almost doubled the total amount. It was not much but it helped.

At last a small buff envelope arrived and, on a flimsy piece of paper, someone who said that he had the honour to be my obedient servant told me he had been commanded to say that I had been accepted by New College, Oxford. I regret not keeping it, but even then I was intolerant of unnecessary paper, (years later one of my chief clerks remarked that my wastepaper basket filled quicker than any other he had known). A subsequent and less pretentious letter instructed me to report on the 10th October to the Depot of the Northamptonshire Regiment for kitting out prior to my six months at Oxford.

My memory of 10th October is of a large gymnasium in which over two hundred young men were changing from civilian clothes into uniform while struggling to make some sense of the complete inventory of soldier's equipment with which each had been issued. I fortunately was in the battledress brought from the Home Guard so at least I had a uniform with matching blouse and trousers, for there were many shades of khaki and qualities of weave in those hairy war time garments mass produced from so many sources. That night most of us slept on the bare boards, as there had been insufficient straw to fill the palliasses, and in the morning queued or fought for the few metal wash basins in the woefully inadequate ablutions. Here, on that first morning in the army, I discovered that the menace of my cut-throat razor would secure for me more than my fair share of washroom space. Later that day the twenty one of us destined for Oxford were fallen in and, festooned about with unaccustomed equipment, dispatched first by road and then rail to our destination. Our journey to Oxford and our movement from the railway station to our various colleges is now a blank, but I remember very well my arrival in New College. It was early evening and the new undergraduates had been assembled in the dining room for the dean's opening address. He was on the point of saying that no firearms were permitted when through the double doors burst half a dozen soldiers, their hobnails rasping on the ancient boards and their rifles and accoutrements clattering against the refectory tables. There was a momentary silence as we stood exhausted amidst our paraphernalia and then laughter from the assembly. We thought it was a better than average entry.

During the bitter winter of 1944 life for the undergraduate at Oxford was very comfortable. The college servants, shared one between four rooms, lit the coals in the iron grates late each afternoon so that by the time the occupants had taken tea and toast in the common-room their quarters were warm for the evening. Public houses being out of bounds, and with nowhere else to go, most evenings were spent in college.

In the morning the servants arrived with tea and hot water and during the day scurried about on whatever domestic chores needed doing. On the short course we had a relatively easy academic life pitched only at matriculation level. I never understood the point of it and cannot pretend I gained much or enjoyed it. Indeed, I felt uneasy that I should be spending my time so comfortably while other young men of my age were fighting their way across Europe, parachuting into Arnhem or slogging through Burma. Fortunately the military part of the course enabled me to retain a sense of proportion.

For military purposes we were based on the premises of The Oxford University Senior Training Corps, a collection of green huts around a tarmac parade ground on Manor Road. We learned a good deal from our troop commander Captain Morgan who, having lost an arm at war, had been relegated to instructional duties. We were also well taught by Sergeant Major Slatter, a martinet who took us at gun drill. Our daily routine was under the close scrutiny of Sergeants Cope and Webb, both of whom had seen active service, Webb still carrying a bullet in his lung. The regime was rigorous, particularly when the sergeant major was involved. Lateness on parade, and that meant not being fallen in five minutes before the due time, was rewarded by a copy of the 1939 handbook of the 25 pounder gun, together with a thick sheaf of amendments resulting from four years of war, and the admonition to have the book amended by the next day. A yawn by one of us during a lecture earned a jog round the sports field with a 25 pound shell under each arm. Against this background of discipline we quickly matured and within six months became extremely competent gunners, able to cope, at least technically, with all of the jobs in a troop of artillery.

By March, when our course ended, we could each with credit have joined an active regiment but this was the moment when we were all to begin again, for it was now time to become basic recruits. For me it was a relief which my old college servant could not understand, the war being in a different world to his. He thought it incredible that I should leave my academic gown hanging unwanted behind my door. And with some justification he must have thought me unbalanced to decline a taxi as I left to go on leave, setting out on foot with my rifle, kitbag and pack bearing me down. Luckily an old lady and her grandchild took pity on me and insisted they accompany me to the railway station with my kit athwart the child's bicycle.

A week later, reassembled in a hutted camp at Bury St Edmunds, where there were a thousand men under training, we found ourselves split among the raw recruits. The training, under the auspices of the Suffolk Regiment, was dedicated to the mass production of young soldiers at a time when the shortest commodity in the British army was infantry. The whole process was no better illustrated than on the occasion when the intake of which I was a part was inoculated against tetanus and typhoid. It took place in the gymnasium where a hundred of us filed slowly forward towards two medical officers, who attacked from each flank as we passed between them. Tetanus in the left arm and typhoid in the right. Each syringe held six doses and, the needle being replaced only when the syringe was refilled, there was a certain amount of shuffling in the queue as men tried to avoid the fifth or sixth shot by which time it was thought the needle would have become a little blunted. (These were the days before disposable syringes or any apparent concern over diseases which might be transmitted through a shared needle.) The days were filled, with not a moment wasted. I had done most of the training before, either with the Home Guard or at Oxford, but it was fun for an energetic eighteen year old to have absolutely no responsibility except for himself and to test how close he could sail to the wind of authority without being caught.

We were still in recruit training when the European War ended on May 8th. There was considerable merry making and I still have the Union Jack which I removed from the upper reaches of Woolworths in Bury St Edmunds by shinning up a drainpipe. The intention was to fly it in Japan when the war took us to that country, for that was surely our lot, none of us having an inkling that the fighting in the Far East was also about to end. When it did, on 15th August, I had just finished my training as a gunner at Watchet in Somerset and, in company with a few others, was moving in a three ton truck to a camp called St Austell a mile or so along the coast. I felt little elation and certainly no relief that the war was over but rather a sense of being cheated of my fair share of the experience. However, St Austell, in the warm summer of 1945, provided amusing diversions. It was a collection of huts, taken over years later by Butlin's as a holiday camp, but occupied in my time by about fifty potential officers who were left largely to their own devices while awaiting the officer selection board. For some time I had been known to my friends as 'The General', a misnomer in the view of one pompous major who, while conceding it was an amusing nickname, was at pains to explain the impossibility of my ever approaching such a vaunted rank. However, he trusted me to run day-to-day administration. Much of this I was required to delegate as part of the potential officers' education and I managed to leave myself with only the distribution of mail and the typing of daily orders, so that I had plenty of time, in the company of friends whom I had excused duties, to explore the Quantock Hills and scramble down the cliffs and over the rocks for a daily swim. All of us who had started at Oxford were now at St Austell, from whence most of us passed our selection tests and moved on together to officer cadet training.

Our first officer cadet training unit was housed in a collection of dank Nissen huts in the woods at Wrotham in Kent. The aim of the training, we said unkindly, was to bring everyone down to the level of a corporal of infantry. The duration varied for individuals between two weeks and six months, depending upon the reports from the selection board. I was given six weeks during which time I learned to ride a motorcycle, became adept at assault courses and acquired an intensive dislike of blanco, the green powder which mixed with water was used as a cosmetic on webbing equipment. Each day our equipment became thoroughly muddied and each evening had to be restored with blanco, a seemingly pointless procedure based on universal and apparently unquestioned attitudes which caused me to ponder a good deal about discipline in its various forms. As a result I later became careless of spit and polish except when there was a specific need and, after becoming an officer, irritated some of my superiors who thought more about the internal appearance of barrack rooms than the fitness for war of their occupants. From Wrotham we moved to basic officer training, first to Foremark Hall in Derby and later to Aldershot. Apart from a battle camp in North Wales, which involved live ammunition and a realistic crossing of Lake Bala in assault boats, it was pedestrian. A good deal of the activity centred on a very senior and well known regimental sergeant major who, although having served for many years, had not a single active service medal to complement the coronation and long service ribbons which decorated his rotund figure.

After this barren period it was a delight to arrive at the Royal Artillery officer cadet training unit at Deepcut in Surrey. For the first time in a year we were housed in reasonable comfort. We were in brick buildings, Belisha blocks, named after the minister for war under whose regime they had been constructed in the 1930s. No longer was there a need to brave the outside air to reach the ablutions or steal coke to keep warm. There was still the possibility of failure or relegation but it was less obtrusive in what was unquestionably a more balanced atmosphere. Gone were the drill sergeants with their pace sticks and shrill commands, dedicated it seemed to discovering trivial mistakes. Gone too were the officers of limited outlook who had been off-loaded by regiments who had no use for them. In their place were a set of officers and NCOs with values we could respect, and none better than our battery commander, Major Frank Weldon who later managed the British Olympic equestrian team. Sport played an important part for the first time and our teams spent enjoyable weekends competing at home and away. I captained the boxing team and ran the quarter and half mile, thus enjoying more than my fair share of these outings. As a troop of artillery we covered a good deal of Surrey and Sussex during our training, in the aftermath of war using common land with a freedom unthinkable a few years later. Now as I drive around southern England I sometimes come across places which bring amusing incidents to mind. There is the pavement in Guildford where an old lady in black did a remarkable hop, skip and jump to avoid one of our lorries skidding out of control. On a twisting country road an irate motorist, scared witless by a motor cyclist overtaking on a bend, demanded to see the person in charge and was told that he had just departed on a motor bike. That was my first recognisable near miss on two wheels.

Eventually on 10th August 1946 our cadet training ended. Of those who had gone to Oxford two years earlier, only two or three failed to gain commissions, an unusual collective achievement. Four of us were to become regular soldiers: Bill Green, whose father was a brigadier and who left in the rank of major, Dick Norton whose father was a general and who left as a lieutenant colonel in order to join the civil service, and Tim Streatfield who retired as a major general. All of us, less one who had died and one or two living abroad, met again for a reunion dinner in 1982. To one another we had changed but little and the event, like our passing out parade thirty six years earlier, ended in considerable disorder.

Chapter 2

Subaltern at Large

THE army in 1946 was a huge machine in which the thousands of subalterns were like so many small cogs, largely interchangeable and pushed into place as expediency dictated. A young officer, on commissioning, could express a preference for posting but only in broad terms, Europe, the Middle or the Far East. The trouble spot in the news was Palestine, then still a British mandate, where the Jews were impatiently seeking to establish a homeland, using terrorism and illegal immigration as their principal methods. As a result a large number of British troops were deployed there, constantly in action against well trained and highly motivated guerillas. Palestine, I decided, was the place for me and as a first step I asked to be sent to the Middle East.

After embarkation leave, I spent a few days at the regimental depot in Woolwich where a draft of officers and men was being assembled. On the second day I found myself as orderly officer, my main task being to ensure that the guards at half a dozen installations in the neighbourhood were properly mounted and remained alert. In the middle of the night I approached what I thought was the Old Academy building and, finding it incompetently guarded, turned out all the men and gave them a thorough dressing down. While in full flow I noticed that they were wearing a strange cap badge and realised I had come to the wrong place but, being far too committed to admit that the men I was rebuking had nothing to do with me, I continued and dismissed them with an admonition to do better next time. They had deserved it, had escaped a rebuke from their own officer and that, no doubt, was why they marched meekly away. It was the first of many errors from which this young officer was to learn.

The draft, of which I was part, crossed France on the hard wooden benches of an old railway coach and then spent several days at a transit camp in Hyères on the Mediterranean coast. In comparison with

Britain, food seemed plentiful but there was an acute shortage of soap and cigarettes, and small amounts of these, which for us came with the rations, would cover an evening at the casino. We crossed from Toulon to Port Said on a liberty ship, one of the merchantmen welded together in a record few days in American shipyards during the war. The officers slept in a draughty hut on the lifeboat deck. The troop decks, in the bowels of the ship, suffered no excess of ventilation; here was an overpowering smell of humanity and seasickness. Then came a few days in a transit camp at Port Said with nothing much to do except to see the sights. There was shopping in Simon Artz, which before the war had catered for the cruise liners and was to do so again, but which had now for several years made handsome profits from the sale of handbags and ill fitting lingerie for the wives and girlfriends of British soldiers. Next came a camp on the outskirts of Cairo and, each evening, the brown tram into the city, the return journey with a British officer in high spirits trying his hand at the controls after a night on the town, the Egyptian driver apprehensively standing by. At last, three weeks after leaving Woolwich, we arrived at the headquarters of Middle East Command, a huge camp at Fayid where our ultimate destinations would be decided.

I lost no time in making my preference known but our names had preceded us and we had already been allocated to regiments. The major who had made these arrangements was obdurate; there could be no change. I said that I was volunteering to be shot at and it seemed extraordinary that no one would take up my offer. He thought it was the offer, itself, which was extraordinary, his opinion being based upon a wide experience of being shot at. There was no point in further argument and I arrived in the autumn of 1946 in 7th Field Regiment, Royal Artillery, stationed on the bare, dusty shores of the Little Bitter Lake, through which flowed the southern reaches of the Suez Canal.

I was only the second officer to join the regiment since the war had ended in Europe well over a year before and the other one had at least seen some sort of action in Palestine. It was somewhat daunting to be surrounded by so much experience. Even my batman had driven a tank across the Normandy beaches and on through France and Belgium into Germany. However, there was much to be learned and for this I was in the right place, serving among people who had recently been to war. On exercises with live ammunition in the desert, the regiment was handled with a professionalism acquired only in action, while among the soldiers around me I observed many tricks of the trade picked up in battle.

Some of the older campaigners were being demobilised and replaced by men recently conscripted so that the regiment now comprised an uneasy mixture. The war time conscripts, still awaiting demobilisation, were bored with playing soldiers in the desert and impatient to get home, while the recent arrivals needed convincing that their stint in uniform was necessary. Morale dropped and the regiment became listless, illustrating Napoleon's dictum 'There are no bad men only bad officers'. Not that the officers were bad, as a Distinguished Service Order and several Military Crosses testified, but they were tired, overdue for home and incapable any longer of exercising the leadership required. Salvation from this sorry state came in early 1947 when the regiment was moved along the North African coast to Tripolitania where it changed its role, equipment and title, becoming 73rd Heavy Anti-Aircraft Regiment.

None of us knew anything about anti-aircraft artillery and, to remedy the deficiency, several of us spent six weeks at the school of artillery at Acre in northern Palestine. I had arrived at the hot spot I had been seeking several months earlier but, being there only for instructional purposes, was no more than a spectator, confined to the camp and the local town of Haifa. I overcame this frustration, at least in part, by co-opting others into forming organised recreational parties which, with official approval, visited places of biblical or historic interest. We found the synagogue at Capernaum largely in ruins but the surroundings and the fishermen with their nets along the shores of Galilee were little changed since the time of Christ. The same could be said of Nazareth. Bethlehem was disappointing, geared for tourism even before the days of mass air travel, with tawdry souvenir shops lining the street opposite the Church of Nativity in which, for the appropriate fee, a priest would bless whatever had been bought across the road. Jerusalem, a modern city, retained a dignity befitting its biblical history. We travelled as an armed party, for terrorism was never far away and sometimes erupted before our eyes, as on a day we returned from Tiberias. Approaching Acre, we heard an enormous explosion followed by the rattle of rifle and machine gun fire. We sped to the scene to find four jeeps, immaculately painted with Scottish regimental signs, bullet riddled and with what appeared to be the bodies of Scottish soldiers being removed. Fortunately it was not as it seemed at first sight. A party of terrorists, dressed and equipped as British troops, had driven up to the jail and by blowing a large hole in the wall had released the prisoners, among whom were a number of terrorists awaiting trial. Unfortunately for the terrorists, a company of troops swimming on a nearby beach had heard the explosion and rushed into action with a vengeance.

When, after two months, the course ended, I set out to rejoin the regiment in Tripolitania. Passing through Port Said, I was made draft conducting officer for a party of ATS girls (now called Women's Royal Army Corps), thirty privates and a sergeant. On arrival in Malta we were detained for some days in an almost empty transit camp at the deserted end of the island while awaiting a corvette for Tripoli. With no duties of any sort, the sergeant and I took the local bus into Valetta each day for lunch, exciting the imagination of the camp commandant, a fussy little major who mumbled about King's Regulations. He need not have fussed over us for the sergeant was more interested in her military career than in me and was not inclined to break any regulations on my account.

Rejoining the regiment I found it dispersed throughout Tripolitania but with morale vastly improved. In Egypt there had been a lack of purpose and, apart from sport, little for the troops to do in their spare time. Cairo and the Pyramids would occupy one weekend but no more. Tripolitania was quite different and the new commanding officer, Lieutenant Colonel Francis Gore, had taken advantage of the change of environment to infuse a new spirit throughout the regiment. He was a man of high integrity who led by example and the first of several officers under whom I served whose standards I took as a bench-mark for my own.

The battery to which I belonged was stationed in an old Italian ordnance depot which had remained derelict since the end of the war in Africa several years before. The soldiers slept on rows of bunks in a large warehouse and while the officers and NCOs enjoyed more privacy, living in what had been the administrative buildings, a good deal of self help was needed to make all ranks tolerably comfortable. All doors and windows had long since been stolen and the only furniture issued was a bed and a camp chair apiece. We therefore allowed a local manufacturer to remove as much timber as he liked from the roofs of the unhabited parts of the barracks, in exchange for doors, windows and furniture. There was not much we could do about the inadequate plumbing but otherwise we were eventually living in reasonable style.

Tripolitania was an enjoyable station. A large number of settlers remained from the days when it had been colonised by Italy and the culture owed more to the southern Europeans than the indigenous Arabs. This twentieth century colonialism, with its neat settlements, efficient irrigation and well ordered orange groves, was only repeating, on a less grand scale, what had been achieved by the Romans. In those earlier times Tripolitania had been the granary of Rome and the ruined watch towers, which we sometimes came across as we drove out into the desert, showed how far cultivation and civilisation had once spread. In the city of Tripoli the culture was more mixed; the corniche was undeniably colonial but the gharries, with their emaciated horses, in which British officers raced from their club to the night life at the Delmahari Hotel, were as Arab as those in Cairo. The Vittorio Emmanuele could have been a street in Naples, yet a few yards away, through an archway into the old city, were smells, spices, beaten copper and wares of a traditional Arab *suq*. Peace and relative prosperity had returned since the war but there were many signs that Libya had been a fiercely contested battle ground. The harbour was still littered with wrecks and here and there in the hinterland were large numbers of unexploded shells, the remnants of German and Italian ammunition dumps. The poorer Arabs, dealing in small amounts of scrap metal, would not infrequently blow themselves to pieces while attempting to remove the brass and copper from the fuses and driving bands. Perhaps the most obvious indication that these were still early days of peace was the British military administration which governed the country.

I was now in command of a troop comprising two other officers and sixty men. We were equipped with four heavy anti-aircraft guns, two radar sets each about the size of a removal van, an early electronic computer which filled the inside of a small caravan, and about twenty vehicles of varying sizes. Our days were spent in training, in the barracks, in the country around Tripoli or sometimes in the hills a hundred miles inland. With a large number of troops deployed throughout Tripolitania there were plenty of sporting fixtures to occupy those so inclined and I began to take athletics and boxing seriously enough to achieve some modest success.

The considerable turnover among officers had brought in a number of national servicemen, some of whom begrudged their time in the army. Among the eight of us there was one such whose arrogance and intellectual pretensions infuriated his fellow national servicemen. He was known as Snog because, given the chance, he would be early to bed and late to rise. A colleague conceived a prank to teach this officer a lesson and arranged for a fake telegram to be delivered to the lunch table. This communication, purporting to come from regimental headquarters ninety miles away, summoned Snog to report there by nightfall to become the regimental education officer. Snog should have smelt a rat for there was no such appointment, but such was his excitement that he proceeded immediately to pack his belongings and dispose of the few sticks of furniture which he owned. At tea time, with his baggage on board, he climbed into a truck for the drive to Gharian and we photographed him with his foot on the running board and an arm full of books. The driver had been carefully briefed to drive out of the barrack gate and go immediately to the front entrance of the officers mess which, being set in the barrack wall, was normally locked and barred. As the truck drew up the doors were flung open and a roll of carpet sent bouncing down the steps. 'Welcome home!' we roared in unison. We immediately felt sorry for the victim, returned his furniture, helped him unpack and treated him to a very good dinner in town. It was undoubtedly his making.

In September 1947 I went home on a month's leave during which I became engaged. Anne Barry was the daughter of a chief petty officer retired after many years' naval service. We had originally met when she was a war time member of the Women's Land Army and I was working on a farm during the school holidays. We had seen one another during my leaves from officer training and corresponded since I had been abroad. We were faced with a long engagement because I was due for no more home leave until the end of my overseas tour in two years' time, but that seemed a better option than starting married life with a long separation.

While I was on leave a telegram arrived from the regiment telling me I had been granted a regular commission. I had achieved my immediate goal and if anyone at that moment had probed my further intentions they would have thought me a singularly unenterprising young man, but promotion during the next decade would depend more upon age than performance—I could not become a captain until my 27th birthday in just under six years—which in those days left plenty of time in which to develop healthy ambitions. I had, however, to the delight of my parents, stepped permanently from one walk of life into another.

Soon after I returned from leave the batteries vacated their separate stations and the regiment assembled at Zavia, a small town on the road between Tripoli and Tunis. It was the centre of the main wine producing area in Tripolitania and had the atmosphere and architecture of rural southern Italy. The barracks had been built years before for an Italian infantry battalion and consisted of a number of low white-washed buildings around a large dusty parade ground of impacted earth. There were no garages, the original occupants presumably having marched wherever they went, so that the parade ground became a vehicle and gun park on which, every morning before breakfast, the entire regiment could be seen busy at maintenance. Near the barrack gate was a somewhat more imposing two storey building, shaded with eucalyptus trees, in which the regimental headquarters were housed on the ground floor with the officers' mess above. Behind it, overlooked by the mess verandah, were tennis courts and a dozen married quarters, as yet unoccupied.

In the centre of Zavia was an Italian social club which welcomed the officers as members and a small cinema which, when it showed English films, was well patronised by the regiment. There were also girls. There had been girls in Tripoli but here, in a smaller community, they seemed more friendly. Yet however enticing their smiles, they remained unavailable. In matters of sex British soldiers are not easily defeated but in Zavia they failed to outflank the chaperones or penetrate the protective screen of local youth. There was no trouble between the troops and the locals which might easily have been the case with eight hundred and fifty young men swamping a small town. The only occasion during which our regimental police had any difficulty was during the weekend of the annual grape harvest carnival when, for a few lira, a soldier acquired a paper cup and the right to sample as much wine as he could drink from any of the many barrels ranged around the town square. Undoubtedly on our arrival business picked up at the local brothel but although it was checked periodically by the orderly officer, in company with the orderly sergeant, no one was ever caught out of bounds.

In addition to commanding my troop, I was now the senior subaltern, the mess secretary and the messing officer. Being the senior subaltern added little to my responsibilities, I was simply expected to ensure that the other subalterns behaved themselves in the mess. My duties as mess secretary were altogether more onerous as they involved running what amounted to a five star hotel, for those were the standards expected. I had no qualms over the domestic administration or the accounts but, not being a gourmet, the meals were a nightmare. As messing officer I was responsible for the regimental cook house which, in those days, was more a matter of organisation than culinary appreciation but it meant, under the exacting standards of Francis Gore, being present at the start of every meal except on Sundays.

Breakfasts in the officers' mess were always difficult. If the cooks were not having trouble with the antiquated ovens, the officers were moodily grumbling about the way their eggs were done. I was prepared for many complaints but certainly not one to do with newspapers which, coming out by sea once a fortnight, had nothing to do with me. Therefore, when the colonel one morning complained that he had found jam on The Times, I felt no tinge of alarm until he suggested that, as senior subaltern, I should call the others together and read the riot act. Confiding in a friend and fellow officer, Nick Cameron, that I was not much looking forward to administering an admonishment on such a petty matter, I ordered the subalterns to assemble in the ante-room before lunch. Word got out and I was clearly in for a rough ride, with my friend doing nothing to help. However, the tables were neatly turned for me when a telegram arrived mid-morning informing Nick that his regular commission had been granted. As seniority depended upon age, he now became the senior subaltern and I was able, in one breath, to offer congratulations on his promotion and commiserate with him over his lunch time task.

Our routine life was interrupted when the British mandate in Palestine ended in May 1948 and fighting broke out between the new state of Israel and her Arab neighbours. The Egyptian army received a severe mauling and, when it appeared that British interests in the area might be threatened, it was decided to deploy anti-aircraft defences on the Suez Canal at Ismailia and Fayid. My troop, being one of the two selected to form a composite battery, found itself, at twelve hours' notice, embarking in Tripoli docks on a large landing ship. This vessel, originally designed to discharge tanks and vehicles across beaches during assault landings, was loaded through the bow doors, had a lower deck for the heavier equipment and an upper deck, exposed to the elements, approached by a steep ramp from the lower deck. Obviously, the loading of the top deck had to be completed first in order to remove the connecting ramp obstructing the deck below but the latter needed partially filling at the outset in order to maintain the stability of the ship. It was a complicated process of which neither the staff who organised the move nor any of us taking part had previous experience. The loading proceeded empirically and took a good deal longer than any one had expected, almost twenty four hours. The captain had been ashore during this time and, when he returned, declined at first to put to sea as we had exceeded the weight limit permissible on the top deck. As a junior officer I was not party to the wrangling which then ensued but we eventually cast off at daybreak and the troops bedded down for a long sleep. They did so wherever they could for the ship was crammed with many times the number she was intended to take. My troop leader and I erected our camp beds on the top deck under the funnel, where there was some privacy and a little warmth at night. It was a bad choice, for the wind which followed us during the next five days caused the smoke to linger above our heads and shower us with soot. Later, thinking about what had happened, I wondered why such a shambles had been allowed to occur; there must have been a number of officers in Tripoli whose wartime experience with landing ships could have been put to good use. There are ways of learning other than by one's own mistakes.

On arrival at Port Said we disembarked and set out during the night for Fayid. We arrived as the sun was rising and, understanding that we would be there for some hours, I found a bed and tumbled into it fully dressed. Within two hours my troop was on the road again, driving back over part of the route by which we had just come, to deploy beside the Suez Canal at a place called Ferry Point. We dug in on the banks and languished there for several months after the Israeli threat had receded, if ever there had been a real threat. We amused ourselves by gun position drills, sport and swimming at a small leisure centre close at hand, run by canal company officials. Occasional visits to the French and Greek clubs in nearby Ismailia was the extent of our social life and it was with some relief when orders came for us to return to Tripolitania.

The other officers who had been involved in this Egyptian adventure had previously served only on static gun sites in Britain and, being unfamiliar with the problems of military movement, left me to organise the return of all equipment. They set off with the main body of men, leaving an assurance that a landing ship and all necessary facilities were awaiting me at Port Said. The three dozen of us left behind winched the guns and radars out of the sand and set off up the canal road. On arrival at Port Said I found that nothing had been arranged, indeed, no one seemed to have heard of us. 'A landing craft, my dear chap, they don't grow on trees. Besides how do we know you are meant to be doing this?' I pointed out that it was unlikely I would be freelancing to the extent of moving eight heavy guns and a large number of vehicles along the North African coast, said that I hoped he would help and, meanwhile, we would find somewhere to bivouac on the quayside. The week during which we waited for a ship to turn up was put to good use. With baulks of timber and other large bits of bric-a-brac gleaned from the docks, we constructed a driving course to simulate the difficulties of embarking on a landing ship so that when the time came the process went smoothly. The men also trained their pet mongrel to sit quietly for an hour or so in the tool box of a ten ton truck by which means it was proposed the animal would be smuggled aboard. After a few days at sea I gashed my head badly in a companion way and, in the absence of a doctor to put in the half dozen or so stitches which ideally were required, my troop sergeant major chopped off my hair, poured in a generous measure of sulphonamide powder and applied a large plaster. Miraculously the wound healed without ill effects but my hair, where it had been so peremptorily chopped off, grew in spikes and resembled that of a Red Indian brave for many months.

By 1949 regimental life abroad had settled largely into a pre-war pattern. This was not surprising for our senior officers had all been commissioned into the peace time army of the 1930s and, with the hiatus of war behind them, were reverting to their previous, long established ways. Officers were, no doubt, now more involved in the day-to-day administration, due to the relative inexperience of national service NCOs and the increased complexity of equipment, but the demands of parades, drill orders, sport and the mess again ruled an officer's life.

The major difference was the absence of horses but this hardly affected the daily routine for every morning at half past six we held a stable parade, and it was still called that, when, for an hour, the regiment groomed its vehicles so that inside and out they gleamed as new. After breakfast the morning continued with a miscellany of military activity. There would be battery commander's orders for those miscreants who had been apprehended committing some mis-demeanour or another. There would be fatigue parties essential to the domestic life of the regiment, attending to chores in the cook house, sweeping barrack roads and removing the refuse. For the majority the day continued with military training applicable to their particular role. Sometimes I would take my troop into the neighbouring countryside for a drill order—a morning's exercise—deploying, moving and redeploying until no one was slicker than we. Lunch was at half past one followed by a siesta and then, mid-afternoon, sport. At the end of the working day all drivers attended to their vehicles much as their predecessors had bedded down their horses for the night.

Each evening from Monday to Friday all officers were expected to dine in the mess, the only exceptions being those senior officers whose families had arrived during 1948 and who were now living in married quarters. Once a week there was a formal mess night when we dressed in mess kit, passed the port and drank the loyal toast. On these occasions those who lived in married quarters also dined in the mess. In the absence of air conditioning the sweat soon seeped through our mess jackets but no one complained of such small discomforts or thought it incongruous for it was part of a ritual which we all enjoyed. At the weekends, those who were not out on the town were allowed to dine in the mess wearing nothing more formal than a sports jacket.

Early stirrings of Arab nationalism in Libya were inevitably directed against Italian interests and when rioting in Tripoli was effectively handled by British troops, hostility was deflected into the rural areas. When this happened, my troop was one of those deployed to deter further violence against the Italian settlements and I found myself with responsibility for some two hundred square miles inland from Zavia. I drove into a village in the centre of this area and, leaving my sergeant major to requisition the school and welcome the soldiers who would be arriving later, I set out in an armoured car to reconnoitre the countryside and show the flag. On my return the sergeant major informed me, with a smirk, that he had made special arrangements for me to be accommodated with the school mistress in her bungalow across the street. He had obviously anticipated my reply and, when I said I should remain with the men, he promptly offered to take my place, explaining that it would ease the crush in the school office which otherwise he and I would share with a second lieutenant. I vetoed that suggestion and offered up the second lieutenant but not before meeting the lady concerned, thirtyish and inevitably attractive given our recent lack of feminine company. It had been her suggestion, I discovered, for me to move into her bungalow, my sergeant major having been no more than a message bearer chancing his arm. I wished my veto had been less emphatic but over tea, biscuits and broken English I explained my regrets and accepted on behalf of the second lieutenant who moved in with alacrity. Subsequently, he was remarkably silent about the whole episode leading me to doubt whether he ever got beyond the spare bedroom.

Among our number in the regiment was Captain Harry Simms who had flown artillery spotting aircraft during the war, earning the Distinguished Flying Cross in the process. Like me, he found heavy anti-aircraft less than satisfactory because it tended to operate in isolation rather than as part of the field army and he was determined to return to flying as soon as possible. I found his enthusiasm infectious and when a few years later I decided to spread my wings, Harry's earlier proselytising was a decisive influence. I might have opted for flying at the end of my time in the Middle East but that would have complicated other more pressing arrangements now in the making. I was due home in early October and entitled to a month's leave, during which time Anne and I were to be married. As October approached the regiment was ordered to Malta, whence it moved during September, leaving me in charge of a rear party in Zavia. I was due to embark in Tripoli during the last week of September but the ship was delayed and I arrived home just in time to be married as planned.

In early November 1949 I joined the 64th Training Regiment Royal

Artillery at Park Hall Camp in Shropshire, one of the six regiments which prepared national servicemen for the Royal Artillery. 'We thought you were a bachelor,' they said and I had to explain there had been a recent change. By marrying between regiments I had avoided the need formally to ask permission and the disapproval invariably expressed when an officer married under the age of twenty five. However, I had not avoided the military penalties of early marriage, no assistance with accommodation and a lower than standard rate of marriage allowance. (In those days an officer's pay assumed the recipient was a bachelor and a marriage allowance was granted when he acquired a wife.) I therefore set about finding somewhere cheap to live and moved, temporarily, into the officers' mess. Anne, meanwhile, remained with her sister in Sussex.

The national service training machine in which I found myself reflected the same discipline and methods to which I had been subjected five years earlier as a private soldier and which, in turn, had been based on the pre-war army. During the Second World War the army had been too busy to adjust its attitudes to a citizen intake and when the war ended, the problem of coping with demobilisation, transition to peace, national service, internal security problems in various parts of the world and a war in Korea, had fully occupied those who otherwise might have introduced methods more in tune with the times. Thus, a good deal of what the national serviceman was required to do seemed open to question and he had the inclination to seek answers. In this way national service hastened the change but it was some years before the army no longer required men to make up their beds in the shape of armchairs and prevent their use as such by the display of kit laid out thereon, shirts stuffed with cardboard and ammunition pouches filled out with socks.

However, the wind across the barrack square at Park Hall in 1949 was not one of change and, feeling that too much priority was placed on superficial activities, I was faced with a job for which I felt ill fitted. Fortunately, someone, somewhere, expressed dissatisfaction with the recruits arriving on active service in Malaya and I was tasked with giving these men additional training before they were sent out, the recruits coming to me at the end of their basic training for six weeks of practical soldiering and toughening up. My battery commander still showed an unwelcome interest in my barrack rooms and ablutions and when he found there were no plugs in the wash basins, was unhappy when I explained that my men provided their own as part of their training in self reliance. (Old soldiers will remember how wash basin plugs always vanished.) These small irritations apart, I was now in my element for I alone decided the training syllabus and had my own instructors to carry it out in a manner I prescribed. We marched across the Welsh hills, forty miles in two days carrying all our kit and ammunition. We fired a virtually unlimited amount of small arms ammunition on the ranges at Llangollen and spent a week on the deserted artillery ranges at Sennybridge in South Wales, practising with live ammunition in as near realistic conditions as possible. Only later, towards the end of 1951, by which time I was providing recruits for the war in Korea, did my superiors take a hand in what I was doing, and then only to join the fun.

Private accommodation was difficult to find but eventually Anne and I were able to set up home in the east wing of a large house in Weston Rhyn, five miles from the barracks to and from which I cycled each morning and evening. Cycling was our usual method of travel, to the market town of Oswestry on Saturdays for shopping and occasionally in the evening to a cinema. After a year we rented a small terraced house on the outskirts of Oswestry where we were living when our daughter Maureen was born in November 1951 and where we remained until the end of our time with the training regiment.

In the early fifties the standard of sport in the armed forces was higher than ever before or since. It was not simply that virtually all young men were in uniform at about the time they were reaching maturity, but rather the manner in which the services took advantage of this. Units in all three services specialised in particular sports and recruited star performers into their ranks. Training organisations were best placed to do this and the men recruited as sportsmen would, on completion of their training, be retained in some guise or other on the permanent staff and given duties which would not seriously interfere with their sport. 64th Regiment's speciality was boxing and I soon found myself captain of the team, not because I was the best boxer—I was probably the worst—but because I was the only officer in it. During the boxing season, the winter, we virtually became professionals, road running in the morning, squeezing in an hour or two at our military duties before lunch and spending the entire afternoon in the gym. In the early part of the season I would usually hold my own and often even win. In the New Year, when the team had progressed to the army quarter finals at Aldershot and was meeting other gladiatorial teams, I was usually on to a hiding for nothing as although the inter-regimental competition was organised on a team basis, boxing is not a team game. It is a highly individual sport and in a competition between two evenly matched teams, some of the individual contests may turn out to be between boxers of widely differing abilities. For this reason, boxing in one of the best teams in the army, I came a cropper a number of times. On one occasion I found myself in the ring with a boxer who, within a year, was contesting the professional light heavyweight crown of the British Empire (although Britain had divested herself of Empire, the title still remained). At the time I met him, Arthur Howard had recently disposed of the American national amateur champion within one round. I lasted longer, a round and a half, before the referee stopped the fight, not because I was better than the American but because I back pedalled more adroitly. On another occasion I was more fortunate. I went into the ring a certain loser against a command champion but, as this huge bruiser moved in to demolish me, he ran on to my left hand, keeled over and was counted out. The surprise of the spectators was surpassed only by mine.

Although I enjoyed boxing, it was doing me no good and I developed an intermittent but pronounced stammer which vanished the moment I gave up fighting in early 1951. I now hold a very different view of the sport and, while acknowledging its character building aspects, I believe it should be banned by law for anyone over the age of sixteen, which is about the time when a tough young man can hit hard enough to knock someone out. Of course, people receive serious injuries when playing other contact sports but physically knocking out the opposition is not the main purpose of these other games and if it occurs it does so only incidentally. Some of the professionals with whom I sparred in the gymnasium at Park Hall were already showing signs of punch drunkenness in their early twenties; their ability to take punches which would have floored most people only increasing their vulnerability to permanent damage.

Having been with the training regiment for about eighteen months, I began to consider what I should do next. I felt I needed a change from regimental soldiering but neither of the traditional outlets, becoming an ADC to a general or polishing a chair as a junior staff officer, appealed to me. Not that these openings would have been available. I did not take easily, as an ADC would have been expected, to the hunt ball atmosphere of Shropshire and, in spite of the responsibilities—considerable for a subaltern—I had successfully discharged, I was still graded only 'average'. I knew I was better than that and was seeking an environment in which my abilities would be measured by something more fundamental than the yard sticks by which I had so far been judged. Thinking back to Harry Simms in Tripolitania, I volunteered for flying.

I nearly failed at the first fence, the medical. In the days before proper earplugs were issued, cotton wool was the only protection against the sharp crack of gun fire but, as it inconveniently deadened all other sounds, I seldom used it. As a result I had become a little deaf but remained unaware of this until, at the flying medical, we sat listening through earphones while someone transmitted a series of dots and dashes at varying frequencies. When I saw the officer next to me scribbling away while I was hearing nothing, the best I could do was to copy what he was writing. When it was found that the two of us, side by side, had made the same errors, I had to own up and a doctor tested me again by whispering across a large room. 'You will have to speak up,' I said, 'I can't hear.' Whereupon he passed me.

Chapter 3

War in Korea

IN the days when I began as a pilot, all army flying was still under the auspices of the Royal Air Force who provided the aircraft and ground crews. The pilots, however, came from the army, artillery officers in the case of those whose primary task was artillery observation, officers and NCOs from other regiments where the flying was of a more general nature. Trucks, radios and military paraphernalia needed on the ground, together with the soldiers to man them, were also provided by the army. Thus, the air observation post flights—air OP for short—, and light liaison flights which were part of the army in the field, were each a mixture of khaki and light blue.

The training of all army pilots took place at Royal Air Force, Middle Wallop, a flying school in Hampshire, and it was here I reported in January 1952. There were no married quarters for junior officers and I moved into the officers' mess until I was able, after a few weeks, to rent a furnished house in Andover. It was a good deal better than our previous accommodation and provided an agreeable base from which to tackle the six months course. Flying is fun but learning in a service environment, with frequent tests and a high failure rate, is a stressful business not to be undertaken against a background of domestic difficulties.

There were some eighteen starters on the course with me and we began on Tiger Moths, simple bi-planes from a previous era. With open cockpits, leather helmets and goggles, we might have been mistaken for World War I fighter aces except that our fledgling efforts were of a somewhat erratic nature. None more than mine in those early days. After only six hours' tuition and an unusually smooth landing which owed more to luck than judgement, my instructor climbed out and waved me off. First solo flights are intended to be no more than a take off, a single circuit of the airfield and a landing—as the jargon goes, a

31

circuit and a bump. Mine was three take offs, three circuits, two bumps, which I failed to convert into landings, and a crash which removed the undercarriage. After an anxious twenty four hours I again went solo, this time successfully. The first hurdle had been passed.

Our days were a mixture of flying and classroom instruction. We usually flew twice a day, being taken up first by an instructor, addressing some new aspect of flight and then flying solo, practising what had previously been taught. The solo flights were fun for there was no one to berate the quivering student and it was possible to enjoy the thrill of an open cockpit among the billowing cloud tops. There were, of course, moments of anxiety, the first solo stall and spin, or becoming temporarily lost because one could not yet simultaneously cope with flying and map reading. After about fifty hours the chief instructor flew with each student and pronounced his suitability or not to move on to the next stage. Already several of our number had failed and left; one or two were now relegated to the following course and the rest of us moved on to the Auster, the aircraft with which operational units were equipped.

The Auster was a high wing monoplane with a closed in cockpit. Built largely of wood and fabric, it was under-powered and did not handle well when landing at slow speed. Rudimentary it may have been but it needed more than rudimentary skills to fly in the role for which it was cast, operating in the forward battle areas. It was for this environment we trained, flying below the tree tops to avoid the attention of hostile aircraft or troops. To observe and correct artillery fire the pilot pulled sharply up, levelling at several hundred feet coincidentally with the burst of the shells, before diving to earth and radioing further fire orders. The radio itself seemed an impediment to communications for it was not the easily operated sort of set now in use but a collection of dials which needed skilful manipulation if contact was to be maintained. There was also the map to read, plotting the positions of targets and friendly troops and finding the way home. Home was usually a field requiring a low and slow approach, low to avoid giving its position away and slow to land successfully in a confined space. It would have been nail biting stuff had we fingers to spare and although we qualified as pilots after some one hundred and eighty hours, it took a further two hundred hours or so before a complete sortie could be performed with absolute confidence.

On completion of pilot training, I asked to be sent to Korea where a United Nations army was engaged in a full scale war. The reply was that only experienced pilots were posted to Korea. I tried all arguments but to no avail. My enthusiasm did not make up for my inexperience in the air. My logic, that we should be using Korea to provide battle experience for those without it, was taken as an affront to authority. I withdrew and, conducting a reconnaissance before my next assault, discovered that a squadron in Malaya was the source of replacement pilots for Korea. I therefore settled for Malaya, which offered the chance of getting to war later and, meanwhile, would involve me in what I thought was the next best thing, the campaign in Malaya against communist guerillas. I was mindful, in arranging my movements, of a wife of less than three years and a young daughter but, as a professional soldier, I needed operational service to make good an omission in my experience. So, in early September, I set out for Malaya with the expectation that Anne and Maureen would join me in about two months.

In 1952 air travel was still in its infancy and the motley collection of passengers who assembled at Blackbush airport one evening were faced with a five day flight to Singapore. We took off early next morning in an Avro York, about a dozen officers all senior to me and an equal number of wives and children en route to join their husbands. We had lunch in Malta and spent the first night in Nicosia. The following day I was invited to fly the aircraft, the captain having discovered that he had another pilot on board. We were crossing Saudi Arabia at three thousand feet and the captain's only instruction was to maintain that altitude and follow the pipeline. In spite of my inexperience this presented no difficulty and when a sharp bend appeared, I threw the aircraft into a steep turn, as if I had been flying a Tiger Moth or Auster. The large machine responded with unexpected alacrity; seated passengers were compressed into their seats while those who had been wandering up and down the aisle found themselves on the floor. There was no doubt that the power to weight ratio of a York, lumbering as it seemed, was far superior to an Auster. On we flew from Karachi, lunching at Delhi and night stopping at Calcutta when the drive from Dum Dum Airport exposed us to what were, surely, the most appalling slums in the world. We eventually arrived in Singapore rather less jaded than the modern traveller who, taking less than twenty four hours, sleeps fitfully en route.

I was welcomed on arrival by the officers of an air OP flight which was positioned on the northern side of Singapore Island and had the task of covering operations in the southern part of Malaya. They had an aircraft which required delivering to squadron headquarters at Kuala Lumpur and I offered to fly it up. The flight commander was concerned over my unfamiliarity with local conditions and lack of jungle survival training, but he agreed I should take the aircraft providing I followed the railway, so that I would not risk becoming lost over the jungle and stood a reasonable chance of a successful forced landing if anything should go wrong. I took off early the following morning and headed north across the Singapore Straits towards Johore. Climbing to two thousand feet in the clear air, the rubber and palm plantations of southern Johore were laid beneath me in a mosaic. On my left the railway ran straight as a die towards the north west while the roads, a few tarmaced but mostly red laterite, wound their way hither and thither as they did at home. Presently, the cultivation gave way to jungle and the forest clad slopes of Mount Ophir rose ahead. The railway took a dog leg and I could see I would save time by simply cutting the corner across the jungle. When I arrived well before expected, the squadron adjutant, a Royal Air Force officer, expressed concern that I had been allowed so much freedom so soon. However, within two days he had conveniently forgotten my inexperience and agreed that I could go on to Korea where the air OP flight was, I had discovered, calling for a replacement pilot. So, within a short while, I was ferrying another aircraft back to Singapore and boarding an air force Dakota for Korea.

Five days later I was deposited on the tarmac at Seoul, the airfield through which all reinforcements and most of the air-lifted war material arrived in Korea. It was the busiest airfield in the world with huge American Globemasters, then the largest aircraft in existence, arriving every few minutes. Small aircraft were unwelcome, so when the Auster which had come to collect me suddenly appeared beneath the tail of one of these giants, I threw my bags in the back and quickly climbed in with the propeller still turning. The tower flashed a series of greens, meaning, 'Will you please go away,' and we were soon airborne, bouncing along in the wake of a huge transport which had taken off ahead of us.

Half an hour later our destination came into view, an air strip named Fort George, the home of 1903 Air Observation Post Flight, the unit I was joining. As we let down into the circuit I observed for the first time the features which for the next year would provide my daily surroundings and which would sometimes be used as land marks when returning in bad weather. To the north west of the strip was the River Imjin, flowing slowly at this time of the year between its steep banks. It curled around the northern end of the strip where it was crossed by a high girder bridge carrying the main supply route to the forward troops. To the south west of the air strip, sheltering behind a long low ridge, were vehicles, tents and huts in sandbag emplacements: the headquarters of the Commonwealth Division. The pilot turned finals over the girder bridge, the bridges were named after birds and this one was called Pintail, and allowed the aircraft to float down the strip towards the vehicles and tents at the far end which, had it not been for the aircraft barely showing above their sandbagged revetments, resembled nothing so much as a gipsy encampment.

The flight was commanded by Major Jack Hailes who expressed surprise and irritation that I should have arrived virtually direct from Middle Wallop. He had been expecting an experienced pilot and his mood did not improve when I remarked that one volunteer was better than several pressed men. However, none of this worried me; I had got myself to war.

The war had started in 1950 with North Korea invading the South. Thereafter, it had ranged up and down the country, with the United Nations arriving to fight alongside South Korea and the Chinese coming in to assist the North, before settling to a stalemate in the manner of the First World War. With both sides deeply entrenched, it was now largely an artillery war with infantry action confined to patrolling and limited attacks. In this situation the mountainous nature of the terrain, which hindered observation from the ground, gave air OP an exceptionally important role to play. For most sorties the pilot would take off briefed to engage enemy artillery. He would be provided with aerial photographs annotated to show where information from sound ranging devices and photographic interpretation coincided to indicate the probable position of camouflaged enemy guns. The guns were well dug in and it was usually impossible to say with certainty what destruction had been achieved, although a bright flash signalling a direct hit, or explosions indicating that ammunition was going up, probably meant the target had been destroyed. We were also briefed for targets such as headquarters and logistics areas, in fact anything important which, to our troops on the ground, was 'over the hill'.

Most of our shooting was done with heavy American artillery, eight inch guns and 240 mm howitzers, whose shells would crumble the thickest earthworks if accurately directed. Other targets, such as men or vehicles appeared from time to time and these we would engage using the twenty five pounders or five point five inch guns of the Commonwealth artillery, or the American 155 mm howitzers. Occasionally, for targets a very long way behind the enemy's forward line, we would use the Long Toms, 155 mm guns which, at their extreme range of some fifteen miles, were so inaccurate we sometimes ran short on fuel before hitting anything. A prodigious amount of ammunition was expended. Thirty heavy shells might be fired against a single enemy gun. I once engaged a company of Chinese infantry, numbering about one hundred men, with the divisional artillery of seventy two guns firing eleven rounds apiece. No one thought it extravagant. On the contrary, Brigadier Peter Gregson, the artillery commander, suggested I should have used air burst fuses, a method I had deliberately discounted as they were in short supply.

As there were no enemy aircraft over the battle area, we could, cloud base permitting, fly at sufficient heights from which the targets could be easily observed. However, the static nature of the war and the fact that the enemy front line and gun areas were subjected to heavy air strikes, had induced the Chinese to deploy large amounts of anti-aircraft artillery in their forward areas. We needed to ensure that our slow flying aircraft did not present easy targets and, whenever possible, we selected altitudes of between six and eight thousand feet which took us above the effective range of 40 mm guns but not so high as to make us unduly vulnerable to the radar controlled 85 mm guns sited further away. These could make short work of a slow flying Auster and there was no alternative but to dive sharply towards home whenever a vicious crack or ball of black smoke signalled the opening shot. Sometimes the weather forced us down to two or three thousand feet where we played hide and seek among the clouds with the Chinese gunners, and occasionally we flew at ten or twelve thousand feet to observe a distant target without venturing too far into enemy territory.

The early morning pilot could well appreciate why Korea is called 'Land of the morning calm'. He had little to do as his aircraft droned upwards to its operational altitude and, while the calm would no doubt be shattered on his arrival over the lines, he meanwhile had at least twenty minutes in which to enjoy it. One element of the calm was constant, the silence sensed above the noise of the engine. In the autumn and winter, except when the snow came, the sky was clear, adding a dimension of space to the silence. The nose swung around the horizon in a slow climbing turn, bringing into view the distant mountains to the north on which the snow lingered until spring. It swept past the precipitous ridges to the east, in shade against the morning sun. Then came the grey pinnacle of Kamaksan to the south and, as the turn continued, a flat uninteresting plain stretching towards the port of Inchon and the lower reaches of the River Imjin flowing into the Yellow Sea. Then it was north again where a lack of any visual activity among the isolated clusters of thatched roofs added to the eerie calm. Closer to the lines the villages were in ruins, the largest, Kuhwari, a blackened skeleton where the thin and meandering Chuam-chon met the wider flowing Chigo-chon. Rice thatch was always an early victim of phosphorous or napalm.

In winter the cold accentuated the sense of isolation and at eight thousand feet the temperature would go down to forty below freezing, causing ice crystals to form on the eye lashes as we sat in unheated cockpits, so puffed out by cold weather clothing that our seat straps had to be specially lengthened. In spring, when the snows had melted, the underlying grey and brown hillsides became tinged with a hue of green. A thin white mist would then hang over the terraced rice fields until the sun was high enough to burn it off. The hot summers brought periods of torrential rain when thick low cloud reduced to several hundred feet the height from which observation was possible. On these occasions, with clouds skimming the cockpit canopy above, ravaged hills all round and the Chinese forward slopes a mere machine gun burst away, the morning calm vanished on take off.

Everyone, after four months in the battle zone, was entitled to five days leave, known as R and R—rest and recreation. The R and R centre was in Tokyo where many traditional Japanese values seemed to have become submerged by the flood of young men from the front. There was not much time for courtesy and charm on the Ginza, where shops, bars, strip shows and hotels catered for Americans with money to burn. Away from the bright lights Japanese society became itself again and I wondered how the people, themselves, reconciled their deferential and obsequious behaviour with the brutal conduct which had characterised their military campaigns only a few years before. Of course, the Japanese can be pretty rough with one another when push comes to shove, as in the rush hour or at a box office, but that emphasises rather than explains their two enigmatic and contrasting faces. I left Japan with no desire to return and when my next leave was due I spent it on HMS Glory, an aircraft carrier operating off the west coast.

My few days on board HMS Glory resulted in the flight adopting a mythical figure, Sir Harry Clampers. On board Glory, whenever the weather clamped down and prevented flying, a cardboard cut-out figure in broad brimmed hat and cloak, used by Sandemans in advertising their wines, appeared on the wardroom bar. This was a sign that the aviators could relax without fear of suddenly being scrambled. I wrote to Sandemans asking if they would send me a similar cut-out and by return received a wooden box within which, packed neatly in straw, was a porcelain version of Sir Harry Clampers. We painted the Korean medal ribbons on his chest and henceforth he stood, fair weather and foul, on the bar in a corner of the officers' mess.

The mess was originally in a small marquee, furnished with a couple of six foot tables and a few folding chairs. Underfoot, several sets of duckboards kept the mud at bay during the wet season and provided some insulation from the frozen earth in winter, when a couple of oil fired space heaters barely removed the chill as their heat vanished through the double tent roof into the arctic atmosphere. Indeed, the warmest place seemed to be between the inner and outer canvas, for it was here that those persistent camp followers, the rats, gathered at night, a number of sagging lumps thrown into sharp relief by the light of a bare electric bulb. Well aimed bottles would send them scurrying down the canvas, but they were soon back.

By the time Sir Harry arrived to oversee the pouring of alcohol, we had built a log hut, named Casa Mitty after its Canadian architect, Captain 'Mitty' Tees. The bar never closed and it was said that we regulated our drinking in terms of feet from the cockpit rather than hours before take off. The story was, of course, apocryphal and although we were a hard drinking lot, our open house was more for the benefit of our many friends in the Commonwealth and American artillery, who came in whenever they were passing, usually en route to the mobile bath unit. They knew us as radio call signs rather than by name, I was Six Bravo, but that was enough to open the door. Pilots took it in turn to ensure a ready supply of refreshment and when stocks were low one of us would collect a fiver all round and fetch a jeep load of replenishments from the Naafi depot. This informal system worked well until a pilot was shot down with the money in his pocket (he survived as a prisoner), whereupon more careful accounting procedures were introduced.

In March, Captain John Hoare arrived direct from Egypt having also, for a wager, defeated the normal reinforcement system. After an initial misunderstanding, when, on borrowing his aircraft, I upset his precise cockpit arrangements by throwing out his maps, chinagraph pencils and pee bottle, we became firm friends. Several weeks later, when he was using my aircraft, the engine cut out just after take off and John was lucky to walk away from the crash. He and I decided we could do better than to live in a tent and, taking advantage of the fact that the American Army had no alcohol in the field, we exchanged a bottle of whisky for one of the crates in which the fuselages of the American S55 helicopters arrived. Cutting the necessary holes, we filled these with a door and window, stolen one night from the control tower built by an American aviation unit, which was temporarily occupying the other end of our air strip. It was known variously as The House with a View, because it afforded a magnificent panorama across the River Imjin, and The House of Laughter because humour was our primary antidote to discomfort and danger.

On Saint Patrick's Day I was the flight duty officer, a task requiring me to man the radio sets in the flight command post. With me was a newly arrived officer learning the ropes. Sitting in the damp dugout, I heard a discreet cough and there, framed in the doorway against the light, was the most gorgeous figure. Blondes look good in battle dress and this one was no exception. She introduced herself as Madame Vivario, a Belgian war correspondent, en route from the Belgian battalion at the front to a Saint Patrick's Day dance which was being held that evening at Army Headquarters. She wondered if we had an aircraft going that way. The light liaison flight at the other end of the strip would certainly have an empty seat that afternoon but I was in no mood to surrender the first woman I had seen for two months. Leaving my colleague in charge of the wireless sets I invited Madame Vivario to accompany me to my aircraft where there was no shortage of volunteers among the ground crew to help her strap in. Half an hour later, I landed on the race course at Seoul and reluctantly delivered my passenger to Army Headquarters. I was not asked in; the staff were brooking no competition.

Sited within four miles of the front line, Fort George seemed an obvious refuge for fighter ground attack aircraft which had been too badly damaged to reach their airfields or aircraft carriers. The first one to try was an American Corsair which appeared overhead, belching smoke. In some difficulty, the pilot mistimed his landing, bounced, turned through one hundred and eighty degrees and slithered to a halt facing the way from which he had come. Major Peter Wilson, the Light Liaison Flight commander, walking with his back to the approaching aircraft, was bowled over and left lying in a ditch. I leapt into a jeep, which was standing close at hand with its engine running, and drove rapidly to where Peter lay, passing the American pilot who was shouting that no one should go close to the burning aircraft as it was still carrying its full load of rockets. Stopping the jeep about twenty yards in front of the aircraft, which was now crackling furiously, I pulled Peter into the back of the vehicle assisted by three others who had come running. With a loud whoosh the first rocket fired, skimming low over our heads and I put the jeep into reverse intent on a quick withdrawal.

In my haste I stalled the engine. The starter button produced no response and I reached beneath the seat, the customary place for the starting handle. There was none there, which was presumably why the vehicle had been left standing with the engine running. Another rocket went over our heads and the ammunition began to explode as we lifted Peter back into the ditch and cowered beside him. Eventually, when all the weapons had fired, the four of us carried Peter across a padi field to a waiting ambulance and, having seen him off, turned back the way we had come. 'Don't walk across that field,' said a sapper officer who had just arrived, 'it's full of old mines.' It seemed unlikely, because four of us had just trudged through it, but we did not take the chance and returned the long way round. Later I discovered he had been right. Fortune had smiled again.

My aircraft was fitted for a camera and, having done a short course with the American Eighth Army, I flew whatever photographic sorties were needed. One of these nearly finished me. The Australian infantry intended to send fighting patrols at night into the Chinese areas and asked if the Air OP Flight could provide pictures of the Chinese positions. If we were reluctant they would ask the air force but that would unfortunately take longer to arrange. It was impossible not to accept the challenge and I planned a sortie for early the following morning when, coming out of the sun, I might catch the Chinese standing down and at their breakfasts. This photographic run entailed flying straight and level, at a height of about two hundred and fifty feet, behind and parallel to the Chinese front lines. It lasted for a little under a minute and at the end of it I raced for home in a steep diving turn, not having seen a single tracer. I then, stupidly, thought I would do it again rather like a man taking a second snapshot in case the first does not come out. Once more I came around the hill and out of the sun. With my heart beating a little faster than normal I settled on course as the sandbags and pockmarked earth flashed past beneath me. Twice a second I heard the rasp of the camera shutter behind me. Then the tracer began, seeming to float lazily up towards me before accelerating as it flashed past the cockpit. Finishing the run, I turned unscathed towards our own lines and was racing low over the trenches when, with a tremendous bang, a considerable hole appeared in the engine cowling in front of me. Something had obviously gone through the engine compartment and out the top. With relief I heard the deep note of the engine continuing normally and when the fire warning lights remained unlit I relaxed. On landing I found that a single bullet had severed both port side engine bearing struts and taken a chunk from the fuel pump.

Had the fuel pump not miraculously remained intact, the aircraft would have ignited instantly in a ball of flame. Had my return flight lasted a little longer, it seemed probable that the starboard struts would have given up the unequal struggle and the aircraft would have broken in two.

Once in a while there was a need to visit the forward troops on the ground. From the experience so acquired, two incidents served in later life as useful examples of behaviour in battle when I was instructing officers under my command. 'What,' I said, 'would you do if shell fire along the road ahead caused your driver suddenly to stop and say that he wished to go no further?' 'What do you do when you are sitting on the turret of a Sherman tank talking to the commander when, suddenly, shells come down all around you and the commander disappears inside shutting you out?' I suggest the right answers are, in the first case you do anything but throw the driver overboard, and in the second anything but get under the tank. Too often in peacetime we ignore the effect of stress on men in battle but if officers in peacetime are introduced to situations concerning the reaction of men in battle they will probably get the right answer first time in war. In the incidents I quote, I scored a mere fifty percent, I threw the driver out but fortunately resisted the temptation to shelter under the tank, which, shortly after I jumped off, slewed round, chewing up all beneath it, and drove away.

One evening there was a considerable commotion at Pintail Bridge and, out of curiosity, John Hoare and I strolled across. On arrival we found a three ton truck loaded with diesel drums and half a dozen Korean peasant girls huddled together under the watchful eye of a military policeman. Several more policemen were scouring the adjacent rough ground for girls who had fled. Wherever there is war there are always women willing to hire their bodies to the licentious soldiery and some enterprising Canadians had moved into the market place. They had cut the tops from some forty-gallon drums and were using these to smuggle girls into the forward areas where, civilians being denied access, there were no girls. Viewed from the ground the truck appeared to be carrying fuel, and raised no suspicions. On arrival at Pintail it had halted, to wait its turn to cross the bridge, where the girls, thinking they had arrived at their destination, jumped out. John and I watched with some amusement as several shrieking, diminutive figures were carried from the surrounding scrub. The round up continued long after we left but several girls remained at large, faced with a long hike home.

The summer rains produced a spate of flood water and in May the river Imjin was brimming its banks, flowing at a fast rate. Somewhere upstream a pontoon bridge gave way. As the wreckage, swept down-stream, was a potential danger to other bridges, I went up to report on its position. The ground crew often accompanied flights in rear areas and my engine mechanic, Senior Aircraftsman Goodfield, was sitting behind me. We were accustomed to flying along the river and aware of the danger from overhead wires, slung from bank to bank to enable the passage of emergency supplies should the bridges become unusable. Seeing what appeared to be several half submerged pontoons and keeping an eye out for cables, which were normally marked with fluorescent bunting, I went down to within a few feet of the water to have a close look. Having verified that it was the wreckage I was seeking, I was about to pull up over Pintail bridge when a set of unmarked cables appeared immediately ahead and above. As I focussed on these in order to go under them there was a loud bang and the aircraft cartwheeled through the air. The wheels had struck a low cable which dipped into the centre of the river for the purpose of catching debris before it hit Pintail bridge. The engine stopped abruptly and there was silence except for rushing water. Goodfield went out of the righthand door and I tried to go through the left but found I was imprisoned in my seat. Well submerged, I now undid my harness and, on coming to the surface, found Goodfield having difficulty in keeping afloat because of his heavy boots. I managed to grasp him but my calf length flying boots, strapped firmly round my ankles, were pulling me down like two filled buckets and my swimming was not up to saving my companion. I eventually got my boots off and, clinging to one of the aircraft wheels which had come to the surface, I struggled ashore.

The sequel was bizarre. In something of a daze I walked back to the air strip where the new flight commander, Major Wilf Harris, sug-gested I should go to the field ambulance unit. I could see no reason for this because I was unhurt but I acquiesced, my wet clothes drying in the hot sun during the thirty minute jeep ride. It was an Indian unit who were, that day, giving a curry lunch party and I was ushered into the officers' mess as a guest. Seated next to the commanding officer, I picked at my food and my story came out. I was a patient not a guest. 'Don't worry,' he said, 'time is the best healer of all. A friend of mine killed three people in a car accident a couple of years ago and he is now as right as rain!' It was an insensitive comment which did nothing to help and I hitched a lift back to the flight where I was flying again the same afternoon.

Brigadier Peter Gregson was on hand when I landed. 'That was a pearler you took this morning,' he said. 'I don't think we need an enquiry.' But we were an air force unit and when the Royal Air Force, from their headquarters in Japan, insisted that an enquiry must be held, they got their way. It sat for a day and a half; its findings were 'pilot error' and the subject was closed. As the Indian doctor said, time heals everything, but if I had seen the wires, my engine mechanic would not have died and few days go by without me remembering it.

We lost a good commander when Wilf Harris was killed on the 2nd June 1953, Coronation Day. He set high standards but was approachable. If he thought someone was taking undue risks he would suggest that he was, perhaps, being too much of a sportsman. On Coronation Day, the war notwithstanding, there were certain festivities at headquarters and Wilf had been invited to signal the start. Driving back to the flight, he was rounding the end of the strip when his jeep was hit by an aircraft, killing him instantly. An American Thunder Jet, severely damaged by anti-aircraft fire, had been attempting to land. Among the rest of us, the senior was Captain Peter Tees from Canada and I assumed he would take command. However, later that afternoon, when I returned from a sortie, he said there was general agreement that I should become the commander. Appointment by election was unusual, probably unique, but the result suited me and it was a few weeks before someone back in England realised that a major's command in war was being filled by an officer who was not even a proper captain. (My substantive rank was lieutenant and I was a temporary captain by virtue of being a pilot.) Thus, in the closing stages of the Korean war I enjoyed this wonderful, independent command until, after six weeks, a senior major arrived from home.

Both sides wanted the war to end but it was only after interminable negotiations that a cease fire was agreed. Shooting stopped midmorning on the 27th July. I had spent four hundred and thirteen hours over the front, flying two hundred and fourteen sorties and engaging four hundred and seventy targets.

In the days immediately preceding the cease fire, the Chinese had mounted a number of local attacks in an attempt to secure more advantageous positions before the cease fire took effect, and had suffered severely in the process. When on 28th July I went out into what had been no-man's-land and passed a number of Chinese troops searching for their dead, it seemed natural to exchange a slight wave of the hand, a nod, a tentative smile. I was reminded of a conversation some months before with a visiting chaplain who felt sure, or at least felt he had to persuade us, that we were in Korea to fight for a cause. Not so we said, trying to explain that for whatever personal reason we were risking our necks, the common factor was that we were soldiers. And so, in a dried out padi field, a few British and Chinese soldiers acknowledged a common bond.

In late August I flew Peter Gregson into Panmunjong to meet some of the returning prisoners of war. There were chaotic, emotional scenes as United Nations prisoners of all nationalities came through. This reflected the success of the Chinese and North Koreans at breaking the indigenous discipline of national contingents in prison camps as a prelude to political indoctrination. The British regiments resisted this more successfully than most and it showed in their bearing on repatriation. I can see now the regimental sergeant major of the Gloucesters, who had been taken prisoner two years before, standing impassively, sipping tea from an enamelled mug, while all around him swarmed dozens of men not sure whether they were cheering or crying.

The war over, we needed to occupy ourselves and the brigadier turned to the river. The early summer rains were past but the water was still flowing fast. Lilo racing became the British sport and each day I would be ordered to reconnoitre a stretch of fast flowing river to which a column of jeeps could consign their officers early in the afternoon and recover them from downstream some time later. The air mattresses on which we normally slept now carried us down through the rapids, except for the brigadier, who had an aluminium canoe constructed from an aircraft drop tank. He led the water cavalcade carrying a red parasol but, as far as I remember, no paddle. Having, myself, barely escaped drowning three months before, I found the whole business rather frightening but it assisted in my rehabilitation.

With the advent of peace, things had to be tidied up and the American corps commander took exception to our gipsy encampment. There was even a danger that John and I would need to move from our helicopter crate into a regulation tent. The satisfaction of having done a good job during the war remained but it was with no regrets that I left Fort George for the last time on 1st October when John flew me to Seoul where I caught the train to Pusan. I had seen enough of Korea from the air and the train journey would provide me with a different perspective. In Pusan I embarked on the troop ship Empire Fowey for Singapore.

Chapter 4

Flying in Malaya

IN late October I was back in Malaya. Although, in 1953, the emergency there had been going for five years, the terrorists, in the main Chinese, had never attracted a sufficient measure of public support to make them credible as a revolutionary movement. Nevertheless, their aggressive tactics of ambush and surprise attack had threatened the fabric of government, prompting the deployment of an immense number of British, Ghurka and Malay troops. Although the high point of danger had passed, the terrorists continued to intimidate the rural population from whom, in spite of rigorous security measures, they often obtained food and information. There was a long haul ahead before they were finally defeated.

656 Squadron, which I was joining, had a crucial operational role, for it provided the only means of reconnaissance over deep jungle. Having located terrorist positions, light aircraft pilots were also frequently essential to the subsequent action, helping the infantry find their way through difficult country, marking targets for air strikes, dropping emergency supplies and observing artillery and naval bombardment. The crucial nature of this role was illustrated when the ageing Austers developed a serious defect some months before new aircraft could be made available. Metal fatigue was causing the engine shafts to fail in flight with the result that a number of pilots suddenly found their aircraft without a propeller. In normal circumstances the Auster would have been taken out of service pending a proper solution or the arrival of new aircraft.

As it was, the same Austers had to continue until new machines arrived many months later and, until then, the problem could be no more than alleviated by frequent inspection of the crank shafts and an order prohibiting us carrying passengers. Fortunately, by a combination of skill and good luck, all the pilots who lost propellers walked away from their wrecked aircraft.

The squadron headquarters, where I reported, was housed in a collection of huts beside Noble Field, a laterite air strip about two hundred and fifty yards long on the northern outskirts of Kuala Lumpur. 656 Squadron consisted of four flights positioned throughout the length of Malaya and it was to one of these that I assumed I would go. I was looking forward to flying operationally again and was disappointed and displeased when I learned that I was to be retained at squadron headquarters to fill the vacant position of intelligence officer. I had not taken up flying to pilot papers across a desk. Major Sandy Robertson, the squadron commander, sought to alleviate my disappointment by explaining that I would probably get enough flying to satisfy me, but it was with no high hopes that I took up the job.

There were two Austers in squadron headquarters and, as there seemed little for the intelligence officer to do, I turned my attention to these. They were used to support Headquarters Malaya Command, a large hutted establishment on a hill behind the air strip from whose sizeable complement of staff officers there was a ready supply of passengers who wanted to travel. However, I did not intend to become a taxi driver and looked around for other opportunities. I found there was a large jungle and rural area in the state of Selangor where no proper affiliation existed between the squadron and troops in the jungle and over which no regular surveillance was flown. I soon rectified these omissions, sharing the tasks with a sergeant pilot. Soon there was more than enough for the two of us to do and I enlisted the aid of the squadron commander and second-in-command and asked for a third aircraft. My activities resulted in an invitation to join the Selangor State War Executive Committee which was a feather in the cap of a mere captain, for this gathering, chaired jointly by a brigadier and the head of police, and attended by senior state government officials, coordinated all anti-terrorist operations in Selangor. My job, which had begun so unpromisingly, was turning out well, but I then caught jaundice.

It kept me in hospital for three weeks and off flying for six. Lying in bed I became concerned lest the progress I had been making in my new job should receive a fatal set back in my absence, as I had long since discovered that fresh ideas from eager young men invariably attract opposition. However, I need not have worried for, as soon as I was deemed fit to approach a telephone, I learned that Sandy Robertson had already decided to make me the commander of a new flight, Squadron Headquarters Flight, for the support of operations in Selangor.

My morale received a fillip while in hospital when I discovered I had been awarded the Distinguished Flying Cross for service in Korea. I say discovered because the official system had forgotten to tell me and I learned of the good news through a telegram from my mother who had been interviewed by a reporter from a local newspaper. The award had been published in the London Gazette a week earlier. Later, when I was shown a copy and considered the citation, I felt that the writer had done me proud. However, as I now look back over a span of thirty years, I see it all in a rather more sober light. As a young aviator, thriving on excitement and danger, it was with gay abandon that I did things which would now demand a good deal more conscious resolve.

When I left hospital, Anne and Maureen were on their way to join me. I had obtained a couple of rooms in one of the small government hotels known in Malaya as rest houses. Kuala Lumpur was filled with staff officers from headquarters Malaya and a house was difficult to find, but after fifteen months apart and with a daughter I barely knew, a rest house would do for a start. They sailed out on the troop ship Dilwara, arriving in mid-December. We spent several days in Singapore as an introduction to the sights and smells of the Far East before catching the night train to Kuala Lumpur and the rest house on Penang Road, then a pleasant residential area beside the race course. Pleasant or not, we hoped it would not be for long but the end came quicker than expected when the landlady announced she was closing within forty eight hours. The squadron rallied round, as service communities always do, and each of the officers living in Kuala Lumpur went on leave in turn, giving us somewhere to live whilst searching for a more permanent residence. With our heavier boxes in the quartermaster's store at Noble Field, we moved with minimum belongings every fortnight, a wearying process for Anne who was pregnant and feeling the heat. After three months we found a bungalow on a small estate whose occupants were a mixture of English, Chinese and Indians. It was approached down a rough track which twisted its way under tall coconut palms between the attap huts of a Malay kampong, before emerging at the half dozen white bungalows, situated in a bend on the Klang river, whose brown muddy waters drifted slowly past. Number 57 Jalan Penghulu Mat was to be our home for the rest of our time in Malaya.

Meanwhile, I had been flying again since the first of January. I had three aircraft and two other pilots, Captain Gerry Refoy and Staff Sergeant Walton. I could enlist the aid of the squadron commander and the second-in-command, both of whom were glad to help out in order to keep themselves in flying practice. Well over half of our flying was spent on visual reconnaissance, searching for evidence of terrorist activity in the jungle below. Viewed from above, the treetops merged into a single green canopy, mile after mile in all directions, casting a perpetual twilight over the jungle floor beneath. Every now and then something suspicious would flash past below, it was never more than a glimpse between the trees, visible only for a moment. It had to be pinpointed instantly with reference to whatever terrain features were on hand and its image retained in the mind, for there could be no circling to ease the difficulties of map reading or identification. Terrorists would flee, never to return, if a circling aircraft suggested they had been discovered. Having flown on to a distance at which the engine would not be heard, the pilot could circle, map in hand, and determine the exact grid reference. Evaluating what had been spotted was more difficult for it was seldom anything as positive as the sight of an attap and bamboo hut. A small patch of clear earth was probably all that had been seen and only an inspired guess would correctly identify whether it was caused by a fallen tree, cleared by animals or man made. A row of tapioca plants sometimes gave the game away but the terrorists were careful to conceal their cultivations even when there was an abundance of green all around. Such a sighting might occur at half hourly intervals but only once every ten hours was a report made of suspected terrorist activity, and not infrequently even these would prove to be spurious. Over the featureless north and south swamps of Selangor such flying was extremely boring, entailing hour after hour of straight and level flying at about a hundred feet above the level treetops. In the mountainous areas, flying entailed constant manoeuvring, turning, climbing and descending according to the shape of the forest below. Whether over the swamps or in the mountains, it was a tiring business, not helped by the buffeting air currents from mid morning onwards when towering white clouds began to build up as a prelude to the inevitable afternoon storms.

Having provided the infantry with a terrorist objective we would frequently assist them in making their attack, using a technique called contact reconnaissance. With visibility in the jungle seldom more than a few paces, accurate movement relied more upon navigational techniques than traditional map reading. It was unlikely that after a day's march a platoon could position itself with sufficient precision to attack an objective, invisible through the jungle thicket, only a few yards away. They would therefore put smoke up through the trees and we, knowing where the objective was, would give them a bearing to advance on and an approximate distance. In this way the attacking troops could quietly surround the terrorist hideout and the assaulting party plan their movements with certainty.

When something was needed in a hurry, we also provided assistance in the form of small supply drops, such as explosives or tools to cut a helicopter landing zone for the evacuation of casualties. Supply dropping from an Auster entailed removing the wireless set, a rectangular box some eighteen inches long, which normally sat to the right of the pilot, and also the right hand door. The supplies to be dropped could sit in the empty space beside the pilot and be pushed through the gaping door frame at the appropriate moment, the parachute being opened by a static line tied to one of the wing struts. Supply dropping was fun even in the flat swamps, while in the mountains it was positively exciting. Making a low, slow approach at half flap, the pilot would descend towards the white phosphorus smoke coming through the trees. If the infantry were in a valley the approach might well entail some difficult manoeuvres in the last few seconds. With the trees a few feet beneath the wheels and the sky momentarily obliterated by the smoke, the stores were pushed through the door. In an instant the pilot's right hand was back on the throttle, now slammed wide open as the aircraft lurched skywards. At fifty knots the flaps went up and the aircraft was once more in its natural environment.

Because of their emergency nature, supply drops were often unusual. I once dropped a three inch mortar which, due to its shape and size, could not be fitted entirely inside the aircraft. I therefore flew with the barrel beside me, stretching back into the fuselage, and the base plate swinging on the end of a line beneath the right hand door. While the base plate presented no problem, getting the barrel through the door with one hand while controlling the aircraft with the other was alarmingly difficult. On another occasion I almost came unstuck when dropping a large box of phosphorus grenades. They, also, would not fit inside the cabin and a considerable portion of the package projected into the slipstream causing a good deal more drag than I had anticipated. On take off the aircraft was reluctant to leave the ground and I passed the point at which I could safely stop before I recognised the danger. At the last moment the wheels lifted but I was still faced with the bamboo scaffolding of a tin mine which obstructed the northern aspect of Noble Field. I had insufficient flying speed to turn and it was only with a large element of luck that I skidded to the left of the obstruction. Potentially the most disastrous supply dropping sortie occurred when I was attempting to drop a consignment of explosives. The static line of the parachute failed to part, leaving fifty pounds of gelignite and their associated detonators swinging beneath the Auster. Of course, the detonators and the explosives should, for safety, have been in two separate drops but one takes short cuts in emergencies; they were going down gently by parachute, were well wrapped up and the recipients had been warned to stay well back just in case. I reached for the machete, carried in every aircraft, to cut the static line but someone had removed it. I tried violent manoeuvres but the package declined to part company. Having no wireless on board I was unable to warn my ground crew of the approaching danger and I therefore orbited the strip a couple of times to exhibit the problem. As I lined up on the approach, I could see the ground crew crouching in the monsoon drain, heads and knuckles above the parapet, ready to duck. The package beneath me hit the ground but the only bang was caused by my aircraft being brought suddenly to earth. Two new standing orders resulted: detonators and explosives were henceforth always to be dropped separately; the daily inspection of aircraft would ensure that a machete was always in position.

On Sunday the 13th June I completed a thousand flying hours. I do not know how the Royal Air Force would have rated my experience for I had flown nothing but very simple machines. On the other hand I had operated in conditions which would have been taxing even in far more sophisticated aircraft and was by now graded above average both as a pilot and a navigator.

Terrorist camps, positively identified as such by huts or cultivation beneath the trees, were sometimes dealt with by air strikes before the infantry were sent in. To ensure accuracy of bombing, the target was marked by a smoke flare dropped by the pilot who had discovered it. Target marking was another exciting activity as, in order to avoid alerting the occupants of the camp, there needed to be the shortest possible interval between the marker going down and the bombs falling. With a count down coming through his earphones from the bombing leader, the Auster pilot would orbit at a sufficient distance from the target for his engine to remain unheard and then dart in to release the marker thirty seconds before the bombs were released. The excitement came not merely from the necessity for precise timing but also from the need to fly unerringly to a target only seen once before.

In mid-July I discovered a large camp in the south swamp and a decision was made to mount a bigger air strike than ever before. It was to be part of a combined operation involving eight Lincoln bombers, a similar number of Hornet ground attack aircraft and follow up infantry.

It was scheduled for ten o'clock in the morning and would require a weather reconnaissance over the area several hours before, to confirm that conditions were suitable. Because Noble Field was sometimes covered by mist in the early mornings, I decided to position myself at Seremban the evening before the strike. Here I encountered the first hazard. John Hoare had recently arrived from Korea and was operating from Seremban, where the flight shared an officers' mess with the 11th Hussars. On the evening of my arrival, they were holding a mess party and it was two in the morning when I fell into a camp bed in John's hut. My alarm woke us at five, when, pulling on only shirt, shorts and sandals I stumbled to the aircraft and took off. Thirty minutes later I landed, reported by telephone to the air force in Singapore that the weather was clear and went back to bed, my alarm set again. Just before ten o'clock I was again aloft and in the target area, this time in proper order with the adrenalin pumping round, as accurate flying, clear vision and sharp reflexes would be required if I was to mark the right spot in the flat, featureless swamp. When, several days earlier, a brown patch of earth and four bashas had flashed beneath my wings, I had kept straight on, noting the compass heading and hoping that some recognisable feature would soon appear. There was a flame-topped tree after a few seconds and then nothing but the undulating green canopy until the grey fork of a dead trunk emerged from the background a minute or so later when I turned on a compass course to the edge of the jungle. These were the steps I had to retrace while through my earphones came the countdown. At 'Bombing in three', the grey fork appeared ahead and I pulled into a steep turn, holding it and circling until 'Bombing in two', when I levelled out into a shallow dive for the target. There was no flame-topped tree to be seen but, as my heart sank at the thought of failure, the huts appeared for the second time. I pulled the marker release, a trifle late but certainly near enough for the bombing pattern to obliterate the target. Breaking at right angles from the bombing run and with throttle wide open I raced across the tree tops until the reverberation of the exploding bombs overtook me. Then, with stick hard back, I pulled around and headed towards the pall of smoke and dust. An area of jungle several hundred yards each way was completely stripped of foliage. As I flew across it, branches and leaves were falling around me. I called in the Hornets who began to strafe the surrounding jungle, presumably in the hope of catching anyone who might be fleeing. When they had finished their task, I watched the string of Whirlwind helicopters set down a platoon of infantry in the cutting of an old logging track some miles away. Having sometimes accompanied them,

I knew they had twelve hours of hard slog ahead, much of it thigh deep in water and rotting vegetation.

By all accounts that air strike killed no enemy. There was no one at home when the bombs came down and although the infantry ambushed the remains of the camp and the equipment therein, its erstwhile occupants obviously decided not to return. In the context of Malaya, such operations played their part by reducing enemy morale and enhancing that of the civilian population, but whether they were cost effective is a moot point. For someone who was later in life to direct other anti-guerilla campaigns, it was an early lesson that in counter revolutionary warfare, fire power is less important than other more subtle operations concerning intelligence, psychological operations, and hearts and minds.

The Auster with which we were equipped was not designed to fly in bad weather, having only a very limited set of flight instruments which did not even include an artificial horizon. Officially, we were cleared to operate only under visual flight rules which required a clear view all around of some three miles. If we had followed the rules, we could not have fulfilled our many commitments and it was necessary to fly in conditions which nowadays would be considered unthinkable, given only our limited instrument panel. The new pilot started warily but, after a few months, his intimate knowledge of the country and recognition of the regular weather patterns behind the sudden tropical storms, enabled him to cope in almost all conditions. But no matter how experienced, he would still experience uneasy moments when a solid layer of dark, turbulent storm cloud above forced him to navigate the rain filled valleys at tree top height. In such circumstances one remembered the saying, 'There are old pilots and there are bold pilots but there are no old bold pilots', and prayed that if the weather ahead proved impassable, it had not also closed in behind.

Getting above the weather would solve one problem but create another for, without direction finding equipment, navigation above solid cloud depended upon rudimentary dead reckoning by compass and wrist watch. The brilliant white blanket turned to a murky grey as the aircraft sank into it and the descent became alarming when the ground remained unseen at a lower altitude than the hill tops surrounding the destination. Fortunately, my usual destination in such circumstances, Noble Field, was only twenty minutes from the coast and it was possible to get out over the sea and try again. When the blue-grey water became visible through the thinning cloud, I could turn for the shore and, under the lowering cloud, follow the road from Port Swettenham to Kuala Lumpur and home. If the weather was really bad, I could put down at the old, deserted Japanese air strip near the port and sit it out. My log book records one such occasion with the comment, 'Even the flies were walking.'

Domestically, Anne and I were placed like most other people of junior rank. Our bungalow was reasonably furnished with the bamboo and hardwood furniture typical of the Far East but was barely equipped to alleviate the heat and humidity. Air conditioning was a rarity not found in private houses. A single, clanking ceiling fan moved air around the living room while table fans propelled a flow of air through the mosquito nets at night; it was a matter of enduring a draught to keep cool in the hope that it would not also cause a chill. Isolated as we were, it was for Anne a miserable introduction to overseas service. With a Chinese amah looking after the household chores, there was little to fill the long days except an occasional coffee party or shopping expedition by taxi into Kuala Lumpur. The daily boredom was broken only at the weekends when there was time for dinner with friends or a visit to a cinema and restaurant in the Batu Road. In such circumstances, the Cameron Highlands, where we spent five days in a leave centre, seemed a world apart. The days were cool enough for a walk to be enjoyable and the evenings sufficiently cold to warrant a log fire in the bungalow. It was too short, however, to provide more than a temporary uplift.

Soon after returning from the Camerons Jane was born in the British Military Hospital Kinrara. I took off in the early morning on the 1st November and, on landing to refuel, I learned that in my absence, Anne had given birth to our second daughter. When she returned home, Anne now had a good deal more to do but there was too little recreation and I can understand why she disliked her time in Malaya as much as I enjoyed mine.

By the end of 1954, aerial activity in the jungle was forcing the terrorists to vacate their camps by day and we began to undertake reconnaissance at night, in the hope of seeing cooking fires beneath the trees. Most of the strips from which we operated were short, with difficult approaches, so that landing an Auster at night was a tricky undertaking. Even Noble Field had its hazards, with power lines across one end and a tin mine at the other. While the ground crew could adequately mark the runway with a flare path of cigarette tins filled with petrol-soaked cotton waste, they had no means of indicating a flight path which safely cleared all obstacles. I therefore devised a simple arrangement which became known as the Perkins angle of approach indicator. It consisted of two poles, positioned beside the air strip about three yards apart, on each of which hung a hurricane lamp. The lamps were coloured red and green and were so arranged on the poles that the line of sight between them pointed well above all obstacles on the approach. As the pilot came in to land he could be assured of a safe flight path providing the red light, which to him was the more distant one, always appeared higher than the green. This arrangement worked remarkably well until it attracted official attention by its very success one difficult night. I was approaching Noble Field during a particularly violent thunder storm and having great difficulty both in controlling the aircraft and seeing where I was going. Rain streaming over the windscreen reduced the flare path and red and green lights to an impressionist picture, while my night vision was impaired by the forked lightning which fractured the inky black every few seconds. I was about to touch down when there was an immense blue flash seeming to emanate from the aircraft itself. Simultaneously the lights in northern Kuala Lumpur went out. I had forgotten to wind in my trailing radio aerial which had caught the power lines as I passed over them. The incident attracted some publicity and the air force commander, being impressed with the performance, asked for technical details. A possible commendation turned to an expression of displeasure when he heard of the two poles and this unauthorised method was henceforth banned. Instead, we were issued with proper angle of approach indicators which, requiring a three tonner to transport them and a surveyor to install them, were of limited use to us.

My flight had a pet monkey which lived on the end of a tether and scampered around the verandahs of our offices. I returned one day from a sortie to find everyone at lunch and the monkey sitting beside several sacks of mail stacked outside the squadron office. When I walked out to take off again a few minutes later he was still there. I should have been suspicious of his contemplative manner for on my return the office area and the aircraft park were strewn with torn paper, while the clerks were attempting to piece together what they could from a fortnight's consignment of mail. At least half was beyond retrieval and we never knew what opportunities we had missed or whose questions we failed to answer. I only know that no one ever wrote asking why we had not replied.

As one of the squadron VIP pilots, I flew a number of interesting passengers. Lieutenant General Sir Geoffrey Bourne, who directed operations in Malaya, was a frequent and amusing passenger. He had lost an arm yet seemed not in the least inconvenienced. He played tennis and golf to a very high standard and it was only the simple act of putting on his wrist watch for which he required assistance. He would invariably order me to divert from our planned route, sometimes to view the result of an air strike or to study the nature of a particular piece of ground. Whatever the reason it meant we were breaking the rules for VIP flights which were supposed to follow roads and railways and adhere to strict flight plans. Lieutenant General Sir Hugh Stockwell and his dog were also my passengers, their combined weight causing us narrowly to miss the officers' mess roof on take off from Seremban. I also flew Duncan Sandys, Minister of Supply in Churchill's government, whose daughter, then only eleven, was to change the pattern of my life thirty years later.

We all flew at intense rates with an average each of between sixty and seventy hours a month. My log book shows that I flew ninety five hours and forty minutes in December 1954 and one hundred and thirty three hours fifty minutes in January 1955, the latter a record for army flying which I imagine has held to this day. The ground crew worked for long, hard hours in uncongenial circumstances to keep the aircraft serviceable and every so often there was a need to provide a change of environment. On these occasions I chose the east coast of Malaya, where, from Kuantan northwards, the coastline was particularly beautiful, free of terrorists and almost deserted.

The ground crew would set off in a small convoy of vehicles carrying tentage and all our requirements for a week. It would take them two days to negotiate the tortuous track to Kuantan and a further day on the coast road north to Trengannu, on which part of the journey several river ferries added considerably to the time taken. I followed with an Auster in which, droning through the sky at three thousand feet, there was nothing to do except keep the nose in the right direction and enjoy the magnificent view of unrelieved jungle forest in every direction. Once through the Bentong Pass, with its winding road leading north from Selangor to Pahang, a compass course could be set for Trengannu to the north east. From six thousand feet, an altitude chosen to skim the central mountain range ahead, the jungle took on a bluish tinge so that to the right, looking into the sun, it was difficult to perceive where sky and earth met. To the left the ground rose and fell in a series of undulating mountain ridges until it was lost in the foothills of the Cameron Highlands. Ahead was the sharp ridge line of the central range with here and there a rocky outcrop showing through the green. The individual trees became distinct as the ground rose sharply in front and within a few minutes the highest point in Malaya slid past beneath. It was marked by a metal cone, about the height of a man, carried there by intrepid surveyors from a previous generation, before helicopters eased the burden of such expeditions.

With the central range but a few feet below, it would have been an unimaginative pilot who did not give a thought to the consequences of engine failure, for engines did sometimes splutter to a stop. The drill, if that happened, was to glide as slowly as possible into the branches, pointing the nose between the tree trunks. With luck the wings and the petrol tanks therein would be torn off, leaving the fuselage and cockpit to slither to the jungle floor. It would be a long walk out but, if the pilot was uninjured, not unduly difficult for the jungle is well supplied with food and water. The danger would come at the jungle edge where, moving through the undergrowth in a proscribed area, the returning aviator might be mistaken for a terrorist. A number of pilots came unscathed through such adventures. On one occasion a staff sergeant pilot and his passenger, the latter a police officer, dressed smartly in starched shirt, shorts and Sam Browne, turned up after a fortnight, the police officer's knees rather the worse for wear. Pilots lost without trace were probably the victims of altogether different mishaps, crashing at full power while manoeuvring near the ground or hitting a hill in bad weather.

Two and a quarter hours out of Noble Field, Trengannu came into view, a sleepy little town beside a coastline of coconut palms and silver sand. It had a long grass strip, originally constructed by the Japanese during the war and now used occasionally by Malayan Airways who employed a man on a motor cycle to chase away the goats whenever one of their Dakotas wished to land. In our case we would buzz the strip and the goats would run off into the bush.

The beneficial effects of a week on the east coast came more from a change in activity than environment. The time was spent swimming, close inshore because of sharks, exploring the east coast by Land Rover and observing, from the air, the abundance of marine life. There would be giant rays, more than six feet across, basking on the surface and plunging to the depths with a mighty splash when the engine noise disturbed them. There were sharks appearing as sinister shadowy shapes beneath the surface. Giant turtles lay motionless on the surface, often ignoring our approach. The sea was sometimes like a sheet of glass. At these times, many other fish, the smaller in shoals and the larger singly, could be seen well below the surface. During the week, the pilots would change over and other flights would frequently find an excuse to send a visiting aircraft. At the end of a week, everyone returned with new vigour to Noble Field.

Throughout the length and breadth of Malaya there was a great variety of airstrips but almost all had one thing in common, some hazard which made landing difficult. At Port Dixon it was a crosswind which often reached twenty miles an hour. At Kuala Kubu Bharu, where we landed frequently to liaise with the infantry, the short airstrip nestled under the mountains and had a considerable slope. Irrespective of the direction of the wind it was necessary to land uphill, with the knowledge that there could be no last minute attempt to overshoot and try again if the approach was misjudged. At Bahau, the undulating nature of the fairway and the bunker before the fifth hole were well known hazards, particularly when landing at night. There were other more unusual difficulties like the crowd which gathered when I put down on a narrow track and were reluctant to give way when I wished to take off. I taxied slowly forward so as not to decapitate the nearer ones with my propeller but, as the front ranks parted to let me through, I came upon others still arriving. The process was repeated and by the time I had driven through the gathering throng and could surge forward for take off, I had come to a series of bends in the road. Fortunately there was a T-junction into which a number of helpers backed the tail of my aircraft to allow me to turn around.

In one or two places, when advantage was taken of the overnight hospitality of local planters, the hazard was usually impaired judgement and slow reaction the following morning. These hardy men lived a lonely life behind barbed wire, a gun always within reach, and were invariably pleased to see friendly faces. Isolation bred eccentricities and one evening, after supper with the manager of a particularly isolated plantation, I noticed an extraordinary ornament on an aspidistra stand in the corner of the room. There, highly polished and gleaming white, with a light inside so it shone like a halloween lantern, was a skull. It had a bullet hole in the centre of the forehead. I asked about it, unsure whether the brandy had affected my vision, and was told it was the skull of a terrorist who had been killed outside the manager's house, buried and later exhumed for display.

The Royal Navy added considerably to the weight of munitions expended in the south swamp, or, as I sometimes felt, on the swamp itself. I was frequently involved in this bombardment, controlling from the air the six gun broadsides from the six inch guns of HMS *Liverpool* and *Newcastle*, and smaller, but still significant amounts from the frigates HMS *Comus* and *Concorde*. The huge shells whistled through the air like so many express trains, sometimes bursting in the treetops, scattering lethal fragments over wide areas, and at other times hitting more solid trunks lower down, smashing the forest to matchwood. As with air strikes, the most significant effect was upon morale. Captured Chinese terrorists testified that the bombardment kept them on the move and drove some to surrender.

The ships were normally anchored and one day, when the shells were falling inaccurately, an unknown voice explained over the radio that this was because the ship was swinging at anchor and the plotting mechanism which normally allowed for this movement had gone wrong. I asked why an anchor could not be dropped at the other end and received the sharp reply, 'You do your bloody job and I'll do mine!' Thirty years later, when Admiral Sir Henry Leach was staying with me, I learned what caused this acerbic rejoinder. In the course of discussion on naval bombardment, I told him of this incident. He remembered it well for his had been the unknown voice. The reverberations caused by all guns firing simultaneously had broken the crockery in the captain's day cabin and upset arrangements to receive the Sultan of Selangor who was about to come on board. Henry, the ship's gunnery officer, having just been the subject of the captain's wrath, was in no mood to treat with a mere pilot.

In May 1955 I was awarded the Selangor Distinguished Conduct Medal which had been awarded to a foreigner only once previously, posthumously to the head of special branch. The generous citation was a considerable boost at a time when I was tired and rundown.

I ended my flying career on 2nd August 1955 having, a few days previously, passed my two thousandth flying hour. At the end of my last flight I stall-turned above the airstrip for the benefit of the onlooking ground crew, left too little space to recover in comfort and only by pulling very hard back on the stick avoided hitting the ground, almost blacking out and passing between two palm trees. The ground crew thought this near miss had been put on for their benefit. I thought that two thousand flying hours in three years had been almost too much.

A week later we were on our way home, twenty eight days from Singapore to Liverpool on the troop ship Empire Clyde. It was built for the Atlantic run and had no air conditioning or laundry. The husbands shared cabins at one end of the ship and the wives and children at the other. Anne fell out with the ship's commandant who objected to Jane, then nine months old, sleeping below decks during the daily inspection. It was a dreadful journey but there were two months of accumulated leave ahead and three good years under my belt.

Korea and Malaya had enabled me to climb out of a rut into which the peace time army in Europe had settled, overburdened by the national service sausage machine in which bullshit counted for more than battle training. Fortunately where I had just been, the national servicemen, who mentally rebelled against such anachronistic inanities in training as polishing the studs of their boots, went into action with a will. It was a different army in Korea and Malaya, one in which my enthusiasm at last gained recognition. I had been graded above average for the first time in my annual assessments.

There was a postscript still to come. While on leave I received a letter inviting me to Buckingham Palace to be presented with the MBE and DFC. I had, of course, expected a summons to receive the latter but the MBE came as a surprise and I wrote back asking if there had been an error. There was no mistake; someone had again omitted to tell me.

Chapter 5

Aldershot, Pakistan and Ball Buttons

AT last I seemed to be a desirable military commodity for, when I reported to the War Office to discuss my next posting, the people dealing with me announced with some surprise that the officer cadet training unit at Mons Barracks, Aldershot, had asked for me. This was most unusual, they said with some pique, as the selection for such a coveted appointment was usually made by them. What had happened was that John Hoare, already at Mons, had mentioned me to the chief instructor there who, having looked up my record, had arranged my posting. I was to report on a Thursday, with a view to taking charge of a troop of field artillery cadets who were assembling the following Monday.

My recent gunnery experience had been concerned exclusively with controlling fire at the sharp end, in sight of the enemy, and, as I was somewhat rusty in the calculations required on gun positions, I spent some time during my leave refreshing my memory and learning the latest procedures. Thus, I arrived feeling absolutely confident and looking forward immensely to the task ahead. I then learned that plans had changed as there was an urgent need for light anti-aircraft officers. In this branch of gunnery I had no experience and I decided that all I could hope to do was to learn enough to keep a day or two ahead of my cadets. It was hard work but when they were commissioned four months later, none had guessed at my predicament—there was no doubt that teaching a bunch of intelligent young men was a very good way to learn, particularly when assisted, as I was, by several experienced NCOs.

The cadets, all national servicemen, came from varying back-grounds, split fairly evenly between public and state schools. Between these, the former were more likely on arrival to fit the traditional military mould but by the end of their time at Mons any residual difference tended to be largely superficial. Some cadets had delayed their national service in order to complete their university education and by reason of their greater maturity and experience usually did better at Mons but those who obtained their degrees after national service probably benefited most in the long run. With thirty young men rigorously selected before arrival, it would have been surprising to have many failures and, although sometimes a cadet's leadership qualities seemed doubtful, it was always worth looking for reasons and giving him a second chance. Leadership qualities could easily be undermined by an inability to master some technical aspect of the work and would burgeon once this confidence sapping problem had been mastered. Some of the instructional staff took a less tolerant view and attempted to apply a further measure of selection based on their own high standards but failing to allow sufficiently for inexperience or immaturity. I saw myself more as a tutor put there to develop qualities which a previous selection system had perceived these young men to have. I thought it a highly rewarding job.

All the courses—both anti-aircraft and field artillery, to which I later returned—ended with a week at practice camp. The anti-aircraft practice took place on the Welsh coast at Aberystwyth, which was new to me, while the field artillery practised at Sennybridge where I already felt I knew every blade of grass. At Aberystwyth we fired over the sea at a canvas sleeve, about the size of a small aircraft, towed by a very long wire behind a jet aircraft. It was not easy to hit but the shooting was usually good enough to send it fluttering into the sea several times during the week so that when, after several days of a particular camp it had not been hit, I told my troop in no uncertain terms that they needed to do a good deal better. It was not, I said, that as officers they would be doing the shooting but that their men would certainly expect them to know how. The troop joker suggested that I should demonstrate how it should be done, knowing that, unlike them, I was not in practice. A reprimand for insubordination, merited though it was, would have been an inadequate answer so I stepped into the gunner's seat. As the target came into view I fired one burst, paused and was about to fire a second when, to a loud cheer from behind me, the target fell into the sea. I had established a reputation which, I learned later that day, was entirely unfounded. When my troop sergeant recovered the target, there were thirty yards of towing wire still attached to it; I had missed the target by a wide margin but a freak shot had cut the wire. My sergeant kept the secret and I retained my reputation as a hot shot.

Although an indifferent shot with the light anti-aircraft gun, I still retained my skill with the rifle, carbine and pistol and represented Mons in various shooting events. I had not retained my speed as a sprinter, at least in comparison with the fit young men in their early twenties with whom I was surrounded, and in athletic events had to content myself with a place in the relay teams. I scraped a place in the unit rugby team playing in the second row alongside a Cambridge blue who, in a very short time, added considerably to my knowledge of the game. Riding was another recreational activity available at Mons but the members of the saddle club were all experienced horsemen and I, never having ridden before, felt inhibited from joining. However, the sight of my fellow officers on horseback led me to believe it was an experience to be sampled and I joined a short equitation course with the King's Troop at St John's Wood. Here, assisted by a horse called Watchman, a recent winner in the pistol, sword and lance event at Earls Court, I learnt the rudiments of horsemanship in a fortnight. By the time I was thrown and spent two days in bed, I could jump a five bar gate and ride bare back, admittedly with what was described as a poor posture and an indifferent seat.

Wherever the Brigade of Guards hold sway there are impeccable standards, a good deal of shouting and stamping of feet. So it was at Mons where, with their pace sticks tucked smartly beneath their arms, drill sergeants were to be seen moving briskly in all directions. No aspect of barrack life escaped their attention. The path between the officers' mess and the parade ground was heavily strewn with leaves in autumn and, as soon as it was swept, more fell from above. In order to solve this problem on the occasion of a VIP visit, the sergeant major in charge of arrangements arranged for a party of cadets to attach ropes to the tops of the trees and then, chanting in unison to ensure coordinated movement, shake down the leaves once and for all.

When a young private soldier failed to salute an officer from afar, a drill sergeant was on hand. Distance was no excuse and the offender, on being marched in front of the company commander, was confined to barracks for seven days. I thought this was remarkably savage punishment, particularly as the soldier was married, but was told to mind my own business. A day or two later the soldier's young wife appeared in barracks pushing a pram. She walked boldly up to the company commander, told him that as the army had taken her husband, it could also take her baby, turned on her heel and vanished. She was eventually traced to her mother's address in the north of England but meanwhile the soldier had to be allowed home to care for the baby.

During the previous three years I had begun to look ahead and think of the army in terms of a career to higher rank rather than, simply, as an exciting life. I needed a place on the staff college course, which lasted a year and was essential for anyone who wished to get on. The first step was to obtain a recommendation from my commanding officer, then to pass an examination to make me eligible for selection and finally to have sufficiently good reports to be among those chosen. The examination, which took place annually, comprised six papers, three in tactics, and one each in military law, military history and current affairs. Candidates were allowed three attempts to achieve a pass in all papers at one sitting but, leaving nothing to chance, I worked hard and was relieved to find I had passed the exam on my first attempt in 1957 and had been selected to undergo the course in 1958.

The Staff College is known to the British Army as Camberley, for that is where it is situated, but each year two students were selected to attend staff colleges in Commonwealth countries and candidates were invited to state a preference. My personal preference was for the Staff College at Quetta, in Pakistan, where the course was based on the Camberley syllabus but offered the exciting prospect of seeing the North West Frontier and other interesting places. However, since domestically Anne and I were enjoying life in a comfortable house in Farnham, a stark contrast to the three years of her first overseas tour, she was in no mood for a further foreign adventure. I therefore opted for Camberley but fortune was again on my side and I was selected as one of the two British students for Quetta. Getting there with enough provisions to last the year required considerable planning as many day-to-day commodities were not available in Pakistan at that time, while others were scarce and commanded exorbitant prices. I calculated how much would be required to last a year, down to such items as coffee, cornflakes, boot polish and soap, and commanded the Army and Navy stores to deliver the necessary crates to the dockside at Liverpool for loading on the Caledonia, the ship on which we were to travel out at the end of the year.

After troop ships and liberty ships, a stateroom on the Caledonia was a luxury, indeed. As travelling companions we had the Hanson family, Dave, Lee and their two children, who were to be the Canadian Army representatives at Quetta during 1985. Christmas 1957 was spent at sea, the festivities enjoyed by all except Maureen and Jane who were confined to their cabin with chicken pox. I sent a telegram to the British Defence Adviser in Karachi advising him of this illness and received a somewhat alarming reply to the effect that if the Pakistan authorities discovered this, the children would not be allowed to disembark. We therefore acquired two wide brimmed hats and the girls went ashore with the brims well pulled down and held in place by large scarfs tied under their chins. We explained that they had delicate skin and were unused to the fierce sun.

Our destination, Quetta, was some four hundred miles north of Karachi, a twenty four hour journey in a bare railway compartment with pull-down bunks. The defence adviser had kindly provided us with blankets, pillow and a hamper of food and drink, giving us strict instructions not to buy food at any of the railway stations for fear of tummy trouble. The first day's journey, across the Sind desert was hot and dusty, and it was a surprise to awake on the second morning to a chill in the air. We were now within a hundred miles of Quetta and climbing through the foothills towards the Bolan Pass, at the entrance of which the train acquired a second locomotive. With one pulling and one pushing, we zigzagged our way upwards between the bare brown crags which, as we approached Quetta, were covered with a recent fall of snow, for we were now at five thousand feet. On arrival we were met by Colonel Donald Hildick-Smith, one of three British instructors at Quetta, and by mid-day had arrived at the staff college. It was a low sprawling building with verandahs typical of that part of the world, dominated by a square, yellow brick tower, and was situated on the edge of the Quetta cantonment. Vaughan Road, on which we were to live, was no more than a track on the very periphery, so that our bungalow afforded an uninterrupted view across a couple of miles of rocky plateau to the magnificent mountain peak of Murdar which overlooked the whole of Quetta.

From the very beginning, I recognised the atmosphere of British India, reflecting the impressions I had acquired from books and films of the Raj. As a captain I had a full retinue of servants headed by Francis, the bearer, whose book of chits began when he was a mess boy with the Lancashire Fusiliers and included a recommendation from when he had been a general's butler. He was now a little past his best but still spritely and smart in a long blue coat with brass buttons. Next in seniority came the *khansama*—the cook, followed by the *mali*—the gardener, the *ayah*—the children's nurse, and the sweeper. The *ayah* apart, they were a good humoured lot and a great success but they could have taught even the British trades unions a thing or two about restrictive practices. The *ayah* was a failure, her method of keeping the children quiet was to allow them to do as they wished and we dismissed her, not to be replaced, after she had given them the boot polish to play with.

I had allowed a fortnight in which to get to know the Pakistan Army before the staff course started and I spent this time visiting infantry, armoured and artillery units in the Quetta area. The Pakistan tribesmen, being tough and hardy, made excellent soldiers. The Pathans, from the North West Frontier, where any man of stature served some time in the army, had the most fearsome reputation, but the Baluchis and Punjabis matched them in martial qualities. The more senior officers, lieutenant colonels and above, had all served in the Indian Army when it was part of the British order of battle and most of them had extensive wartime service. The younger officers were relatively inexperienced, having had no active service of any sort, but they were keen and well trained. Again there was a whiff of the Raj, for their traditions, demeanour and attitudes towards their soldiers were exactly as described by Kipling when he wrote of an earlier era.

The course, totalling eighty, provided a good international cross section of students, all in their late twenties or early thirties. There were about sixty from Pakistan itself, an Australian, an American, Dave Hanson from Canada, two of us from Britain, a couple of Indonesians and a variety of Arabs. We were split into syndicates of ten each guided by an instructor, a lieutenant colonel who had commanded a regiment and in most cases seen action in the Second World War. In the early stages, some of our work was done individually but, as the course progressed, we worked entirely as syndicates, either in discussion of particular topics or, with each of us playing a particular role, producing the solution to a variety of war gaming problems. We spent long days in the countryside on tactical exercises. On these occasions, as we assembled after breakfast to await our vehicles, I would arrive laden with a map case, shooting stick, thermos and a haversack, while my Pakistani friends sauntered forth quite unencumbered. We would stand around chatting in the morning sun until the vehicles arrived and then, timed to perfection as we boarded, servants would come running from all quarters bringing map cases and haversacks for their masters. As in Kipling's time, officers were not expected to carry things in public. The course was hard work but fun and, as one of the few students who had been to war, I could speak with the confidence which comes only from experience. I found myself, increasingly, playing a leading part in the proceedings and felt that it was certainly the most intellectually stimulating period in my military life so far.

Pakistan was a country with no middle class. It was still suffering from the effects of partition eleven years earlier when the Indians, who had filled most administrative posts, left for India and were replaced by some eight million Muslim refugees. The founder of the nation, Mohammed Ali Jinnah, had intended that Pakistan should become a modern secular democracy with sovereignty vested in the people and equal rights for all, regardless of creed or caste. However, without the industrial base which India possessed and with no middle class, Jinnah's aspirations remained unfulfilled at the time of his death. Since then, lethargy and corruption had become widespread so that, for example, the pursuit of a sugar or flour permit would entail hours, possibly days, of queuing, a process circumvented only by a five rupee note. A gun licence cost more, only a rupee and a half for the official piece of paper but ten rupees unofficially for the official who signed it. Dressed in threadbare jacket and baggy trousers, he sat in a sparsely furnished office decorated only by the files stacked around the walls and permeated with the smell of curry warming on the stove, the pipe of which was draped with chapattis being cooked for tiffin. Bribery, an inevitable concomitant to this environment, had led to a black market which monopolised all imports so that a bar of chocolate, which cost three pence in Britain, fetched seven shillings and six pence—if it could be found in the bazaar. To the newcomer, it seemed that integrity was confined to the armed forces who, steeped in British tradition, were wary of politics and commerce.

Against such a background, it was not surprising that my fellow officers cast covetous eyes at the contents of my bungalow for they had money to spare and nothing on which to spend it. Over dinner, I would be asked openly if I had yet agreed to sell my crockery, electric fire, bedding or anything else which came to mind. Within a few weeks it was all, less the silver, already sold and paid for at the exact British price of new equivalents, with delivery promised when I left Pakistan at the end of the year. Having arrived with a mountain of boxes we would return home with no more than a few suitcases.

Life in Quetta was enhanced by its healthy mountain climate which, even in mid-summer, escaped the fierce heat of the plains and provided a dry atmosphere. In winter it was possible to sit comfortably in the sun without a jacket when a few feet away, in the shade, an overcoat would be needed. It was an ideal climate for almost everything except brewing, which Dave Hanson and I were attempting as, due to exorbitant taxes, the price of drink was ten fold what it was in Britain.

The horse played an important part in our lives. Back at home I could not afford to ride; here I could hardly afford not to. The horses belonged to an Animal Transport Regiment, ostensibly established against a potential war time requirement but, in fact, maintained for recreation. For seven and a half rupees a month, the cost of insurance, an officer would have the exclusive use of a horse which would be stabled, maintained and groomed by the army. I had two such animals, polo ponies, well trained and sufficiently long in the tooth to be amenable to an indifferent rider like me. Each morning, once the cold weather had gone, a *syce* would bring one of my ponies to the bungalow and I would canter out towards Murdar, returning for breakfast at seven thirty before starting work at eight. Three times a week we played polo and I eventually became first reserve for the staff college team. Each weekend there would be a riding breakfast when we would paperchase to one of the orchards around Quetta where our families would be awaiting us. All this, including the insurance for the two ponies, cost me the equivalent of only thirty shillings a month.

Just as I was beginning to think how good I was becoming, I came a cropper. The warning lights should have lit up when, on a borrowed pony at full gallop after a ball, the animal failed to stop, crossed a main road and carried me far in the countryside before I could bring it under control. When I returned to the ground, in time to join the last chukkar, I thought I had taught the pony a lesson, but he had the last say and two days later deposited me on some rocky ground, necessitating several days in bed. Had I not been wearing a polo helmet, which was ruined by the fall, I might never have recovered.

Squash was a national game and I played in the early evenings whenever I was not occupied with polo. The squash courts were a stone's throw from my bungalow and the professional had introduced himself to me on the day of my arrival in Quetta. He arrived on my doorstep even before the luggage had been unloaded and, confusing me with my namesake, who was the British Army squash champion, challenged me to a game. I immediately hired him to teach me for a rupee an hour. I fell far short of local standards and his seven year old son would stand in the centre of the court, changing his racquet from hand to hand while I circled desperately around him.

I soon found I had seriously miscalculated the amount of provisions we would need, so that, in no time at all, we were reduced to the local economy. It was perfectly adequate and even the children became accustomed to the hot curry produced by the *khansama*—he was from United Provinces in India, where the curry is traditionally hotter than in Pakistan. We had been warned by the defence adviser in Karachi of the dangers to the tummy of eating local food, particularly fruit unless it was washed in pinky-panee, a weak solution of potassium permanganate. Drinking water was also to be boiled. However, we soon became tired of these precautions but no ill consequence befell us when we ceased them. Indeed, we acquired a natural immunity which enabled us to participate in local events without suffering the after effects which some other Europeans always used to dread. We even ate at the restaurant in Quetta where, if you wanted cutlery or napkins you took your own, and if not, and you ate your meal with a chappati in the manner of the locals, there was a tap outside where you could wash your hands and face.

There was a fair amount of rough shooting to be had and, although I never counted it as one of my sports, I joined in as a means of seeing the country and meeting people. Sometimes it was simply a matter of an afternoon's walk while on other occasions it was organised with some style, as when I joined a shikar arranged by a local brigadier. There were a dozen of us with guns and we first shot *chikoor*, a fast flying bird rather like a grouse. For beaters we had a company of soldiers, about a hundred in all, who ran hither and thither along the hill tops, shouting and clapping their hands, to scare the birds into the wadi along which we were concealed. On this, my first outing, I found that the conventions of shooting which were rigorously applied at home, were not always observed here. It was not a question of whose bird it was, simply who fired first, and one needed to be alert to what the guns on either side were doing for fear of getting in the way of one of their low shots. Moreover, when the party gathered together for a break or prior to redeploying, not everyone unloaded their weapons. Having exhausted both *chikoor* and soldiers we drove on and, after crossing a vast expanse of salt flats, arrived for tea at a square, squat, white painted fort near the Iranian border. We were first invited to inspect the Vickers machine gun, its ammunition belt blancoed white and each cartridge highly polished, pointing across the empty plain as if a cavalry assault was imminent. The three inch mortar was next on our itinerary, every part gleaming. Even the row of bombs, laid out ready for instant action, were so highly polished that I wondered if they were still of the right calibre. Then it was tea and, as we sat at a long table attackng sandwiches and sticky cakes, a soldier with a fan stood behind each chair to prevent the flies attacking us. Leaving the Kiplinesque scene behind, we soon arrived at a small encampment which, although erected only for our overnight stay, was lacking in neither comfort nor ceremonial, having armchairs, white jacketed waiters and a smartly dressed quarter guard which lowered the flag at sunset. We awoke the following morning to find a detachment of camels, bedecked in regimental colours, waiting to transport us to the lake where we were to shoot duck. When the convoy set off, each animal was followed by a bearer carrying the rider's gun. At the end of the day my bag of no more than two or three birds was a meagre response to the logistics behind our shikar and a small contribution to the numbers shot, but at least I had hit mine on the wing. All around me there had been a continuous fusillade as the birds, paddling unsuspectingly past the butts, were blasted out of the water. The weekend had been laid on in the style of the Raj but I am not sure it would have entirely approved.

Out riding one weekend I fell into conversation with a visiting air commodore who suggested that I should visit Gilgit, a place to the far north in Azad Kashmir, described in the old days as the place where three empires met: British, Chinese and Russian. I thought that it would be a wonderful venture but there would not be time during my leave to get there, for the journey north from Rawalpindi, along tortuous tracks through the Karakoram mountains, would take at least a week in travel. The air commodore offered to fly me and, when the time came, provided a Beverly transport aircraft which was rather larger than necessary, for there were only three of us bound for Gilgit, Dave Hanson the Canadian, David Reynolds the other British student and me. However, we filled it with Pakistani officers going on leave to Rawalpindi and, having dropped these off, we found ourselves flying several thousand feet above the upper reaches of the Indus where it flows out of the mountains of central Asia. The majestic snow covered slopes rose on either side of us, the highest peaks softened by plumes of snow and feathery clouds. Climbing steadily, we passed under the massive form of Nanga Parbat, at 26,660 feet the sixth highest mountain in the world, and soon afterwards saw beneath us the junction of the Indus and the Gilgit rivers, a mass of foam where the waters rushed together. Then, under the nose appeared the small town of Gilgit, nestling in a bowl in the mountains, and the short, one way air strip which reminded me of some of those I had used in Malaya, once you were committed on the final approach there could be no second chance. As we drove away from the air strip, apart from the aircraft which had brought us and two or three military jeeps, we might have been living in the last century. With no electricity and no transport other than small mountain ponies, life was extremely simple if somewhat arduous. The area was garrisoned by the Gilgit Scouts, who would be our hosts during the next week, and we arrived in their mess as they were giving a cocktail party for the Mir of Hunza, the ruler of an adjacent part of the territory. Cold drinks were being served from a large ice chest and, without much thought, I asked one of my hosts how they obtained their ice. He said he would show me later and the following morning as we sat at breakfast he pointed through the window to a party of men climbing the mountain side, 'There goes the ice fatigue'.

We spent the next few days walking in the mountains or exploring further afield by jeep. Several of the important tracks radiating from Gilgit, originally no more than pony trails, had been widened to take a jeep. Along these our driver bounced at a fair speed, confident that there could be no vehicle approaching around the next bend, which was never more than fifty yards away. There was a frightening, unimpeded view of the valley floor several thousand feet below. Occasionally there was a fissure in the mountainside, a yard or two across, crossed by a couple of hefty planks; here we would get out and guide the driver over. Sometimes there were rock falls which we needed to clear before proceeding. All around us was breathtaking scenery of incredible beauty on a gigantic scale.

Gilgit was the place through which polo had been imported into the British Empire from Persia and in this remote mountain area it was still played in its original form. I had been warned not to participate by a polo playing colleague and close friend, Fazle Haq. He admitted that even he, consummate horseman and polo player though he was, would hesitate before playing at Gilgit but I feared it would be difficult to decline an invitation. However, the local players were engaged in a tournament during our stay and I was saved from the risk of ignominy or injury. Watching the play I understood why Fazle had been so emphatic in his warning for it was played, virtually bare back, at break neck speed on small ponies who seemed to have mouths of iron. It was a game designed for a community where almost every man owned a horse, but only one horse. With a field that was long and narrow, perhaps a hundred and fifty yards long and thirty across, the sport could be played at speed with less sustained galloping than in modern polo so that a single pony could last an entire game. There were no saddles, at best there was a cushion held in place by a surcingle, while the bridles and bits were equally rudimentary. The polo sticks were cut from local trees where a thinner branch left a thicker one, providing a natural mallet head and shaft. These not infrequently broke and small boys equipped with an armful of replacements ran among the horses offering a new stick whenever it was required. There were no rules and, while no one played dangerously with intent, it was obviously a good deal more hazardous than the modern game and one in which I would not have lasted for more than a few minutes. The number of players varied, depending upon who wanted to play but it seemed usually to be about six a side. Play was started, and after a goal restarted, by a player taking the ball in the same hand as his stick, throwing it forward into the air while at full gallop down the field, and attempting to hit it further on its way. A spectacular stroke when it succeeded. It seemed that the whole district turned out to watch, crowding onto the dry stone wall which surrounded the pitch. It could be hazardous even to watch and sitting on the dry stone wall we had frequently to lift our legs sideways and out of the way as ponies came thundering past, or when one player put another into balk by riding him into the wall. Throughout the game the local band wailed and beat their drums, the noise rising to a crescendo whenever a goal was scored. It was a game which created an imagery of Mongol horsemen, a spectacle created by men who thought nothing of it and who doubtless had learned to ride as soon as they could walk.

While we were in Gilgit we heard that General Ayoub Khan, the head of the army, had staged a coup, placing the country under martial law. It was with reluctance he had done this, having virtually been forced into it by the corruption of politicians and the parlous state of the economy. There was an immediate improvement, as we discovered on our return to Quetta. Prices were pegged at reasonable levels, bribery had vanished and even the taxi drivers were reluctant to take tips for fear of being accused of over charging. I felt sad in later years that the promise of those early days had not been fulfilled but at least the coup enabled Pakistan to survive with a reasonable average standard of living. Without it the country would have gone one of a number of ways all less preferable to the actual outcome, whatever its imperfections.

My other major excursion in Pakistan was to the North West Frontier, going there with Ghulam Yazdani, a fellow student who, as a leading member of the renowned Peshawar Vale Hunt, was well fitted to introduce me around. We planned, first, to travel to Rawalpindi by train but on arrival at Quetta railway station found all seats booked for that day's train. Rather than delay our departure we opted to go third class which meant travelling in a large compartment with no seats, surrounded by people, their chickens and their cooking. We each secured an inviolate space by spreading out our bedroll, that piece of baggage varying between a peasant's bundle of blankets tied with hemp and an officer's valise, which seemed to accompany every traveller on the sub-continent. It was an experience best savoured in retrospect: chappatis and curry from station barrows, shaving under a running tap at a wayside halt and listening to interminable stories from fellow travellers who all, a decade after partition, seemed to have a soft spot for the British.

Yazdani and I (he preferred to be called Yazdani, there being no general rule in Islam concerning the use of family names and given names) spent several days in the officers' club in 'Pindi, an old, single storey building where life seemed still to be ordered in a colonial style with officers snapping their fingers for a whisky and soda and smartly dressed waiters sporting starched pugrees. A bearer was appointed to look after me. He appeared at half past six with early morning tea and, if I was not already awake, would rouse me with a gentle shake and whispered, 'sahib'. He would have shaved me in bed had I desired but, preferring not to trust my neck to his cut-throat, I used the Victorian jug and basin in what passed as a bathroom and then splashed about a bit in the galvanised hip-bath before seating myself on the highly burnished pot with its mahogany seat. Meanwhile, my shoes were being polished and my clothes for the morning laid out in the bedroom. In the evenings there was a somewhat similar ritual when preparing for dinner. From 'Pindi we caught the train, this time having reserved our seats, to Peshawar where we used the artillery mess as a base for our further expeditions.

We took a jeep through the Khyber Pass, that north western gateway to the Indian sub-continent which features so largely in British regimental history, stopping first at Jumrood to visit the massive fort of yellow stone which guards the eastern end of the pass. We then drove, our jeep seldom out of second gear as the road twisted and climbed, to the garrison headquarters at the top of the Khyber, passing the regimental crests, set in the rock face, of the many regiments which had served in this area. Then it was downhill to the frontier at Landhikotal and the broad valley which leads into Afghanistan.

On another day we drove off the beaten track into the tribal areas, accompanied by one of Yazdani's soldiers who, as a local, could guarantee us safe transit. The tribal areas were administered by the tribes themselves and government law pertained only on the highways. Tribesmen firing across the government road might well excite the attention of the police or military, but when people shot each other on the land on either side, the tribes themselves administered justice. We stopped for a meal at village where the headman was delighted to welcome a British officer, not having seen one for many years. His vocabulary was unmistakably British. 'The last time I saw one of you chaps', he said, 'I was shooting at him!' We moved on to Durra which had a thriving cottage industry in armaments. Here, in thatched huts, using the most primitive tools, craftsmen were making weapons of all sorts: pistols, rifles, even Bren guns. They were exact replicas of those made in the ordnance factories at home and if anything gave away their tribal origin it was only the slight irregularities of the hand stamped registered number and, perhaps, the slightly heavier weight. There were no power driven tools, simply files, hacksaws, hand drills and hand turned lathes. Small boys were undergoing their apprenticeship at some of the simpler or more repetitive tasks, like operating the pull-push rod which cut the rifling in barrels. The weapons, due to the inferior quality of the steel, would not last long in constant use but the tribesmen were not in frequent battle. If, however, a more durable weapon was required the solution was to sneak into a military establishment and effect a substitution.

During this leave Yazdani and I also went north to Murdan where we visited Fazle Haq at home and met a number of old soldiers and senior officers from his regiment, the Guides Cavalry. We returned through Lahore, the bustling, busy centre of the Punjab.

The year at staff college was a testing time for those Pakistani wives who used this period to break out of purdah. Since the age of puberty the vast majority of them had kept their faces heavily veiled when in the presence of men; their marriages had been arranged and their only adult conversation with the opposite sex had been with their husbands. Not many years ago they would have continued in this manner all their lives but there was now a tendency, particularly among those with successful husbands, to come out of purdah when in society, although they would cover themselves when returning to their own families. At dinners and cocktail parties in Quetta one therefore come across a number of extremely attractive, well educated women who for the first few months were at a complete loss in mixed company.

The course ended in December. We spent Christmas in Quetta, the New Year in Karachi and boarded the Circassia shortly afterwards for the voyage home. It had been a good year, not least because Anne had enjoyed it and would no longer automatically equate overseas tours with the dreary life she had led in Malaya. I felt that in Quetta I had touched the origins of much that was good in the British Army and I was now thoroughly versed in all aspects of my profession. Moreover, I was returning to join an excellent regiment, 3rd Regiment Royal Horse Artillery, and would be entitled to my first married quarter.

Not long after arriving at Quetta, I had written to the War Office asking if I might go back to a regiment when the course finished, rather than to a staff appointment. I had no desire to be a staff officer just yet—

I would presumably have enough of that later in life. I was a little surprised to find myself selected for horse artillery because this meant I had found my way on to the special list from which officers to these elite regiments were appointed. Not having been posted to the 'ball button gunners' as a subaltern (horse artillery, like some cavalry, wore ball buttons), it seemed unusual that they should want me now. Years later I was to have a hand in changing the system of selection but right now I was happy to sample it, albeit with a few reservations which I expressed to the commanding officer on my arrival at Perham Down, on the edge of Salisbury Plain.

Lieutenant Colonel Philip Tower, another senior officer from whom I was to learn a great deal, welcomed me by asking how it felt to be in horse artillery. I had the temerity to reply that he would have to wait for my answer; horse artillery had managed without me for thirteen years and I wondered why they wanted me now. Had I known the commanding officer better I would not have risked such an audacious reply but he took it well and by the time he asked again, the quality of life in the regiment led me to give him the answer he expected.

Philip Tower ran his regiment with flair and it was impossible not to learn from him. I was second-in-command of J Battery under Major Mervyn Janes whose style also suited me for he ran his battery with a sure and light touch. We worked and played hard, establishing a reputation both as gunners and sportsmen. As one of the latter I featured with some success in the regimental rugby and athletic teams—on a good day I could still manage a hundred yards in ten seconds. I fared less well when I returned briefly to the ring to deputise at short notice for the regimental heavyweight and, giving away ten years and two stones, was badly beaten. I took up motor cycling again and in 1960 set the course for the Royal Artillery motor cycle trial.

As always there was amusing trivia. I ran the imprest account from which the soldiers were paid and on which the auditor each month made some trivial comment. I had some ready replies printed which explained: 'The oversight is regretted; it was due entirely to the exigencies of the service'. One day the Command Secretary, who audited all accounts, pointed out that my books did not balance and, while I was still seeking the source of the error, my pay corporal sent off one of my printed replies. The ready made forms were not meant for such occasions but no more was heard. The Command Secretary had joined the monkey in Malaya in demonstrating the futility of much routine paperwork.

I had begun to write military articles for professional journals and also occasionally entered the correspondence columns in a provocative manner. At this time most artillery regiments were, for tactical reasons, within the structure of the infantry brigades leaving the artillery brigadiers with somewhat attenuated commands. Very few gunners were given commands other than of artillery formations and it seemed to me that career planning in the Royal Artillery left a good deal to be desired. I therefore wrote a letter in the Royal Artillery Journal suggesting how it could be improved and, as it was unlikely that anyone would take much notice of a captain writing on this subject, I signed myself 'Downsman', sparking off such a controversial exchange of letters over the next six issues that the Journal, thereafter, ceased publishing correspondence for some time. The initial reaction came from two senior officers, a major general and a brigadier, who used the height of their official positions from which to pour scorn on me. Two other brigadiers attacked me for sheltering under a nom-de-plume, one of them suggesting that I was frightened of 'blighting my brilliant career'. In the next issue a brigadier and three colonels sprang to my defence, supporting my use of a nom-de-plume, expressing horror at the letters from the two senior officers who had written under their official titles, and suggesting it was sinister and obnoxious for them to do so. One correspondent, by the name of Jock Hamilton, wrote an amusing little ditty including the following lines:

'Two brigadiers appear to fume
At types who use a nom-de-plume.
They do not fear to use their name
To saddle soap their way to fame.'

Two years after the correspondence had started I signed it off with a short letter which ended, 'Let us encourage rather than stifle professional thought . . . I remain, Sir, a happy gunner.' This set the tone for my subsequent forays into journalism.

My next appointment would be to the staff. I had resigned myself to a couple of years during which, no matter how prestigious or interesting the appointment, life would have less fun and sparkle than in a regiment. I was therefore delighted when Philip Tower arranged for me to go as the brigade major to the Maltese artillery. It would obviously be an agreeable spot—people paid to go there on holiday—while the job I was getting was hardly run of the mill. I had a few months left with the regiment during which time my battery commander moved on, leaving me in charge. This was a welcome, if short, assignment for it gave me a taste of the major's command which I could not normally expect for another two years even though I had automatically been promoted to that rank on my 34th birthday. I had, of course, temporarily held a major's command six years earlier in Korea but progress up the peacetime ladder was slow.

Chapter 6

Brigade Major and Battery Commander

EARLY in 1961 I drove through France, Italy and Sicily to Malta, the Morris 1000 Traveller loaded with household belongings and well down on its springs. Booked for speeding on the open road in the south of France—I was surprised the car could go that fast—and being fined on the spot, my immediate plans were threatened by a shortage of cash. I had intended to stop and paint, a recently acquired pastime, but could now not afford bed and board, even in the cheaper hotels, and still have the fares for the ferries across the Straits of Messina and from Sicily to Malta. However, with my paints and canvases temptingly at hand, surrounded by landscape bathed in constant, Mediterranean light, there was an opportunity not to be missed, so I slept in the front of the car for several days and lived on spaghetti while painting in Calabria and Sicily. On arrival in Malta, I booked into a hotel which would provide family accommodation when Anne and the girls arrived, until we could find a house or a flat, and reported to Brigadier Arthur Trevor whose brigade major I now was.

Having found a flat in Sliema we settled down to an agreeable life. In those days Malta was not yet full of tourists and we picnicked and swam at deserted beaches. Marine life was plentiful and there was interesting snorkling to be had in the many rocky coves. The architecture, landscape and light provided an ideal environment for an aspiring artist and I painted a great deal. Through their connections with the Maltese regiments we became friendly with some of the oldest families on the island, so that when Nicola was born in November, she was christened in the tiny Crusader fort at St Elmo and her godfather was Lieutenant Colonel Freddy Borda, who commanded one of the Maltese regular regiments.

Soon after my arrival a political storm broke between the Maltese government and the opposition over the proposed posting of Maltese soldiers to Germany. When it was thought that the government's case was being inadequately reported in the press, I was told by the general to write a piece for the Maltese Times. In the process I received a lesson in journalism which I have applied to all my writing ever since. As a practised staff officer, my article began with an introduction, continued with some paragraphs of discussion and finished with a conclusion so worded as to leave the desired impact, all in line with the conventions of service writing. The editor was also practised—at judging column inches—and to fit my piece into the page he snipped off the conclusion. In fury I telephoned the newspaper and found myself speaking to the proprietor, Mabel Strickland, a legendary figure in Malta. In no uncertain terms I was told how foolish I had been to leave the important points to the end. No one was prepared to read several paragraphs in order to discover what it was all about and long before the readers had reached my conclusion they would have been sidetracked to the cartoons. Continuing her lecture, Mabel Strickland said that once I had hooked my readers by putting the important points at the beginning, I should woo them with ever increasing detail so that they would be left with a balanced picture whenever they chose to stop. I replied that I thought such an approach would be difficult without undue repetition. 'Young man, good journalism is always difficult,' and with those words in my ears Mabel Strickland rang off.

I reflected that the conventions of service writing usually resulted in a lengthy introduction and the need for the reader to sustain his interest through several thousand words of subsequent discussion if he was to arrive alert and receptive at the conclusions. People often avoided this drudgery by starting at the end which, it had to be admitted, was a strange way to read anything. The approach I henceforth adopted was to put the nub of my message at the beginning but this, not sitting easily with the conventions of bureaucracy, caused me some difficulty, at least until I became more senior. However, I persevered and my valedictory article to the British Army Review, when I retired from the service twenty years later, concluded: 'Readers of serious newspapers have similar needs to those burdened with official papers and there is no difference between unit officers detained reluctantly at their desks or Whitehall warriors for whom the written word is the largest part of their work. All wish to extract the maximum information with the least effort and in the minimum time, for there are other things to do. Good journalism does all this agreeably, kept up to scratch by a need to sell the written word to those who can select their source and please themselves how much they read. Warriors in Whitehall and elsewhere, who have no such choice, would do well to adopt the newspaper style and make life easier for one another. Tell the whole story in a few sentences and then develop it in detail.'

My newly discovered approach to military writing preceded by many years the 'executive summary' now often attached to the front of long documents, and was much welcomed by the commanders to whom I wrote, for they were no longer detained unnecessarily at their desks on my account. Of course, their adjutants still had to pore over a great deal of paperwork which, it seemed to me, often had more to do with the ego of the writer than any other apparent purpose. Our paper-shredding monkey in Malaya had surely demonstrated that. My first attempt at reducing the vast amount of paperwork was a considerable success: rubber stamps saying 'answered by telephone'. Having encouraged the use of the spoken word, I then thought I should consolidate the position by reducing the number of typists as, in the days before word processors and photocopiers, the volume of paper was easily contained by reducing the numbers of nimble fingers poised above typewriters. I had, unfortunately, not conducted a sufficient reconnaissance and as soon as I was committed to action I discovered that the temporary typists whom I was seeking to remove were wives working in their spare time. I decided instantly that discretion was the better part of valour and my campaign was abandoned.

My tour of undemanding duty in Malta came to an end in November 1962 when I returned to attend a six months course at the Joint Services Staff College, which I joined at the beginning of 1963. It was situated at Latimer, Buckinghamshire, in a large country house. The students lived privately round about, Anne and I renting a cottage in an isolated spot on the high ground above Amersham.

As its name implied, the course brought together officers of all three services, most of whom, up to this time in their careers, had not been involved with uniforms of different hues. The emphasis was on a joint approach to all problems but the evangelic fervour with which this was preached soon disappeared in the face of serious discussion. The early 1960s were a time of intense rivalry between the three services, in particular between the Royal Navy and Royal Air Force who each argued that they alone were best fitted to provide air cover over maritime and amphibious forces. On this issue the soldiers tended to sit back but they were not entirely unaffected by the competition for resources, being increasingly concerned that insufficient attention was being paid to helicopter support, then an air force responsibility and suffering from the demands of the nuclear bomber force on air force funds.

My own experience in Korea and Malaya led me to argue against single-service autonomy and the doctrine of joint command which avoided placing men of one service under the command of another by having dual command. It was ridiculous, I said, to go to war with two people in charge. It was equally absurd, I argued, to remain in the position in which history had left us, with three uniforms and nine services. Army aviation, which had just come into being because the air force had been unwilling to provide the likes of me in Malaya with adequate arcraft, was simply repeating what had happened before, when the navy produced its own aviation and marines, the air force its own regiment and maritime rescue service, and the army its own landing craft. How much more economical I suggested it would be, both in terms of procurement and training, if each element was taken care of by one service. We could have the light blue looking after things in the air, the dark blue coping with the sea, leaving those in khaki to grovel in the mud and sweat among the sand dunes. There would of course need to be some central direction to ensure the balanced allocation of resources and command arrangements designed to obviate the sort of capricious decision by commanders in the field which had caused mistrust in the past, but the new Ministry of Defence created under the recent Mountbatten-Thorneycroft review should provide the mechanism. However, when the Secretary of State for Defence, himself, came to tell us about the new organisation, he inferred, in answer to my question, that it would be undesirable and altogether too much to expect the single services to subject themselves to the central allocation of resources.

I seemed to be a lone voice advocating more central direction and, being the most junior officer on the course, although I probably had the most operational experience, was, I suspect, looked upon by the instructors as an angry young man. Central direction of defence was a theme I was to pursue for the remainder of my career and one in which I was often the odd one out. Twenty years after my question was summarily dismissed by the Secretary of State, central direction was imposed as the only sensible policy in an increasingly complicated and expensive business.

My image took a further dent when the course discussed Middle East strategy. I wondered aloud, in the presence of the senior army instructor, Colonel 'Shan' Blair, why we maintained a garrison in the Gulf when both the Germans and the Japanese took much more of the oil from the area than the United Kingdom yet seemed to see no need to garrison it. 'After all', I said, 'the Arabs can't drink the oil: they have to sell it.' It was simply a provocative question with no solution suggested but the colonel, who, unbeknown to me, had just been appointed to command that garrison, took me to task for asking it and the rest of the syndicate for not refuting the implications. That may have weighed against me when, at the end of the course, he told me that it was thought I was unsuitable for a joint staff appointment, although it seems more probable that it was my views on central direction which made me suspect. The verdict fortunately carried little weight, but that was not apparent until much later on when, as a brigadier and major general, my appointments involved command or co-ordination of all three services.

At the time I was disappointed but there was little point in pondering the effect on my future for this was already beckoning in the shape of 1st Regiment Royal Horse Artillery. I joined them at Hildesheim, in Germany, where Lieutenant Colonel Mervyn Janes, under whom I had served in 3rd Regiment, was in command. I moved into the officers' mess for several weeks in order to get to know the captains and subalterns, all of whom were strangers to me, and then took over married quarters in readiness for Anne and Nicola to join me— Maureen and Jane now being at boarding school.

They had gone a little sooner than we would have preferred in order to take maximum advantage of whatever financial assistance was available. The army, recognising that the nomadic life of a soldier was inimical to his children's education, paid a boarding school allowance which covered about a third of the fees. On the pay of a major, as it then was, I needed further assistance to help bridge the gap and discovered that some county councils would provide assistance towards boarding education, providing the recipient had established the need for his children to be so educated. I approached Sussex who agreed to provide assistance providing my initial application was made whilst I was serving abroad; as a result Maureen had started at boarding school while I was in Malta and Jane was now going at the tender age of nine. Thereafter, the assistance continued whether I was at home or abroad and although it diminished as my pay increased and ceased just before Jane left school, it enabled an uninterrupted education for my two elder daughters within the limits of an overdraft which my accommodating bank manager could accept.

After several months commanding Headquarters Battery, I took over

E Battery Royal Horse Artillery, equipped with six 105 mm howitzers mounted on Sherman tank chassis, and three Centurion tanks. The operational role of the battery was to support the Queen's Own Hussars, a cavalry regiment equipped with Centurion tanks under Lieutenant Colonel Pat Howard-Dobson. On manoeuvres I commanded the battery from one of my three tanks, close in the wake of Pat Howard-Dobson, whose keen eye for the going saw us across country like a hunt in full cry. My forward observers, each in one of the other two tanks, moved with the cavalry squadrons and controlled the fire from the guns which were deployed about three thousand yards behind us.

Days on manoeuvres resembled real war at least to the extent that one ran into the next in a kaleidoscope of time, places and activity. And so, after twenty five years, I retain a grey-green impression of tanks and troops moving freely through the open countryside of Northern Germany or rattling their way in columns through cobbled streets. There were nights of bivouacing in damp woods or smelly farmyards. There were Pat Howard-Dobson's orders groups, usually in a convenient barn where, after a warming glass of cherry brandy, we would learn what was expected of us over the next few hours.

It was E Battery which had fired the first British artillery shell in the First World War. On the fiftieth anniversary the battery returned to the gun position in Belgium which it had briefly occupied half a century before and, with the original gun as a centre piece, staged a well attended ceremony to mark the occasion. On the 16th August, on a warm day, under a brilliant blue sky, one of the Old Contemptibles who had manned the gun in 1914, pulled the lanyard so that the air reverberated and gun smoke drifted across the open ground as it had so long ago. A trumpeter sounded the Last Post and, after a minute's silence, Reveille. Then with a much louder crash, one of our present guns fired and the party began. About a mile in front of the gun position was a coal mine and at twelve o'clock, when the shift changed, scores of miners began to pedal past us and, on seeing that champagne was being dispensed from a large marquee close to the road, dumped their bicycles on the verge and made towards us. We could hardly refuse and within a few minutes there was a generous leavening of grimy working clothes among the resplendent uniforms, smart suits and elegant dresses. Several times people asked me how certain I was that I had rediscovered the actual gun position. I could only refer them to Mr Docherty, who, as Driver Docherty, had galloped into action on that August morning in 1914. Standing beside me with a glass in his hand, he surveyed the landscape and noted a field of mangold-wurzels some fifty yards behind the position I had chosen. 'You're spot on,' he said. 'We galloped into action through mangold-wurzels.'

In mid-1965 1st Regiment were due to go to Aden and it was planned that I should leave at that time and take up a staff appointment. I was disappointed to hand over my battery as it was leaving for active service and not at all enthused with the prospect of two years at a desk, but fortune smiled again. I learned that I was to be appointed to the Staff College at Camberley as an instructor, a staff posting on paper but far from it in effect. I accompanied the regiment to Netheravon, where it prepared for its tour in the Near East, moving to Camberley in late 1965, when the regiment had left for Aden.

Chapter 7

Teaching at Camberley

THE instructors at Camberley were normally selected from among its own graduates and apart from those on exchange postings from other countries, I was only the second to be appointed who had not been there as a student. Arrival as an instructor meant promotion to lieutenant colonel; it was a local promotion only, bringing no extra money but auguring well for an officer's career. Each instructor looked after a syndicate of ten students who changed at the end of each of the four terms of the year's course. Although the job was referred to as teaching, it was more a matter of directing syndicate studies and discussions, and the less an instructor needed to speak the better he was doing his job. Hence we were called directing staff, shortened to DS. In addition to leading the syndicates, each of the DS was responsible for setting up the instruction for the subject in which he specialised, a considerable task involving writing and supervising the printing of precis, notes and exercises. I learned with dismay that my speciality was to be staff duties.

In a nutshell, staff duties are concerned with the procedural side of military life and I knew that at the Staff College a good deal of attention would be devoted to the small print. The prospect of immersing myself in this did not appeal at all. It seemed to me that I was far better suited to the pursuit of tactics, the love of my military life, and after only a few days was able to persuade the colonel who arranged these things to reallocate responsibilities accordingly.

I approached my new task with eager anticipation and was not surprised, having recently been exposed to tactical discussion in Germany, to find myself at odds with some of the doctrine which seemed to owe more to expediency than the hard won lessons of war. It was a situation which had arisen as a result of recent changes in the political background. In the 1950s tactical doctrine in NATO had been

84

based upon the absolute nuclear supremacy of America and envisaged an immediate nuclear response to the merest Russian incursion. The staying power of the troops on the ground had to be no more than was required to identify the enemy's threats and delay him sufficiently for subsequent congestion in his ranks to produce worthwhile nuclear targets. This trip-wire strategy remained valid for only a limited time and when the nuclear balance became such that a doubt could be cast upon American resolve to risk its very existence in defence of European territory, the doctrine of flexible response was born. This meant matching force with similar force so that an attack by Russian conventional forces would be met with a conventional defence, a strategy which required far stronger forces than were made available. The army did its best, planning and exercising with what was at hand, but in the process a generation of its officers had been brought up on conventional tactics at only trip-wire strength and had grown to believe the doctrine was viable. Few, it seemed, had analysed what had happened and argued that recent improvements in communications and mobility together with the increased distances over which conventional weapons could fire, would bridge the gap between what was available and what had been found necessary when we last went to war. When I explained why the improvements would not close the gap and harked back to the Korean War as the closest point of reference for reliable examples of conventional war, I was accused of falling into the old trap of preparing to fight previous battles. It was said that the doctrine I was questioning had been proved during exercises. I suggested that testing tactics in peace time was like testing an aircraft on a drawing board, to which came the answer that the computer war games now in vogue supplied reliable answers. The argument had come a full circle for I was questioning the basic wisdom underlying the computer programmes. 'Rubbish in, rubbish out,' I said and the discussion continued until the commandant, Major General 'Tubby' Butler, a parachute soldier with considerable combat experience, told me to gather the DS together in order that my views could be debated in his presence. As a result the Staff College teaching on defence was modified and a major exercise, which occupied a week walking the ground near Basingstoke, was rewritten, an undertaking which I accepted with alacrity.

Teaching at Camberley was a rewarding experience. The students, representing the best in the army of their age group, were ambitious and bright. In chairing discussions or leading students through an exercise, I worked on the assumption that what I had to offer was simply my wider experience and, as they were ten to one, I would be failing in my job unless the vast majority of innovative ideas came from them. The students worked hard with a good deal of reading and preparation in their spare time. The instructors worked even harder, for at least as much preparatory effort was required to chair a discussion as to participate in it, while to read and comment on ten written exercises took longer than writing each of the exercises themselves.

Some of the instruction took the form of presentations, each of which might combine a lecture, short play, film and slides. These were produced in the Alanbrooke Hall, a spacious and well appointed auditorium the architect of which had incorporated the best features from a number of London theatres. The student body was a critical audience and, as the writer and producer of a number of presentations, I found it difficult to strike a balance between good theatre and good instruction. If all the facilities were used, with lecturers speaking alternately from podiums each side of the stage, with actors—from among the instructional staff—popping out of the wings and even descending like Peter Pan, with films and slides—simultaneously if desired—showing on three screens, there was a danger that the message would be lost in the medium. If, on the other hand, imaginative use was not made of the facilities, the students would think it dull. The same critical appraisal was directed at visiting lecturers who received a rough ride at question time if they had relied too heavily upon a script or obviously not given much thought in advance to their performance.

A highlight of the course was the battlefield tour during which the college spent a week among the Normandy battlefields of the Second World War. Standing on the ground they had fought over twenty years before, a number of specially invited officers and men, both British and German, explained the course of the battles. Thus we had, for example, an ageing general explaining his concept of an operation and his reactions to events as it developed, while a wartime NCO, now with a middle-aged spread, recounted what it had been like as a lean young platoon sergeant to find himself in command of the frightened remnants of his platoon. Bravery, the way men react to good leadership, cowardice and the contagion of panic, were all vividly described.

The majority of those listening had not been to war and for them, I think, it was the muddle and mistakes which occur when people are tired and frightened which was most striking and sometimes unbelievable. When we stood in a narrow lane being given a vivid description by an infantry major of how his battalion had been reduced to a shambles by our own shells, the senior gunner on the college staff questioned whether such a calamitous mistake could occur; there were procedures, he said, to prevent such errors. The major, who had won a DSO in the event he was describing, had no doubt whose shells had caused the damage. A heated discussion seemed in the offing and I diverted it by remarking, in a stage whisper, that a similar thing had once happened to me. As a forward observer in Korea I had given all the correct orders only to see the shells fall among a squadron of Centurion tanks. Encased within their armour, our troops had suffered no casualties and, blissfully unaware of the mistake, had reported incoming Chinese shells and asked me to look for the offending guns.

In addition to providing a valuable insight into the reaction of men in battle, the battlefield tour was a test of stamina. After an early start and a long day tramping the French countryside, there would be an evening of French cuisine rounded off with a glass or two of calvados. Anyone who found himself in the same restaurant as 'Tubby' Butler would be fortunate to manage more than a couple of hours sleep for his parties invariably continued into the early hours.

The students benefited greatly from their time at Camberley and in the process considerably sharpened up their instructors. For this reason, teaching at Camberley was an ideal job before taking command of a regiment, which was the next appointment for which I hoped. Although due, it was by no means certain that I would get a command, for competition was stiff but, judged on my recent jobs, it seemed very likely and I was somewhat on tenterhooks. There were a variety of regiments, all desirable, some more coveted than others but none more than the three horse artillery regiments. I was therefore highly delighted when one Saturday afternoon John Hoare's wife, Gritta, telephoned to congratulate me on being nominated to command 1st Regiment Royal Horse Artillery. I said that no one had notifed me and, being unable to believe my good fortune, questioned her closely. It was true, she assured me; everyone at the School of Artillery, where John was an instructor, had seen the list and there was no doubt that my name was at the top. It was an unusual way to receive the news of my most important job so far but it was the substance that was important and I was not going to quibble over the source.

The regiment was still in Aden and I persuaded the air force to fly me out and back in order that I could pick up the threads of regimental life and arrange with Lieutenant Colonel David Baines, the commanding officer, the details of our handover. I had always thought the barren rocks of Aden an unappealing place but my judgement had been based on no more than a view from a steamship passing through and a single, brief, trip ashore. It was, as I discovered in my week there, one of those

places which benefits from being lived in. The regiment was in fine
fettle, busy on anti-guerilla operations and deployed throughout the
Aden protectorate in various positions. I visited a number of these, in
one place standing on a bare dusty hilltop looking into an area of North
Yemen which the guerillas used as a secure base from which to mount
operations against the Protectorate. Fifteen years later the situation was
to be exactly reversed. I would be standing in North Yemen looking at
this very hilltop, which would be used by the South Yemenis as a
vantage point from which to control their activities against North
Yemen, the government of which, so many years later, would be
seeking British advice.

I flew back home, much refreshed by my contact with the troops.
David Baines and I had discussed most of what was necessary and
agreed that I would assume command of the regiment on their return in
June 1967.

Thus, I left Camberley after only eighteen months but having
achieved some worth while changes in tactical doctrine and fortunate to
be moving on while teaching was still fun. Academic life for me is like a
party, best left while still in the mood.

Chapter 8

Commanding 1st Regiment

I ASSUMED command of 1st Regiment Royal Horse Artillery over a cup of coffee in the Army and Navy Club on a morning in June. It was one of those fine days when London feels at its best and the ambient vigour reflected my own buoyant mood. Outside, yellow sunlight filtered through the trees and fell on the windows overlooking the quiet corner of St James's Square. Inside, David Baines and I, sunk deep in leather armchairs, went over the various personalities in 1st Regiment. There was little else to discuss, for the regiment, coming home from Aden, was starting afresh in a new environment with a clean slate. I was being offered a chance to shape the regiment's training and arrange its programme, unimpeded by prior commitments. It was a rare opportunity of which I was determined to make the most.

Command of a regiment is the first opportunity of independent command at a significant level. Entailing complete responsibility for a community of several hundred families, it is at once enjoyable and testing. In everyday terms the accountabilities encompass the operations of a multi-disciplined, mobile workforce and their varied sophisticated equipment, and the health, welfare and behaviour of them and their families. There is no other job, military or civilian, quite like it. Certainly no job in civilian management, where the workforce is welcomed and waved goodbye at the factory gate, can begin to compare.

The regiment reassembled at Kirkee barracks, Colchester, where it took over equipment and accommodation from 19 Regiment which was departing for Germany. 1st Regiment comprised a headquarters and three gun batteries: The Chestnut Troop, B and E Batteries. On its rolls were some thirty officers and six hundred men who, within a few days of arrival, were set to tackle their new role as part of 19 Infantry Brigade, a formation designed to fly anywhere in the world at short notice in support of British strategic interests.

There was a great deal to do before the regiment would be operationally fit. Twelve years in an armoured brigade in Germany had bred attitudes which were alien to its new task and which two years in Aden had not eradicated. In Germany there had been no shortage of transport and the regiment embarked on manoeuvres on a lavish scale. Now, when it took to the field, it would need to be lean so that it could be moved strategically by air and deployed tactically by helicopter. It would need to live entirely out of Land Rovers, and with not too many of those. There would be no room for the frills, officers' messes and cook houses that trundled around Germany. In addition, to modify its operational procedures to suit its new shape, the regiment would also need to master the detailed procedures for moving by air. Having discussed the requirements with the commander of 19 Brigade, Brigadier Bill Scotter, I said that we would be operationally fit in a month and a half.

Meanwhile, it was necessary to introduce ourselves to Colchester, for which purpose I decided we would hold a regimental dance. Having been abroad for some years, we also needed to invite a number of senior officers to dine in the officers' mess and for administrative and financial reasons—the cost of these events falling upon private regimental funds— it was decided to have the dance and the dinner on the same night.

The dance was boosted by Radio Caroline, a pirate radio station the like of which had recently been proscribed by an Act of Parliament. This caught the eye of the Sunday Telegraph, prompting the Chief of the General Staff, General Sir James Cassels, to demand an explanation. I am not sure whether my entirely truthful denials of any deliberate involvement with the radio were believed, particularly when the Daily Telegraph kept the story alive, but it was welcome publicity which led to Anglia television giving the regiment a three minute slot after the six o'clock news. We were represented by 2nd Lieutenant Bill King-Harman, a bronzed, good looking officer who, dressed smartly in his best uniform, explained who we were and issued an open invitation to the dance. He was deluged with replies, even from young ladies regretting that they would be unable to attend. When letters began to arrive from all over the country, it became obvious that our regimental hop had become a national event requiring more attention to music, lighting, decor, catering, transport and policing than we had so far intended.

The dance, which took place in the regimental gymnasium, was probably the biggest, most pulsating and successful any of us had ever attended. Coaches came in from the surrounding towns while others met the London trains. The beauty queen of East Anglia arrived on a gun carriage. When dinner in the officers' mess was over, the officers and their guests, including the Master Gunner, General Sir Robert Mansergh, trooped in, all resplendent in mess kit and medals, and were immediately engulfed. The mayors of Colchester and the midland towns with whom the regiment was associated, could be identified only by their chains of office as they struggled through the milling throng. The soldiers behaved impeccably; they wasted little time drinking for there were many more girls than men and the plans for dealing quietly with those who became the worse for wear were superfluous. 1st Regiment had launched itself into East Anglia in style.

The senior guests who needed a bed for the night had been accommodated in my quarter—Reed Hall House—a fine Georgian farmhouse in the barrack area. They were the vanguard of many for, as the senior regiment of artillery, serving at home for the first time in some years, we had a backlog of entertainment. Anticipating that my time in command would prove expensive, and with an official entertainment allowance covering no more than a stiff gin and tonic a day, I sought an increase in my overdraft. I said that if I succeeded in command, promotion would follow and my bank manager would get his money back, otherwise I might find it difficult to refund what I already owed. 'In that case,' he said, 'you had better take twice what you have asked for.' I took it and thoroughly enjoyed spending it.

The regiment's first real test came when it accompanied 19 Brigade on Exercise Overdale in the Eifel area of Germany. It was universally acknowledged that we acquitted ourselves well on this testing and imaginative exercise but, delighted though I was with our performance, I knew that there was insufficient logistic backing for us to survive in battle. At that time, the airlift available for our deployment overseas limited the regiment to taking only twenty rounds of ammunition for each of its eighteen 105 mm howitzers and there was considerable uncertainty over the manner of replenishment and the amounts that could be expected. Certainly none for many hours.

The situation reflected the position into which artillery had allowed itself to be relegated since the British Army was last at war. I addressed myself to the artillery headquarters which had endorsed the air movement plans for 1st Regiment. I suggested, not entirely facetiously, that it would be better to deploy only one of my three gun batteries and use the remaining airlift for extra ammunition. I failed to raise much interest and, seeking a wider audience, I wrote an article for the British

Army Review entitled 'The Power of the Gun' and one for the Royal Artillery Journal called 'The Influence of Artillery'. Possibly because it was critical of the Royal Artillery itself, the journal declined to publish this article which was then picked up by the British Army Review. It caused a minor upset at a senior level in the artillery but there was no doubt that the reason for the decline in the influence of artillery could be laid partly at its own door, and the situation would not be remedied unless it was honestly acknowledged. Fortunately, it was not a problem which directly affected 1st Regiment for I had a brigadier who did all he could to foster our position within his brigade, and subordinates with the personality and drive to ensure that we were listened to. Moreover, we now acquired a second role, one which made us the centre piece of NATO's mobile reserve.

The ACE Mobile Force, as it was known—ACE standing for Allied Forces Central Europe—was designed as a deterrent to Russian adventures on the flanks of NATO. Some half a dozen members of the Alliance were pledged to deploy troops in the face of any threat so that an attack on the ACE Mobile Force would mean an attack on the major member countries of NATO. To be effective, the deterrent needed to be militarily credible and to this end exercises were periodically held in Northern Norway, Greece and Turkey. Although the composition of the force varied according to the deployment area, an unchanging and ubiquitous element was the artillery headquarters which was always provided by a British regiment, one of whose batteries was also assigned to the force. It was a role which gave the commanding officer considerable influence, was one for which 1st Regiment had been mooted and which, after some prevarication among those who decided, I secured.

The ACE Mobile Forces Commander at the time we joined was Major General Gilles Turcot, a French Canadian infantryman, on whom I lost no time in calling. His headquarters in Heidelberg was always a pleasure to visit both because of the intrinsic appeal of its setting, a charming medieval university town on the River Neckar, and the warm welcome from the general's polyglot staff. Most of my detailed business was conducted with Major Tony Clay, a British gunner, who ran the operations section and who, with his wife Jenny, always ensured that I was comfortably accommodated and enjoyably entertained.

Our Mobile Force commitment in Northern Norway required us to become proficient in Arctic warfare and early in 1968 my headquarters and E Battery spent several weeks training in Norway under the guidance of the Norwegian Army's specialists in Arctic warfare. We could never hope to match them on skis and we contented ourselves, except for recreation, on the more pedestrian snowshoe, but in other skills the average British soldier was their equal within a week or two. Our instructors were very surprised that troops with the sand of Arabia scarcely out of their boots could take so readily to living in the snow and be so little distracted from their tasks by the inclement surroundings. 'It's because you are real professionals,' confided a Norwegian major over a cup of steaming coffee early one morning as we stood in the lee of a line of spruce trees in a temperature well below zero. I had just spent a fitful night in a slit trench, an escapade which originated in a discussion the previous day. Sitting in the comfort of an Arctic tent I had remarked that, while the Norwegian Army had inherited all the splendid hall-marks of the wartime resistance, a swish of skis and they had come and gone in the night, I doubted their defensive ability. They lived either in Arctic tents or snowholes, man-sized rabbit warrens, both of which gave comfortable protection from the elements but were unsuitable as fighting positions. Defence of Northern Norway, I said, would require the holding of certain key positions astride the few passable invasion routes. If the attacking forces were to run the gauntlet of our defence, a large proportion of the latter would need to be more exposed to the elements than was apparently planned. The hazards of war were usually in inverse proportion to the discomforts. I would, I said, demonstrate what I meant. Taking an axe and a shovel, watched with curiosity by some of my own soldiers, I cut a slit trench, laid a few conifer branches across the top and, wriggling into a sleeping bag, bade the major, 'Goodnight.' My regimental sergeant major, Mr Coward, later des-cribed what followed. Having visited my trench several times and, by the aid of torchlight, observed my inert form, the Norwegian major suggested that he should wake me to ensure that I was alright. Fortunately Mr Coward thought otherwise. 'If he is frozen to death we can't wake him. If he is asleep I won't try.'

The regiment's first exercise with the Mobile Force was in the summer of 1968 when, on flying into Bardufoss, in the far north of Norway, I found myself with a Canadian field battery, an Italian alpine battery and one of my own. Exercising command from a helicopter I had more chance than most to appreciate the majestic grandeur of our surroundings. Long fingers of sea reached for miles inland between the snow topped mountains whose grey sides dropped steeply to the glassy fiords, pausing at the water's edge to provide a ribbon of green, a narrow winding shelf of useable land. In the distance, the high plateau of Finmark glistened white to the northern horizon. By helicopter, I had an easier passage than others between the variously inaccessible positions of the force artillery: the battery commanders and their forward observers clinging to the mountain sides, the batteries under their camouflage nets along the water's edge, the collection of Land Rovers comprising the fire direction centre tucked into a valley, and the lonely radio relay stations—each two men in a small tent well above the snow line.

The endless daylight of the Arctic summer introduced me to a new dimension of soldiering when my helicopter flight commander announced that I had flown both his pilots and his machines out of safe flying hours. The situation was also reflected on the ground where there was a tendency to pursue objectives without the benefit of a change of pace which nightfall usually brings. On one occasion I turned up at a battery position for supper to find they had eaten five hours earlier, being reminded that it was now one in the morning.

Recalling the scepticism with which, as a senior captain, I joined horse artillery, I was determined, now that I was in a position of some influence, to improve its credibility. Selection in all ranks was now made from all officers graded above average, an improvement on the virtual closed shop which had persisted until recently, but the Royal Artillery as a whole, seeing so much talent concentrated within three regiments, still questioned what it was getting from its investment. I felt the returns needed to be more deliberately organised. The issues also involved the sergeants' mess, most of the occupants of which had joined as recruits and, growing up within horse artillery, had benefited considerably. Seldom were any posted away and arrivals from elsewhere were accepted only if highly graded. It seemed to me that the system needed putting into reverse; we should be promoting warrant officers and sergeants for appointment elsewhere.

I discussed the subject with the appropriate selecting and posting authorities, saying that no single regiment within the Royal Artillery *needed* to be filled with above average officers, as did the horse artillery of old which dashed about the battlefields and required quick-thinking individuals. If we were to fill particular regiments with officers of high calibre, it should be for a specific purpose which, I suggested, should be to raise standards within the Royal Artillery as a whole. I also addressed the officers' and sergeants' messes along these lines for if horse artillery was to gain wholehearted and widespread approval, the individuals within it needed to acknowledge the responsibilities they were incurring. Although I would not claim more than a small part of the credit for improvements to the system and its more easy acceptance by others, my efforts came at an opportune time when it was under review.

Commanding a collection of stars was not the easy task that some other commanding officers imagined. If given their heads my battery commanders would have bolted in different directions. What was required was an easy rein which enabled each of them to develop their own potential to the full while still remaining part of a well co-ordinated team. I therefore encouraged the battery commanders to exercise independence, not that they needed much encouragement, and pulled them together periodically for regimental exercises. One such venture was 'Grand Prix' which took us, clockwise, around England and Wales in ten days, firing our guns as a regiment on every artillery range and indulging in various side activities including a long weekend recruiting.

Although the exercise was designed to try the regiment, on occasions, close to its limits, it was meant to be enjoyable rather than testing. I said that we would assume a very adverse air situation and that vehicles were to move singly or in pairs, with NCOs map reading their way no matter how far the destination or difficult the route. In war I would have concerned myself with the routes they took but on this occasion gave them complete discretion saying only that I wished them to move as quickly as possible without incurring the wrath of the law. They responded magnificently; no one got lost and the only adverse involvement of the law was when Major Joe Lawrence, who commanded the Chestnut Troop, was caught speeding on the A1. Out of courtesy we notified the police of our intentions and they were delighted by the manner of our movement. A police sergeant and I stood on a pavement beside the Bank of England watching the regiment move through the City late one evening. The sergeant, with a row of ribbons from army service, was at first somewhat critical of the apparently haphazard progress as, at this confluence of streets, the vehicles did not always approach from the same direction and might well have been departing for different destinations. It had been different in his day but he conceded that it demonstrated an unusually high standard of training.

The regiment's itinerary took it first to Salisbury Plain for a couple of days shooting then via Dartmoor to Sennybridge in South Wales for a comprehensive exercise in fire planning. Next was Towyn, in Wales, for a ten mile march and small arms competition before admiring the illuminations at Blackpool en route to Warcop, in Cumbria, for an anti-tank shooting composition. Then it was over the spine of England to Otterburn and the Cheviot Hills for a rapid fire and movement exercise where the batteries raced one against the other with me spurring, and sometimes goading, them on. From Otterburn we launched ourselves into a recruiting drive through the regiment's home ground of Nottingham and Sheffield. For this purpose we rearranged our vehicle crews so that each Land Rover, containing men from the same part of town, could literally be taken home to mum and parked in the street outside. I spent the weekend touring the area, visiting the soldiers' homes, in some cases finding a whole gun detachment accommodated in the parlour of a terraced house while, in the road, a howitzer was deployed as for action and a swarm of children were playing soldiers under the watchful eye of an NCO. In every house on which I called, the best china was brought out and I was awash with tea when we moved on to a training area near Thetford, in East Anglia, where we practised the use of helicopters with live firing going on all around. Then it was back to Colchester with the batteries again going their different ways.

In order that a commanding officer should not be unduly distracted from his responsibilities, a batman was provided to cope with some of the domestic chores. Mine was known throughout the regiment as 'Twiggy'—on account of his slender build. He was not a natural soldier and found that being a batman ameliorated the discomforts of a military life. Thinking that a volunteer would be better than a pressed man, I took him on. He looked after my uniforms, helped when I was entertaining and did odd jobs but, largely because I did not instruct him in the finer points of his duties, he was not the gentleman's gentleman at least one of my guests thought he would be.

I had invited Major General Peter Gillett, an old friend of the regiment, to dine in the mess on his last night in the army. We were sitting in my house chatting before changing into our mess uniforms. When I offered to top up the general's drink, he accepted on the assumption that 'your man has boxed my spurs'. What he meant was that Twiggy would have prepared his uniform. This form of dress was not the easiest to climb into quickly and preparation included fitting the tight trousers over the wellington boots so that the lot could be pulled on simultaneously. There was also a stiff fronted shirt requiring studs and cufflinks; there were medals and other paraphernalia. Leaving the room, ostensibly to refill the glasses, I took the stairs two at a time to discover the general's suitcase had not been unpacked. Feverishly I arranged everything as it should be: trousers over boots, medals, cufflinks, studs, spurs, boot-pullers, even hair brush and razor placed to hand. I then reappeared with the drinks, making some excuse for the delay.

The following morning the general left early. Twiggy was on hand, having loaded the suitcase into the car. Turning to him and passing over a crisp note, the general said that not since his time in India had his uniform been so expertly prepared or his kit so conveniently arranged. Quickly, before Twiggy could let us down, I said that in 1st Regiment we aimed to be the best at everything.

A commanding officer relies heavily upon his adjutant if he is going to achieve his full potential in command. I was extremely fortunate in Malcolm Hord, a young captain whose appetite for responsibility and work was leavened by intelligence and wit. Mistakes are inevitable if people are going to learn and on such occasions Malcolm placated the superior authorities who would otherwise distract me to no purpose. There was the amphibious vehicle which sank in the River Trent during a recruiting demonstration because an enthusiastic NCO had attached an outboard motor to improve its performance. Malcolm somehow headed off the witch hunt which usually attends such accidents and persuaded the authorities to accept my cavalier explanation: 'The NCO was using his initiative in seeking to improve the performance of a somewhat underpowered vehicle. It is fortunate the accident occurred in the River Trent. It might just as easily have happened in the Lingen Fiord where, in an Arctic winter, the consequences would probably have been serious.'

I played my last game of rugby in 1968, leading the regimental scrum against the Welsh Guards, a team packed with league players from the Valleys. I normally played in the middle of the back row but on this occasion deputised for a prop forward who had broken his collar bone. I found myself in an unfamiliar position, pitted against a massive guardsmen who bore down on me like a pile driver each time the front rows met. After a while I felt a pain in my side and, when it became unbearable, Malcolm Hord drove me to the military hospital. My ribs were displaced and the doctor sent me for an X-ray. I did not go through the painful process of replacing my shirt before returning to the consulting room and as, in my mud caked boots and dirty shorts, I clip-clopped along the polished corridor, I encountered the hospital sergeant major. Fixing me with a glare, he enquired why I was 'wandering about in an undressed state'. Feeling too wan to explain the circumstances or who I was, I made a weak excuse and walked on—to his evident surprise, as regimental sergeant majors are usually treated with more deference. Some time later, lying on a couch with my eyes closed awaiting the doctor, I heard the stamping of feet beside me. Opening my eyes I saw the sergeant major hovering over me in the salute. 'I am extremely sorry, sir, I did not know who you were.' Some years later at a cocktail party in Kenya I learned what had caused his return. Across the room I caught the voice of a senior military doctor telling a group of people how, when he was the commanding officer of a hospital, his sergeant major had come to him saying that he had just administered a severe rebuke to someone who, he realised on second thoughts, was fairly senior. The doctor was recounting how he had sent the sergeant major to apologise but never discovered the identity of the senior rugby player, when I wandered across and solved the mystery.

All regiments, wherever they may be garrisoned, do their best to maintain cordial relations with the local people. Occasionally an incident would occur which cast a cloud and called for remedial action, particularly if the press had made something of it. Thus, when the regimental ration truck crumpled a bicycle beneath its large wheels, severely injuring its young rider, Garry Wilson aged 10, it was appropriate that I should become involved. When the boy emerged from hospital, fortunately fully recovered, he was invited to the regiment for a day, given a conducted tour of its activities, lunch in the mess and a helicopter ride with me to the training area where he fired one of the guns. At the end of the day I presented Gary with a cheque for a new bicycle. The remedial action was successful and attracted larger headlines than the accident which had prompted it so that when the Ministry of Defence tried to take me to task for giving the boy a ride in one of the regimental helicopters, I was able to make light of their strictures.

The most enjoyable ACE Mobile Force exercise in which the regiment participated was 'Olympic Express' in north eastern Greece. It was preceded by the large conference and reconnaissance essential for the mounting of an international exercise on such a scale and which, attended by numerous officers from the participating countries, was all part of the process by which NATO demonstrates its political will through military means in peacetime. During these meetings in Thessaloniki, I met Major General Li Gobbi, an Italian who had taken over the ACE Mobile Force. I took an instant liking to this stocky, swarthy general, his drooping moustache giving him the appearance of a modern Ghengis Khan. His dashing style was also in the manner of that Mogul leader but, unfortunately, the battalions gathered temporarily under his command were unused to his methods and, much to his frustration, often failed to react as he intended. I was more fortunate, having been able to take the entire force artillery through a two week live firing exercise in Denmark, so that, irrespective of nationality or previous training, my units knew what was required and were able to produce it.

1. My first uniform 1931.

2. My Mother and Father.

3. With my Grandfather 1929.

4. 2nd Lieutenant Home Guard. Seaford, 1944.
Author in shirt sleeves.

5. 2nd Lieutenant. Egypt 1946.

6. Army pilots in Korea 1952.
Left to Right: Captain Tees (Canada), Author, Captain Deacon (Australia),
Captain Joyce (United Kingdom). (Photo. *Flight*)

7. Auster under fire. Korean War.
(From an original painting by the Author)

8. Quetta 1958. Author and Yazdani second and third from left.

9. Malaya 1954. Author briefing Captain Stuart Whitehead for a sortie.

10. Military wedding 1957. With Captain John Hoare.

11. Malaya 1955. The Sultan of Selangor presents the Distinguished Conduct Medal.

12. Malaya 1954.
Jane's christening – with
Anne and Maureen.

13. Nicola. Aged 5.

14. Colchester 1968. The author and Garry Wilson. (see page 98)

15. Caribbean 1972. The author, and right, Major General Glyn Gilbert.
(Photo. *Soldier*)

16. Muscat 1975. The Sultan and his Council of Ministers.
Extreme left: Qais Zawai. On the Sultan's immediate left: Sayid Faher.
Author right (in beret). (Photo. Mohammad Mustapha)

17. Dhofar 1975. The author and Sultan Qaboos share a joke.
(Photo. Mohammad Mustapha)

18. Muscat 1975. Left to Right: Jim Treadwell (H.M. Ambassador),
the author, Roy Mason (Secretary of State for Defence), John Mayne
(Private Secretary).

19. Muscat 1976.
Commander The Sultan's
Armed Forces.

20. Woolwich 1982.
My last parade.

21. London 1985. With Celia after our wedding.

22. Chieveley 1987.
Celia with
Alexander.

The exercise began in an assumed period of international tension caused by sabre rattling along the Bulgarian border. Advance elements of the ACE Mobile Force flew into Thessaloniki and deployed across the Strimon River valley. For the participating elements of 1st Regiment, my headquarters and the Chestnut Troop, it was a long wearying journey: by road to the airfield at Lyneham, loading, an eight hour flight, and a fifty miles drive after unloading. Beneficial sleep in a Hercules transport aircraft is virtually impossible. The best that can be managed is a series of catnaps. There is considerable vibration and noise which earplugs do little to alleviate. With the centre of the aircraft filled by vehicles, guns and equipment, the passengers, sitting along the sides in canvas seats, are hard put to stretch their legs. I usually pulled rank on such flights and sat at the front where I could stretch my long legs between the bumper of the leading Land Rover and the forward bulkhead. An apparent disadvantage was that my seat was beside one of the two urinal tubes but I overcame this potentially inconvenient hazard by writing 'out of order' in chinagraph pencil on the lid!

After twenty-four hours of travelling and a short fitful sleep in the open on the banks of the Strimon, the manoeuvre phase of the exercise, lasting a week, began. When it was over, the whole force paraded along the promenade of Kavella, the citizens of which were given a day's holiday to mark the event—for this was the time when Greece was ruled by the colonels. While the parade was forming up under the NCOs, the officers gathered in a cinema to be addressed by the prime minister, Mr Papadopoulos, and hear a few words from General Li Gobbi. The latter, on this occasion, decided to dispense with the red beret and parachute smock, which he habitually wore, and put on his best uniform. However, despite my protestations that there would be insufficient time, he insisted on returning to his hotel to don his combat clothing before leading the parade. As a result, the cheers of the large crowd signalled the start of the march past before he and I had returned to the promenade so that the two leading vehicles, in which he and I should have been standing rigidly to attention, were empty, apart from the drivers. Fortunately, the streets were deserted and, having rushed frantically to a point just short of the saluting base, the general and I fought our way through the spectators, vaulted the crush barriers and, cheered on by the crowd, sprinted across the road and jumped into our vehicles. Once past the saluting base the general peeled off to join the prime minister, leaving me in the lead. The spectators, massed either side of the road, were applauding vociferously, their cheers drowning the noise of the vehicles. I was basking in this unaccustomed public acclaim when an object was hurled from the crowd. It was as well that I restrained my instinct to duck for I was hit by nothing more weighty than a rose, the first of a shower which continued for some time. Whatever they thought of the military regime, there was no doubt that the people of Kavalla enjoyed a military parade.

The regiment played a good deal of sport but, being continually on the go and seldom together, displayed no outstanding team talent and I was content for the batteries to enter their own teams in the minor military and local civilian competitions. There was, however, one sport which I pursued regimentally with some vigour, orienteering. This combination of cross-country running and map reading had not yet become widely popular in Britain or a recognised army sport—it would do so later—but it seemed to me an interesting and useful form of competition, and means of taking exercise. I therefore appointed an officer to organise orienteering and declared that I would be the first runner to set off at the first meeting. I hoped that my map reading would compensate for my waning athletic ability but I had not reckoned with the guile of some of my soldiers.

I should have ensured that the first half dozen or so who followed me at half minute intervals were more of my age and that the course had been laid through thicker country. As it was, I was pursued by a group of young soldiers who, with an easy loping stride, kept me in sight. I had not the acceleration to give them a false lead and then race away leaving them lost, a tactic I had found useful in similar circumstances on motor cycle trials. They stuck to my heels and sprinted past me between the final check point and the finishing post, where they gathered to welcome me in.

Cramming as much useful activity as we could into each day, we sometimes seemed to be in a state of continual crisis management. To others we appeared to be moving serenely, if swiftly, with the ability to change direction at will, taking all effortlessly in our stride. Thus, it was that a long since scheduled test exercise was brought forward at short notice to suit the convenience of the artillery headquarters setting it. I protested to the artillery commander, Brigadier Drew Bethell. Of course we could cope but it would mean gathering the various elements of the regiment at the last moment from a number of tiring activities, recruiting, a tattoo and an infantry exercise. Starting in an exhausted state, we would not be at our best for what would no doubt be a demanding exercise. My arguments were in vain. We did not do well and in fury I insisted that we should be tested again. Brigadier Bill Scotter supported me, finding an occasion, even before we successfully tackled the repeat exercise, to write that 1st Regiment was the best artillery regiment he had known. In this period, my only uneasy time in command, it was comforting to be the object of unqualified support from above. Unstinted loyalty to subordinates in need is all too rare.

Gunner regiments are not usually noted for their foot drill. I was always more concerned with gun drill and ensured that whenever we were required to participate in an important parade, we were mounted in vehicles. However, when we were nominated to provide a guard of honour of a hundred soldiers for the Queen I had no option but to take foot drill very seriously, sending a number of warrant officers to the Guards Depot at Pirbright for a crash course in drill and appointing one of my battery commanders, Major John Bettridge, to take charge of the whole project. There could be no half measures. This was the first occasion in some years on which the Royal Artillery had produced a guard of honour for the Queen and the smartest hundred men, with twenty in reserve, were selected from the entire regiment. The guard of honour was supposed to turn out in khaki uniforms, blues being worn only on specific occasions by NCOs. I protested; for an occasion such as this, the entire guard should be in blue uniforms, white belts and the old fashioned, steel tipped army boots. How could 1st Regiment shuffle past in drab uniforms and rubber soled boots? When the Adjutant General's department told me to stop arguing and do as instructed, I turned to Major Leslie Spencer, my quartermaster. He acquired, by means I never discovered, all the blue uniforms, belts and boots that were needed. The actual event went well but was almost ruined when the band changed the step as the first half guard approached the saluting dais. Afterwards it was rumoured that this had occurred because the conductor had passed his baton from one hand to the other. Malcolm Hord approached him in a rage to be rebuffed by the assertion that he, the conductor, had long experience of music and marching. 'Well, you're a bloody slow learner!' said Malcolm, turning on his heel.

Each year I gathered the ACE Mobile Force Artillery for an exercise which went under the name of 'Annual Barbara', after the patron saint of all gunners worldwide. Member countries of NATO took it in turn to play host to the exercise, all attempting to do better than the last. The participating nations each provided well trained batteries with a good allocation of ammunition. Thus, with batteries from America, Canada, Britain, Germany, Italy and the host nation, it was a marvellous opportunity to show what artillery can do. My first 'Annual Barbara', at Borris in Denmark, had been a considerable success but with the benefit of this experience I knew that much more could be achieved. As

'Annual Barbara' 1969 approached, I set myself two objectives: firstly, to make it the liveliest exercse in which any of the participants had been involved and, secondly, to demonstrate realistically and credibly, to as influential an audience as I could assemble, the full potential of artillery.

A prerequisite was a good exercise area without undue restrictions on live firing and I obtained, for the ten day exercise, the exclusive use of artillery ranges in Elsenborn and Braschatt in Belgium, and Vogelsang, just across the German border. The local safety regulations posed a problem. The rules on these ranges required all gun positions to be agreed and surveyed in advance, a strait jacket which would obviate realistic deployment. However, they seemed to ignore the possibility of an accident at the target end. British rules, conversely, assumed that the officer on the gun position was capable of surveying his own whereabouts but were nervous of untoward incidents around the target. I agreed a compromise with the Belgian staff, British rules at the gun end with their rules at the sharp end. It gave me, of course, the best of both worlds enabling a more realistic exercise and a better demonstration than would have been possible in either Britain or Belgium.

The exercise proved a huge success, involving the equivalent of two regiments' worth of artillery. The intense but friendly rivalry between the various national contingents produced extremely rapid deployment and very high standards of gunnery. It was even more extraordinary considering the number of languages involved. Malcolm Hord's fire direction centre, with a bilingual liaison officer from each of the contingents, and ten wireless nets in five different languages, became known as the Tower of Babel.

The exercise entailed a great deal of motoring, often at night. No one travelled further along the narrow roads and twisting tracks than the quartermaster, Major Leslie Spencer, as he delivered ammunition, petrol, rations and all the other necessities required to keep a couple of regiments in action. One night his Land Rover was hit by a Mercedes timber truck and Leslie was taken to a small hospital in Malmedy with severe injuries. On learning of this I drove to the hospital, arriving at about midnight. In spite of my none too clean combat kit, I was taken straight to the operating theatre where, under harsh overhead lights, two surgeons and an anaesthetist were already at work on the unconscious Leslie. They showed me X-rays and, my fractured French not being up to a conversation, let alone a medical discussion, I merely nodded my head, for even I could see the hip was badly displaced. The muscles which hold the hip in place are evidently extraordinarily strong for it took two of us at each end of Leslie, pulling hard in opposite directions, before the hip was satisfactorily back in position. Using a drill rather like my Black and Decker at home, the surgeon then inserted a pin into Leslie's shin and the leg was put in traction before some time was spent on his head wounds. When all was finished, and Leslie wheeled away to a ward, the senior surgeon, peeling off his gloves and removing his mask, opened the refrigerator where the drugs were stored and extracted four cans of lager. It was only as we sat relaxing did I realise I had been mistaken for the regimental medical officer.

I knew that several dozen generals would be arriving for visitors' day at Elsenborn and that some senior British officers would be in a critical frame of mind. I had previously taken the School of Artillery to task, writing in an article that the Royal Artillery should '.....rethink its policy on demonstrations if it is to give other arms more than a superficial idea of artillery support. The demonstration for staff college students, for example, differs little, if any, from that given to the public..... The students invariably come away with a high regard for the Royal Artillery's stage management and thorough approach but are unlikely to have learned much professionally, or acquired a feeling for, and meaning of, close support.' I went on to say that spectators should be 'taken into confidence and shown around the gun areas and observation posts during the adjustment of the fire plan so that . . . they know it has been produced realistically'. I suggested that one or two spectators should be asked to select targets for impromptu engagement. I emphasised that demonstrations should integrate air and artillery in order to illustrate the complementary nature of these two forms of support and suggested where spectators should best be positioned in order to see the great variety of tasks which could be undertaken. Clearly, my visitors would be waiting to see if I practised what I preached. I did, to the letter, and the day was a huge success. In the morning, the visitors were free to go wherever they wished as the artillery deployed, the observers dug in and the fire plan in support of a mythical infantry attack was arranged. They were then whisked off to a good lunch in the officers' mess at Elsenborn and returned in a jolly mood where, as close to the target as regulations permitted, they watched the artillery fire plan unfold, preceded by air attack from two wings of the Belgian air force.

My highly enjoyable time in command of 1st Regiment had come to an end. The sergeants' and junior NCOs' messes dined me out. The officers' mess chartered a boat and we drank, dined and danced on the

Thames until the early hours. I was reminded what a privilege it had been to command these officers and men. No matter how enjoyable or rewarding future appointments might be, none would entail the company of such a lively band.

Chapter 9

Infantry Brigadier

AFTER commanding a regiment, the next job was bound to be an anticlimax, although in my case the disagreeableness of exchanging my regiment for a staff appointment was alleviated by its location in Singapore where Anne, Maureen, Nicola and I arrived in September 1969. Jane, at boarding school, would join us for the holidays. After several uncomfortable weeks in temporary quarters we took over one of the old fashioned married quarters. It was an airy, colonial type house, built before air conditioning, with verandahs and doors designed to make the most of natural breezes. We tore out the air conditioning installed by the previous occupant and, attended by an excellent cook-amah, lived very comfortably. The garden, a lush tropical green, contained a moon flower, a species which blooms only once in several years and, even then, compresses the process from bud to wilted flower in a few hours of darkness. It blossomed for us and we sat out after dinner in the warm, moist air watching the pale yellow flower unfold.

This was my first experience of working in a large headquarters. The job, known as 'G One SD', was the co-ordinating point for a wide variety of activities and I soon became restive over some of the time honoured procedures, in particular those concerned with the written word. Hours were wasted on drafting, a process in which the perfect expression became the enemy of timely communication. My habit of putting the message in the first paragraph disconcerted my boss Brigadier 'Tig' Gray and was a requirement one of my subordinates found impossible to meet. He, fortunately, was soon replaced by a guardsman, Major Malcolm Havergall, who, untainted by previous staff training or experience, was an avid pupil. We got along famously.

My job entailed some travel and I revisited several places in Malaya. I also returned to Hong Kong and while there crossed the wide, brown estuary of the Pearl River by hoverfoil and spent a day amid the faded, crumbling Portuguese architecture of Macao.

After six months of what seemed likely to be at least a two year appointment, I learned that I was to be promoted to brigadier, jumping the rank of full colonel, and assume command of 24 Air Portable Brigade at Plymouth in early 1971. This was good news, more so as I was to be the first gunner in eight years to get what was, in effect, an infantry brigade.

Making the most of what time was left, we crammed into our small Renault 4, and drove along the east coast of Malaya. There was now a motorable road all the way, although rough in places where the high wheel base of the little car was an asset. At Chukai, where, in 1955, I had slept beneath the wing of my aircraft, a few yards from the sea, a motel had been built conveniently on the air strip. Much had changed and I was unable to find the bungalow where I had seen the bullet-pierced skull. The tawdriness of coke cans and tourism was creeping in but, for the locals, prosperity had arrived.

So, escaping to what I regarded as real soldiering, I returned home at the end of 1970 and took over 24 Brigade. Like 19 Brigade, of which I had recently been part, it also was in the Strategic Reserve but vested with the additional and interesting task of keeping amphibious warfare techniques alive within the army. An airportable, amphibious infantry brigade; a formation more suited to my inclinations could not have been devised!

When I assumed command, the brigade comprised two battalions, the 2nd Light Infantry and the Royal Irish Rangers, together with an Army Air Corps squadron and the usual supporting units of ordnance, transport and workshops. Apart from the Royal Irish Rangers, who were at Watchet on the north coast of Somerset, the brigade was concentrated in Plymouth, my own headquarters being in Crownhill Fort on the outskirts of the city at the edge of Dartmoor. We were destined to move to the north of England and, in anticipation of this, the Duke of Wellington's Regiment, stationed at Catterick came under command of 24 Brigade soon after I had joined.

The principles of command are the same at any level. For me they have always embraced maximum delegation, no interference without good cause and the promotion of initiative. If it means subordinates sometimes learning by making mistakes, so be it, so long as mistakes are not repeated. The purpose of delegation is to release the full potential of all concerned and does not imply the abdication of responsibility. Indeed, it often incurs increased liability and those on whom authority sits uneasily usually retain a tight rein for fear of losing control. Thus, as the commander over the next two years, I would decide what could be achieved with the resources available and issue broad instructions to that end. I would calculate the risks and, even though others were being encouraged to manipulate the situation, remain responsible for the outcome. Applying these principles meant trusting my staff to manage the details and in this respect I was magnificently served by Majors Thomas Boyd-Carpenter, who as brigade major controlled the operations staff, and Ian Sprackling, who, going by the confusing title of deputy assistant adjutant and quarter master general, managed administrative affairs.

The first major event was an amphibious exercise in which the brigade landed near Cambeltown in Kintyre and then, with the headquarters and some infantry sailing around the north of Scotland and the remainder going by air, went on to exercise in the Baltic, landing in Denmark. This was the beginning of a fruitful association with *HMS Fearless*, an assault ship under command of Captain Bryan Straker. *Fearless* displaced some 12,000 tons and carried four landing craft, each of which would take two tanks, and a number of assault craft designed to carry platoons of infantry. On arrival in the area of operations, *Fearless* would ballast down in the water and, with her stern doors open, became a floating dock from which the landing craft could ferry to and from the shore. The assault craft were lowered from davits and the infantry used scrambling nets to enter them. *Fearless* also embarked a flight of Wessex helicopters which, operating from her flat after deck, were used to fly men, equipment and stores ashore. To co-ordinate all this activity and direct an assault on a hostile shore, the ship provided a well appointed operations room.

Bryan had only recently taken command of *Fearless* so for both of us this was an initiation into amphibious operations. I soon learned to multiply by two whatever time I had first estimated would be required for any ship to shore movement. As we approached Kintyre the wind was blowing onshore and we had to put about every time we launched the heavily loaded helicopters. In the Baltic a fog came down and the mexi-float, a raft some 100 feet long driven by four powerful outboard motors, was lost for more than an hour in the 3000 yards between ship and shore. Bryan and I also explored the nature of joint command, a subject over which I had voiced misgivings at the joint services staff college. In theory, he was in command afloat and I ashore, the boundary being the high water mark. As a result, when, from my helicopter, I said the assault craft were heading for the wrong beach and Bryan preferred the apparent evidence of his ship's radar, the leading infantry were landed a good way from their objective. Fortunately Bryan and I got on well, enabling us, after a few initial hiccups, to operate successfully in spite of the doctrine of joint command which has always seemed to me to be a recipe for confusion.

A visit to the Royal Irish Rangers gave me the chance to see what had happened to Watchet Camp in the quarter of a century since I had last passed that way. 'Not much,' was my initial thought as my staff car drew up at the entrance and Lieutenant Colonel Henry Howard, the commanding officer, invited me in to inspect an immaculate quarter guard, for the guard room behind them was exactly as I remembered it from the nights I had spent patrolling outside or drinking tea, thick with condensed milk, within. The quarter guard inspected, Henry said he would show me the camp. I said that I could equally well lead the way and proceeded directly to my old hut. Convector heaters had replaced the coke stove I once tended. There were beds and mattresses rather than double tier bunks with straw palliases. Wardrobes had replaced the boxes into which we had crammed our clothes. Otherwise not a great deal had changed as Watchet Camp had been empty for years and only recently reoccupied when the British Army's withdrawal from the East had caused a shortage of accommodation at home.

Anne and I spent some enjoyable months in Plymouth before the move north caused more domestic upheaval. We lived in Fort House which, having been a brigadier's house in the 1930s, meant, for a brigadier in the 1970s, living in unusually opulent surroundings but without the servants and gardeners which such a house required. It provided a setting for Maureen's wedding when she married Paul Cook, a young solicitor whom she had met while we were living in Colchester. Jane had left school and, living with us, was taking a course in fashion design at the Plymouth Technical College. Plymouth is a city with long established connections between the service and civilian communities. As the senior military family in the city, we enjoyed a varied social round in contrast to the somewhat restricted military circle we would later encounter in Catterick.

We moved there in mid 1971, the brigade headquarters going into a camp at Barnard Castle which, like the one at Watchet, had been closed down for some years and was still the adopted home of a number of sheep. In addition to the minor units which had moved north with us, the brigade now comprised four battalions: the Duke of Wellington's Regiment and the 2nd Fusiliers in Catterick, the King's Regiment across in Lancashire and the Argyll and Sutherland Highlanders just outside Edinburgh.

An infantry brigade needs to be particularly fit and I insisted that everyone ran five miles once a week in boots and combat kit. It was not a means of making men fit but simply of ensuring that they were, and I invited myself to run with a different sub-unit each week. Running one day with the brigade workshops I noticed that several men were lagging about a quarter of a mile behind and I said to the workshop commander, Major Christopher Nitsch, that I would drop back to offer some encouragement. When they drew level with me I began to urge them on whereupon, as one man, they sprinted away leaving me trailing by a distance I could not possibly hope to recover. Christopher had tricked me by setting a trap with his best cross-country runners but it was all in good humour and when I arrived, somewhat breathless, at the barrack gate, the unit was lined up on either side to clap me in. They certainly got full marks for fun.

Each unit underwent an annual inspection to verify its fitness for war. I would have been failing in my job if I was not already aware of a unit's current abilities and I therefore used these mandatory inspections as a means of enabling commanding officers to remedy deficiencies which they themselves acknowledged. If, for example, a battalion had been unable, by virtue of its recent commitments, to maintain its proficiency in air portability, I would agree that my inspection would entail the unit preparing to move by air. I always thought that the inspection of a good unit was an occasion to be enjoyed by all, would always include an amusing event and finish with drinks in the sergeants' mess and a late lunch with the officers.

When the time approached for me to inspect the transport unit, I explained to the commanding officer that I thought his young officers should be more proficient on motor cycles and not always leave the shepherding of convoys to the NCOs. I said that my inspection would include a cross-country motorcycle course and I asked Ian Sprackling to arrange this. When Ian replied that he could not find anyone competent, I told him to produce a motorcycle, hoping, after an interval of many years, that I could still at least set a course for novices. The machine was produced after lunch and, watched with amusement by my staff and dismay by the gardener, I circled the mess lawn several times before setting out for the Catterick training area. On arrival there I reconnoitred various hazards and was putting a course together when a swarm of motor cyclists approached at speed, one of their number, a sergeant major, peeling off to inform me that I was obstructing the Royal Signal's motor cycle display team in their training. He had no sooner said this than he realised who I was and, excusing himself on the grounds that it was unusual to encounter a brigadier astride a motorcycle, he asked if he could help. As a result my course was laid out with expert assistance. On the day of inspection it proved rather more difficult than I had intended and we sat down to a very late lunch while a number of broken motorcycles were still being recovered.

Our next amphibious adventure came about by mistake, at least that was the view in the Ministry of Defence. It began over a glass of gin in my cabin on board *Fearless* during our Baltic exercise. I was discussing the venue of the next exercise with Major General Glyn Gilbert, the commander of 3rd Division to whom I reported, and we decided that the Caribbean was a likely spot. A Royal Marine captain present had exercised on an American training area at Vieques, just off Puerto Rico, and, having listened to his description of it, we decided to see if it could be made available at some time suitable to us. I had assumed that the brigade was scheduled for a major amphibious exercise each year whereas the plans in Ministry of Defence were for a large and a small exercise in alternate years, so that in 1972 the resources earmarked would permit no more than minor training around the coast of Britain. Being blissfully unaware of all this, I decided that I would run a full scale brigade exercise with live ammunition on Vieques, followed by counter-insurgency exercises at company level on a suitable Caribbean island. Coincidently, the general commanding the Strategic Reserve, Lieutenant General Sir Mervyn Butler, under whom I had served at the Staff College, was touring the Caribbean and, in a conversation with the governor of Montserrat, agreed that it would be useful for British troops to exercise there. This was all the authority I needed and, with Tubby Butler's tacit support, I began to make the arrangements.

I visited the headquarters of the United States Marines at Norfolk, Virginia, and arranged for Vieques to be made available to us. My hosts volunteered to contribute a squadron of ground attack aircraft and as many marines as could be made available. It was only when I returned to Barnard Castle that I discovered there were insufficient resources available in 1972 for me to mount such an exercise as I envisaged. However, we were by now committed to the Americans and after a certain amount of wrangling, which fortunately went on over my head, my exercise was approved by the Ministry of Defence and christened 'Sun Pirate'. They agreed that I could take two battalions, the Dukes and the Kings, together with supporting armour, artillery and logistics. The Royal Navy would provide *HMS Fearless*, a frigate and three logistic ships. The Royal Air Force would fly the majority of the men out and back, and provide me with an Andover aircraft for tasks around the Caribbean. Thus, the stage was set for the largest British amphibious exercise in many years.

It was now mid 1971; the first part of the exercise was fixed but we still had to confirm the suitability of Montserrat for the second phase. With several other staff officers in tow, Thomas Boyd-Carpenter and Ian Sprackling accompanied me to Montserrat where we learned that the governor had changed and the new encumbent, Willoughby Thompson, was not in favour of a military exercise on his island. We had alternative places in mind but, before going on to look at these, we obtained permission at least to reconnoitre what might, at a pinch, be made available. He entreated us to wear civilian clothes and, thus attired, we drove around in a couple of mini-mokes being welcomed in one village by a group of children with the words, 'Hello soldiers.' So much for our civilian disguise. We moved on and within a few days had settled on Peter Island as a suitable spot. Leaving my staff to make detailed plans with the American headquarters at Roosevelt Roads, in Puerto Rico, I returned home via Bermuda to brief the senior naval officer in the West Indies on what was afoot and enjoy a weekend's water skiing.

The forces assembled for the exercise in early 1972. Part would be transported across the Atlantic in *HMS Fearless* and three logistic landing ships, vessels designed to transport men and equipment, and the remainder would go by air. The force would concentrate at Roosevelt Roads prior to the assault on Vieques. A few days before the exercise was due to start I was summoned by Headquarters 3rd Division to be briefed on a situation which might require my amphibious force for a real operation elsewhere. In order that my staff could do some preliminary homework I enquired where this might be and because the conversation was on an open telephone line, it was carried out in guarded terms. Somehow my informant conveyed to me the impression that the problem was Malta, which made some sense as, at that time, there was a possibility that British interests might need protection and families evacuating in the face of local disturbances. However, it seemed to me that I had the wrong force, a sledgehammer to crack a nut, for that sort of venture. The obvious question which would need resolution concerned the legal framework under which my troops would operate and I instructed Ian to provide me with all the right questions. The followng day, when the map was unfurled for briefing, we discovered that the object of anxiety was Belize, the British dependency at the southern end of the Caribbean which Guatemala was threatening to invade. My mind turned quickly from the niceties of law to the more worrying aspect of ammunition resupply.

In the event, Guatemala backed off and our exercise went ahead as planned. To the accompaniment of a bombardment from the frigate and rockets and cannon fire from the American aircraft, the force landed by helicopter and assault craft. Once the tanks and artillery were ashore, the sound of battle became even more realistic. For most of those participating it was a novel experience. There was more to come, for, in the days that followed, each infantry company, supported by tanks and artillery, went through an entirely free play exercise with live ammunition being fired from all weapons. Experienced American spectators who, after Vietnam, might have taken it all for granted, were considerably impressed, saying they had seen nothing like it in peace time. An American general asked me for a plan of the exercise and shook his head in disbelief when I replied there was no plan but only objectives which the company commander was free to tackle in any manner he chose. Concurrent with these manoeuvres, the counter-insurgency exercises took place on the nearby jungle-clad slopes of Peter Island. Here the American holidaymakers in their many yachts and motor cruisers were treated to a dazzling display of professional seamanship as the Royal Marine coxwains manoeuvred their landing craft with consummate skill in the confined waters, before discharging their troops across the narrow strip of silver sand between water and jungle.

During the second phase of the exercise, *Fearless* cruised off the British Virgin Islands and the governor, David Cudmore, invited Bryan Straker and me to lunch. I explained that the needs of the exercise would prevent me staying for lunch but said I would accompany Bryan and look in for a drink. The radio message conveying the invitation suggested that our helicopter could land on the tennis court at the governor's residence on Tortola. We took off, Bryan resplendent in his white uniform and I more practically dressed in combat green and jungle boots. The high trees around the tennis court prevented the helicopter landing and the pilot selected a spit of reclaimed land close by in the harbour. As the skids touched, it became apparent that the dry surface was merely a crust over soft mud and the pilot remained in a low hover. I gingerly stepped down and sank knee deep, watched by the governor and his wife at the end of their drive. Fortunately I was dressed for the occasion and the mud would hose off. Bryan, however, could hardly hazard his white shoes and trousers and clambered on to my shoulders. Cheered on by a small crowd of stevedores, who had been attracted by the helicopter, I staggered through the mud to firm ground and was persuaded to stay for lunch, padding around in borrowed socks while my own footwear dried out.

Whatever we did during 'Sun Pirate' had been done before, either in peace or war, but it dispelled two military myths which had gained credence over the years. The first was that amphibious operations require specialist troops. The infantry battalions had been too busy to concentrate exclusively on amphibious techniques but as well trained infantry they took them all in their stride. My only instructions on this point had been that every officer was to drive a vehicle through a water tank, that the waterproofing of every vehicle should be inspected by an officer and that I would wish to know the reason for any vehicle drowning during the landing. As a result the only 24 Brigade vehicle which came to grief was a 3 tonner which drove into an underwater obstacle. One other vehicle also drowned—the specialist recovery vehicle manned by amphibious experts which was on hand to help trucks stuck in the water. The second myth was that operations in a tropical climate require a period of acclimatisation. There had been no time for this but, from a force of some two and a half thousand, there were only three heat casualties. Of course, the Caribbean in February is not at its hottest but it still poses potential problems for well laden infantrymen coming direct from the cold of a northern English winter. In our case the solution rested on physical fitness and logistic management. The men were fit and confident. As they skirmished up the dusty slopes of Vieques or through the steamy jungle of Peter Island, they carried only what they needed to fight and their packs and sleeping bags were ferried forward whenever needed by helicopter. Also, water had an equal priority with ammunition for helicopter resupply.

As I flew back from 'Sun Pirate' my remaining nine months with 24 Brigade offered only a dull routine. The brigade's main task would be to provide troops for Northern Ireland where the terrorist situation was as bad as ever. My command would be attenuated and my task reduced to supervising training for a role in which I had no part. There was, however, always a chance that an additional brigade headquarters would be required in Belfast and I deployed all the arguments I could muster in favour of 24 Brigade. What effect these had I am not sure but they were certainly not adverse for in June we found ourselves established, at 48 hours notice, in a porta-cabin headquarters which had been erected in the car park of Castlereagh police station.

My responsibility for the next few months was the maintenance of order in East Belfast, the City Centre and an area called the Markets. For this purpose I had the Life Guards, the Welsh Guards and 42

Commando Royal Marines. Deployed in aid of the civil power, the military would normally expect to be in support of the police with the latter determining the strategy and tactics to be employed, but, in the lawless situation of 1972, it was the troops who played the major role. At my first press conference I described 24 Brigade as the men in the middle, by which I meant they were there to protect each section of the community from the other. It was an understatement, for the troops were assailed from both sides. The Protestants felt that we were insufficiently tough in pursuit of the IRA and formed a paramilitary force intent on applying their own version of the law, thus bringing them into conflict with the security forces. The pursuit of the IRA brought opposition from the Catholic community, determined obstruction from those who saw terrorism as a solution and passive resistance from others who lived in fear of the terrorists in their midst.

There were those in the military who felt that the British Army was close enough to defeating terrorism in 1972 to ride roughshod over the entire Catholic community in final pursuit of the quarry. They argued that people who withheld information or provided support, however passive, must accept the consequences. They were wrong. A military solution alone was never a viable long-term option. Passive resistance and apathy would have turned very soon to outright hostility encompassing the entire Catholic people. Although the British Government refused, publicly, to acknowledge that they were engaged in a counter-revolutionary war, they recognised that the problems required a political solution. It was, in fact, an impeccably run counter-revolutionary campaign in which the military attempted to create conditions under which political forces could operate while politics, involving international opinion, attempted to produce a favourable environment for military operations. That these complementary processes are taking so long is due, simply, to the intractability of the situation and the intransigence of the two communities. The Irish have a keen sense of history which any lasting solution will need to acknowledge.

This sense of history, whether distorted or true, was manifest in the Protestant parades and marches when, with drums beating, pipes playing and banners unfurled, large bodies of marching men would trail their coats along the sectarian divide. These were the flash points for considerable disturbances and at my morning briefings my attention was drawn to any such forthcoming event in order that I might make the necessary military dispositions. One day I was told that a women's band, protesting against the detention of some Protestants, was due to march from East Belfast through the City Centre but, as it numbered only a dozen, I saw no cause for concern and turned to other things. At four o'clock in the afternoon, the commanding officer of the Life Guards, Lieutenant Colonel Simon Bradish-Ellames, called on the radio to tell me that the women had started marching. 'Roger Out', I replied. Simon came back on the air and, with some relish, said that it was not the dozen women who were causing him concern but the 500 men wearing masks and carrying cudgels marching behind. He feared that they would cause a considerable disturbance when they left his area and moved through the City Centre.

My brigade reserve that day was 42 Commando and I immediately instructed the commanding officer, Lieutenant Colonel Jeremy Moore, to use one of his sub-units to block the march on the bridge which carried the road over the river and into the City Centre. I would, I said, meet him there within a few minutes. Standing on the bridge we saw a huge crowd approaching and, when they were within a few hundred yards and there was still no sign of Jeremy's men, I became somewhat alarmed. Jeremy, who was receiving radio reports from his troops, assured me that they would arrive with time to spare as they were travelling in vehicles and had only half a mile to go. What they had not reported was that they were caught behind the crowd, a fact I discovered when I surveyed the marchers through binoculars and caught a splash of green at the back of the parade. Having told Jeremy that his troops had better find another way over the river so that they could fall in behind us, I came face to face with the crowd on the middle of the bridge. Their leaders insisted on their right to 'the Queen's Highway' and I said that I would not deny them that providing they would remove their masks, drop their cudgels and walk in a single file along the pavement. Meanwhile, the one or two policemen present looked on impotently and the band continued its whistling and rattling. At the back, the crowd were becoming restless when, with a squeal of tyres, a row of armoured personnel carriers pulled up behind me and the road was filled with commandos. Jeremy and I withdrew through their ranks, followed by a hail of cobble stones and milk bottles. In retrospect I found it amusing, although not so at the time.

There was genuine humour to follow. The next day, as I drove through Belfast, I came across the same women's band blocking a street in protest over some minor issue and causing a traffic diversion. Although motorists were resigned to the situation and no one was regarding the incident with any concern, I could hardly turn my back on it. Alighting from my Land Rover I casually approached the band leader and enquired for how long they meant to keep this up. They were going, she said, at three o'clock. I pointed out that it was now one minute past three. 'Ahh,' she said, 'this is just an encore for you.' And with that they struck up 'God Save the Queen'.

There were few such amusing diversions and behind the facade of every day life a grim battle continued. Car bombs demolished whole buildings. Housewives, brought to their doorsteps by the sound of shooting, proffered studied indifference to the sight of a young soldier slumped in a pool of blood. I remember the feigned hysteria of a young mother turning suddenly to sullen silence when, the searching troops having lifted her baby from its cot, an armalite rifle was found beneath the mattress. No other soldiers in the world would have behaved so professionally, so impartially and correctly in similar situations.

The most significant occurrence during my time in Northern Ireland was, to me, my confirmation. By no means a zealot or even a regular church-goer, I had always considered myself a sincere Christian and, not having been confirmed when young, felt I had missed something. This was how I put it to my brigade padre, Rex Hancock, as we sat one evening in the brigade operations room, sipping whisky while the radios crackled around us. Some hours later, having meanwhile done my nightly rounds of Belfast, I found several religious pamphlets on my pillow and a note suggesting how we might proceed. As a result, I was confirmed a few weeks later, a solitary figure in a dark suit following a dozen children in white. I imagine it was an unusual experience for the bishop although probably not unique. I doubt, however, if anyone kneeling before him previously for their confirmation had a pistol concealed beneath their jacket. Featuring high on the IRA's hit list, I always carried a gun and a drive to a lonely country church did not seem the occasion to break the routine. For my soldier bodyguard the occasion was unquestionably unique. He had last been to church when christened and the thought of participating in a service seemed to embarrass him. I said that he should sit at the back where he could keep an eye on the congregation behind me—with which instructions he was happy.

I returned with my headquarters to Barnard Castle in the autumn, having only a few weeks remaining before I would hand over. I had some accumulated leave which lasted over Christmas and into the New Year, giving Anne and me a chance to settle into a house we had bought in Haywards Heath.

In January 1973 I joined the Royal College of Defence Studies which is situated in an imposing Georgian house at the corner of Belgrave Square, the elegant setting reflecting the seniority of the students and the unhurried pace of their studies. The syllabus covers the higher direction of public affairs and it comprises lectures, study, discussions and a thesis from each student. Those attending, some eighty in number, are from the armed forces, the civil service and diplomatic corps at the equivalent rank or status of brigadier. About half are from the United Kingdom and remainder from widely differing overseas backgrounds. The nature of its syllabus, the composition of the student body and the venue in London, makes a year at the Royal College of Defence Studies the most sought after government course in the world.

The course included an overseas tour of four weeks for which the students were divided into six groups, each travelling to a different continent. I chose Africa which I thought, during the decade ahead, would exert considerable influence on world affairs. We visited Algiers, Cameroon, Ethiopia, Kenya and Nigeria. In every country we were received by the ruler, president or prime minister and, thereafter, conducted around government and industry by senior ministers. The most striking occasion was our reception by Haile Selassie, the legendary ruler of Ethiopia. A diminutive, aged figure attended by a pair of miniature dogs, his palace gate guarded by a couple of mangy, untethered lions, he was unfortunately no longer the Lion of Africa. Our African journey entailed an exhausting itinerary and we insisted on leisure time at week ends which we spent in such places as a hotel at the head of the Blue Nile, an oasis in the Sahara and a game park in Kenya.

As the course neared its end I was given a choice of appointment and asked for a position somewhere on the central staff in the Ministry of Defence. It was not that I wished to become a Whitehall warrior but simply that it was high time I discovered how the Ministry worked. And so I found myself, in early 1974, appointed as Director of Defence Operations reporting to Air Vice Marshal 'Togs' Mellersh and with a collection of officers from the three services as my subordinates. It was an imposing title but carried little responsibility for the work was done by the people beneath me and co-ordinated by Togs Mellersh who took all the decisions. I came to describe myself as an unnecessary level of supervision and, one day when Togs was away and I found myself reporting to Chief of Defence Staff, Field Marshal Sir Michael Carver, I said that I thought my appointment was redundant. I was surprised that my remark drew no response from someone with a reputation for ice-cold logic, but within a few days I was given the task of writing a top secret report on the Arab-Israeli war. I suspect that he also knew that I was in line for promotion into a job which would require me to learn Arabic so that between the top secret report, Arabic studies and my job as director, I would be too busy to complain of having too little to do.

My job brightened up when, in August, Turkey invaded Cyprus. With Togs Mellersh accompanying James Callaghan, the Foreign Secretary, to peace negotiations in Geneva, I was left running the operations centre in the Ministry of Defence at a time when there was great concern over the safety of the British Sovereign Base Area in Cyprus. The British garrisons were poorly placed to influence events which were being dictated by large Turkish forces operating close to home. When it seemed to us, in the Ministry, that the Foreign Secretary was overplaying his hand, and doing so without his officials having consulted us, I sent an urgent telegram to Togs Mellersh. It was marked for his eyes only and it ended by suggesting that the Foreign Secretary was 'arguing from a position of military impotence'. It may have been marked for Togs' eyes only, but, going via Foreign Office communications, was shown first to Mr Callaghan from whom I received an exceedingly sharp retort.

My appointment, which would normally have lasted between two and three years, was cut short when I was chosen to take command of the Sultan of Oman's Armed Forces in early 1975, a position filled by an officer on loan from the British Army. A year on the central staff had been long enough for me to become versed in the ways of Whitehall and, incidentally, to confirm my view of the need for greater central direction. My thesis at the Royal College of Defence Studies had been on this subject and, with actual experience of Whitehall behind me, I published it in a shortened version. In the concluding paragraph I wrote: 'The success of any organisation depends largely upon the determination of those involved to make it work. In this respect the armed forces are second to none. But goodwill alone is insufficient; it needs to be exercised within an organisation which is broadly arranged to cope with the major problems of the day . . . there is now a need for it to be more suited to the assessment of priorities and allocation of resources.' What I wrote did not find favour with many around me but I felt that time would prove me right—as it did—and, meanwhile, there were more absorbing things at hand.

Chapter 10

General at War

I HAD first set foot in the Sultanate of Oman whilst still Director of Operations, visiting from Whitehall where my job included the co-ordination of military support for the Sultan's Armed Forces. These were engaged in a bitter guerilla campaign and my visit provided a glimpse of the challenge which makes counter-revolutionary warfare such an absorbing subject. I thought that Major General Tim Creasey, who was commanding the Sultan's Armed Forces, had the best of all jobs anywhere and I enthused about this to the British Defence Attache, Colonel Pat Allardyce, with whom I was staying. His lukewarm response was explained months later when he told me that at the time he had just seen a confidential telegram from the Foreign Office directing the ambassador to propose me as Tim Creasey's successor, causing him to react cautiously for fear of letting slip what he knew. I had no idea I was in the running and could hardly believe my good fortune when I was told in mid 1974 that I would relieve Tim in early 1975. It seemed too good to be true that not only was I escaping from a frustrating job in Whitehall but I was being promoted early into a position which, even then, I recognised as being the most fulfilling I was likely ever to have.

The war in which I was about to engage had started in 1965 when Dhofari tribesmen rebelled against the backward and uncaring regime of Sultan Said bin Timour, the Ruler of Oman, of which Dhofar was the somewhat forgotten southern province. The rebels were near to achieving a separate autonomous state when Said was deposed by his son Qaboos in a bloodless coup in 1970. With the advent of Sultan Qaboos, civil development was begun in earnest and the oil revenues, hitherto unused, were deployed to hustle Oman into the twentieth century. Dhofar received at least its fair share and the basis for rebellion vanished. However, the insurrection was sustained by support from the neighbouring communist state, South Yemen, with the aim of toppling Sultan Qaboos and obtaining a stranglehold on the Straits of Hormuz with its tanker routes to the West. In face of this threat Qaboos modernised and expanded his armed forces. In this he was advised and helped by the British government who provided officers and non-commissioned officers from all three services to occupy key positions in the Omani forces. In addition Britain allowed the Sultanate to recruit several hundred ex-service officers and men to fill those positions for which Omanis were as yet untrained.

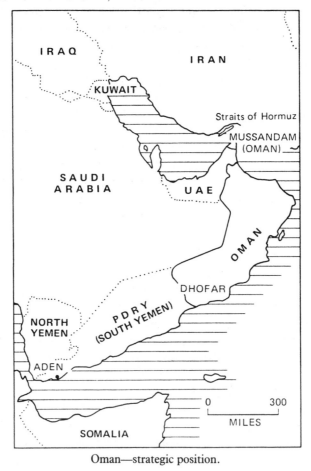

Oman—strategic position.

I arrived, as Commander of the Sultan's Armed Forces, very early in the morning of the 3rd of February accompanied by Anne and Jane. Having been met at Seeb Airport by Colonel Stuart Green, my Chief of Staff, we were whisked away to our bungalow a few miles north of

Muscat. Bait al Alam, translated it means Flag House, was the largest of several whitewashed bungalows on a low gravel ridge. As we approached it along a rough track the few low thorn bushes did little to reduce the intense glare from the bleached rocks. However, on entering the house, the wide verandahs, thick stone walls and typical Omani roof of sun-baked mud, provided a cool welcome. We were met by Sharif, an imposing Pakistani in a white shirt, baggy trousers and Jinna hat. He introduced us to his subordinates: Ayatt and Feroze, the Pakistani house boys, and Francis the cook, a Christian Indian. We were soon to discover that nothing flustered Sharif and his team. The sudden arrival of unexpected house guests and frequent dinner parties at a few hours notice were dealt with like events long planned, even although our deep freeze was filled but once a month when the single cold storage in Muscat stocked up from a visiting ship.

After an overnight flight, I was to be allowed the day resting but being far too excited, I prowled around the bungalow trying my Arabic on the squad of soldiers on guard. I failed to communicate and was rapidly losing confidence in my linguistic abilities when Sharif arrived to translate, explaining that they were Baluch soldiers who spoke only Urdu. Within two hours I was in my headquarters, had taken up the reins of command and made arrangements to fly to Dhofar the following day. My headquarters, a couple of hundred yards across the wadi from my bungalow, was in Bait al Falage Fort, a white, square and solid edifice constructed around a small flagstone courtyard with a central well. Built two centuries ago, to house a few tribesmen, it was now bursting at the seams, my office being on the upper floor in a narrow walled-in verandah cooled by two air conditioners which struggled noisily to reduce an outside temperature of about 100° Fahrenheit to something more bearable. Visitors, who included ministers, ambassadors and other eminent people, must have wondered how we ran a considerable international force and successfully concluded a campaign under such conditions. However, for a proper soldier it matters not from whence he exercises command, be it an opulent office, walled-in verandah, the front seat of a jeep or a helicopter. He does it from wherever he is and the fewer the trappings the better. What a commander needs is a clear notion of his own intentions, reliable communications and good subordinates. I certainly had the latter.

The Sultan's Armed Forces, when I took over, comprised two brigades of infantry, an airforce and a small navy. Brigadier John Akehurst, an outstanding soldier, commanded a brigade in Dhofar, the battle ground in the southern province. Under him were five battalions of infantry, the equivalent of a regiment of artillery, a squadron each of armoured cars and engineers, plus a great deal of logistic support. He also controlled all aircraft operating in support of his troops. Without doubt, in British terms, a general's command. The airforce was run by Group Captain Erik Bennett, an airman who led from the front and whose promotion to Air Commodore I arranged soon after my arrival. He too was under-ranked even after promotion, being responsible in every respect for a force of some sixty aircraft of widely differing types. Colonel John Head's brigade had the task of security in northern Oman and provision of training and logistics to support the war in Dhofar. Under him were three infantry battalions, some armoured cars, artillery, engineers and acres of ordnance depots, vehicle parks and magazines. The small navy, which comprised fast patrol boats, a logistics ship and inshore craft, was under the command of Captain Philip Brooke-Popham. In early 1975 the navy's main concern was to blockade the coast of Dhofar but their role was becoming increasingly more important. In addition to the Sultan's Armed Forces, I had an Iranian Brigade under my operational control in Dhofar, for the Shah of Iran had perceived that the threat to Oman was also a threat to him. The running of this varied force required an alert and industrious staff and in this I was again lucky. Headed by Colonel Stuart Green, it effectively translated my requirements into plans and orders without any bureaucracy; in fact any tendency to the latter would have been frustrated by a shortage of typists, the absence of a photocopier and uncomfortably crowded offices which induced their occupants to get out and sample real life. For me the key figure in my entourage was Lieutenant Colonel Ian Sprackling whose worth I had assessed when he served on my staff in 24 Brigade. I realised that I needed someone of exceptional ability to cope with the immense logistic, administrative and financial problems, and after a little difficulty I persuaded his regiment, the Royal Signals, that he should join me. Like the rest of us, he carried responsibilities well above his rank across a field of unusual breadth and depth. He relieved me of many administrative worries and we developed a close friendship which has endured ever since. My aide-de-camp was Major Hassan Ehesan, a broad shouldered and tough officer whose dark features portrayed a distant African ancestry. Joining as a private soldier many years earlier, he had learned to read and write both English and Arabic and had been awarded the gallantry medal for a particularly brave action at a frontier outpost. He was forever wishing to improve his English and we started with an arrangement whereby I would address him in Arabic and he would reply in

English, a recipe for disaster which we discarded after several unfortunate misunderstandings. Although John Akehurst was my deputy for all operational matters, I had on my staff a deputy commander to look after Omani affairs. This was Brigadier Colin Maxwell who, having lived in Oman for twenty five years as a member of the Sultan's Armed Forces, was a highly respected individual at all levels in Omani society and, to me, a good friend and adviser.

I was to spend about half of my time in Dhofar, at least while the war was on, sometimes staying for a day or two with the Akehursts in their bungalow at Salalah but more often flying there and back in a day in order not to lose touch with opinion and events in and around Muscat. Such days would usually start with half an hour in my headquarters followed by a hair raising twenty minutes in the Mercedes as Salim my driver, unashamedly using the authority of my pennant streaming from the bonnet, raced to Seeb where the daily scheduled BAC 1-11 would already have embarked its other passengers and be waiting with engines running. As soon as my ADC and I had bounded up the steps the door would close and we would taxi for take off. Climbing out of Seeb, our southerly course took us over the bare mountains of northern Oman where the early morning shadows were throwing the razor sharp crags into bold relief. The only colour, and then only in the larger wadis, was provided by the broken green of date gardens and an occasional mosaic of washing laid out to dry on the ground. The clusters of houses, little brown boxes in and around the gardens, were invariably attended by stone watch towers perched precariously upon the peaks around, relics of the turbulent times which had persisted into the 1960s. After a while the mountains slipped down into a flat sandy plain and, when the orange flares from the oil fields at Fahud had passed behind, there was nothing but this featureless landscape for the next three hundred miles. Then, with little warning, the terrain regained its shape and began to turn green as the fertile uplands of Dhofar came into sight. Descending towards Salalah, the view through the small aircraft windows included herds of grazing cattle, clusters of tribal tents and round primitive huts. As the tyres squealed on landing, the scene flashing past left no doubt about the serious business in hand. On either side of the runway were fully armed strike aircraft parked at readiness in their sandbagged emplacements, khaki figures humped green ammunition boxes through the rear doors of drab coloured Skyvans while there was a constant coming and going of helicopters, many with bulging nets swinging beneath. John Akehurst would invariably meet me at the bottom of the steps and drive me in his Range Rover the few hundred yards to the cluster of huts which served as his headquarters, or to a waiting helicopter if I was immediately moving on to visit troops in operational areas.

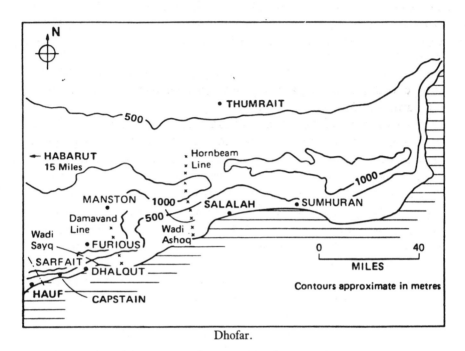

Dhofar.

Dhofar is reputedly the biblical land of Sephar and Ophir, probably where Sheba negotiated with Solomon, and certainly synonymous with the trade of frankincense over the centuries. It would have been a tourist paradise but for the ubiquitous enemy, now you see him now you don't, and the mines he scattered in his wake. Grim little anti-personnel devices, no larger than a cigarette packet, were concealed underfoot where people would be likely to pass and would remain for months after the enemy had been driven away. In a flash they would remove a man's leg and possibly blow away his sex life too. These mines were seldom laid singly and recovery of one casualty often led to more, as when a close friend of mine, Major Peter Isaacs, was even more grievously maimed than the NCO, with a severed leg, to whose assistance he had courageously ventured. Single, larger mines also presented a persistent hazard. We once picnicked with a large party in a reputedly safe area, an ancient place called Sumhuran, where many weeks later the director of antiquities was killed and his assistant wounded when their Land Rover was blown apart. The countryside and climate, which, enemy apart, would have attracted tourists, were also interesting to the soldier for the variety of situations they created. In an area equal to Wales, the terrain varies from empty desert to tropical scrub and the climate between burning sun and heavy rain. The mountains rise sharply from the sea except for fifty miles of coastline where the Salalah plain extends some six miles inland, providing fertile soil and a gently shelving shoreline along which fishing boats can easily be beached. Now the plain is well developed but in 1975 there was just a single road, part metal part dirt, between Salalah and the smaller towns of Tarqa and Mirbat.

For two-thirds of the year the sky is a hard, bright blue but during the monsoon, from June to September, low clouds creep in from the Indian Ocean shrouding the mountains in a blanket of grey mist and rain. The mountainous area, in Arabic the *jebel*, is green where it benefits annually from the monsoon. There is wiry scrub in the west, in places low and sparse but elsewhere thicker with small bushy trees. Underfoot the ground is rock strewn and uneven. In the east there are high plateaux of rolling grassland, scorched brown by the time the monsoon comes around but able nevertheless to support a good deal of cattle grazing. The bush and grazing lands, being the areas which support life and provide cover, were the areas of greatest military significance, although the enemy did sometimes operate further inland. Here, beyond the reach of the annual rain, the vegetation peters out and the sand-coloured mountains descend to the Negd, a gravel plain studded with rocky outcrops. Another forty miles inland as the helicopter flies is a ribbon of gleaming white concrete, once the longest airstrip in Arabia and unquestionably the most expensive, every bag of cement having been flown in from Iran. To one side, in 1975, a building site covering many acres marked the expanding airforce base of Thumrait.

The strategy which I inherited had as its military aim the simple statement 'To secure Dhofar for civil development'. This entailed winning the confidence of the population and protecting them in order that they would disown the enemy operating among them and often living in the villages where, with weapons in the hillsides, they could pass as law abiding inhabitants. This population of jebali tribes posed unusual problems, being nomadic within the wider confines of tribal boundaries and accustomed for centuries to constant movement in search of grazing or water. They would have balked at enforced resettlement as a measure of protection, but the harsh environment had made them extremely avaricious so that they would flock to any centre which promised free benefits. These were accordingly provided at strategic points in the wake of military success. The first step in each case was to drive a vehicle track into the area, in itself a formidable task, in order that well drilling equipment and material for construction could follow. The wells, providing water, became natural centres of gravity for the population. They were consolidated by the construction of water-distribution systems with cattle troughs, and the building of clinics, schools and government shops. To avoid the dissipation of troops on static tasks, protection of the centres was largely entrusted to the Firqa, a home guard recruited from enemy who had surrendered. The success of the Firqa was due almost entirely to the British Special Air Service whose five-man detachments created a framework within which the indigenous population could protect itself, acted as a vanguard of civil development and through their medical assistants brought modern medicine to the *jebel* for the first time.

In early 1975 a mine and wire feature called the Hornbeam Line was still playing an important part in the Sultanate strategy. It was an obstacle some thirty miles long running inland from the sea with the purpose of interrupting enemy logistics into the eastern area. It was manned at intervals by platoons who, by day, covered the obstacle with machine gun and mortar fire from their sangars, emplacements of dry stone walls, and by night could patrol the length of wire. The obstacle caused the enemy a serious shortage of supplies and seriously hampered his movement so that his morale and efficiency in the eastern area fell considerably. Well to the west, on the border at Sarfait, an Omani battalion had been deployed in 1972 in an effort to throttle enemy supplies at source. The enemy strength in the area necessitated the battalion being placed in the only defensible position, a plateau from which the ground descended in a series of sheer scarps to the main enemy supply route running close to the sea some 4000 feet below. It was impossible from such a position to ambush effectively the jeep and animal trains which passed nightly and the battalion remained beleaguered, vulnerable to shelling from South Yemen and dependent upon helicopter resupply. Nevertheless, it diverted a good deal of enemy effort and, sitting on the border, was a demonstration of Omani resolve. At the time of my arrival the western area was still virtually an enemy preserve although it had just been penetrated by the Iranian brigade which had fought its way from inland to a point on the coast half way between the Hornbeam Line and the South Yemen border. Here it had established a series of strong defensive positions in exceptionally thick and rugged terrain between the sea and the northern edges of jebel. These positions, called the Damavand Line after the principal mountain in Iran, provided the potential for further disruption to enemy supplies.

At the end of the first week in February, having visited John Akehurst in his headquarters and had a look at the Iranian brigade, I could see we were in a situation, thanks to Tim Creasey's tremendous drive and ability, from which victory was possible. However, counter revolutionary war is notorious for its classic dilemma: how to avoid alienating the population while crushing the guerillas who live among it. Moreover, the enemy enjoyed a secure logistic base in South Yemen as it was considered impolitic for us to attack installations in a country with whom we were not at war, while the western area contained his forward supply areas and would be contested yard by yard. The end was not in sight although the steps to arrive there suggested themselves.

The first move would be to create an effective obstacle along the Damavand Line whilst simultaneously clearing the area east of the Hornbeam Line. The second required clearance of the remaining enemy from east of the Damavand Line. The third and final step would be to defeat the enemy in the west. Military history as written by generals who directed the events which made it, is usually at pains to explain how closely those events followed the grand design. I have to admit that in Dhofar the design was unfolded somewhat empirically. In war one does what one can!

In the first few days I was continually on the go, hopping by helicopter from one position to the next and becoming acquainted with the wide variety of my command. Dhofar brigade, with its Omani and Baluch battalions, inevitably reflected British army traditions and capabilities as there were British commanders down to battalion and sometimes company level. However, these Arabic speaking commanders acknowledged that an Omani might behave very differently to a British soldier; he would be more likely to question his instructions and inclined to react sharply if he lost confidence in his immediate superior. (I recall that we once had to remove an excellent company commander because, in magnanimously accepting responsibility for an operation which had gone wrong, he was unfairly blamed for the casualities by some NCOs. He was subsequently, on my recommendation, awarded the MBE.) The Omani when well trained was good; he used ground naturally, was alert to his surroundings and, once conditioned to stop chattering, was exceptionally good on patrol. He had considerable stamina and could walk for miles over the rock strewn hills without fatigue. He was also good company, gabbling away and joking while offering a visitor coffee and dates even in the austerity of a weapon pit.

The Baluch was an unusually reliable mercenary, slow to learn but, once taught, a good sound soldier. I had the impression he was a bit dour but that may be because I did not speak his language. Dhofar brigade also had operational control of the Firqa, the erstwhile enemy who, having returned to the fold, were organised in tribal units. These men were suspicious, aggressive, argumentative and extraordinarily skilful in negotiation. They usually surrendered carrying only their rifles, leaving other armaments hidden as a source of subsequent revenue, for there were generous government rewards for the capture or discovery of enemy weapons and munitions. To me they seemed difficult and unreliable often having brothers and cousins among the enemy and being concerned principally with the needs of their own tribe. '*Areed*', Arabic for 'I want', seemed their favourite word.

The Firqa unit which was at once the most notorious and successful came from the Mahra, a wandering tribe equally at home in Yemen and Dhofar which, realising it was unlikely to prosper in South Yemen, had crossed into Dhofar and opted for the Sultan. The financial transactions involved had been masterminded by their leader, Barakat, who had learned his trade as a soldier under the British in the Aden Protectorate Levies. Not long after my arrival, Barakat had a complaint and, when he let it be known he would discuss this only with the Sultan or me, I agreed to see him for we needed no bother with the troublesome Mahara. We met in John Akehurst's office, Barakat looking and behaving like a warlord in a loose fitting uniform, green *shemhag* wound around his head and two full bandoliers of ammunition slung across his chest, one from each shoulder. He admitted no English and Bob Brown, an intelligence officer of great Arabian experience, acted as interpreter. Bob warned me that what Barakat really wanted was the prestige of a 'brick built house' at his base in Shishur and advised that I should not agree to this without exacting considerable concessions concerning the Mahara's behaviour. After about twenty minutes of discussion Bob stifled a chuckle and, translating, announced, 'Barakat says that because he alone is entrusted with mounting cross border operations he has heavy weapons which need a proper building in which to maintain them.' We gave him his brick built house in return for a promise of good behaviour and agreement on certain objectives. It is true we had little more trouble with the Mahara but I was never able to verify the performance against objectives.

When Erik Bennett had taken over the airforce in late 1974 it was, I suspected from evidence still remaining when I arrived, somewhat lacking in professional standards. It had an ideal mixture of pilots.

Those on secondment from the British services brought with them the latest ideas and techniques, while those on contract, many of whom had been flying in Oman for a number of years, had a thorough understanding of the local scene. However, when flying intensely on operations, such a mixture needs skilful handling, particularly when some sixty aircraft of seven different types are involved. As an aviator myself, I expressed concern at some of the things I saw, only to find that Erik already had these and many other items in hand. By mid-1975 the airforce was as efficient and as effective as one could find anywhere. The helicopter squadron was certainly the best of its kind in the world; it worked closely with the army and there was never any need for preliminary discussions and rehearsals of procedures such as I had found necessary in the British Armed Forces.

The Iranian troops were very different from the Omanis. I described them as 'American cardboard cutouts', a reflection upon their American instructors, who seemed to ignore national characteristics and sought simply to impose American doctrine and methods. The natural demeanour of the Iranian troops reflected the feudal nature of their country, tough and brave but quite inflexible. It was difficult to probe the thoughts of the average soldiers; they were clearly unused to being addressed by senior officers and looked apprehensive when being spoken to by their company commanders. An infusion of young officers and NCOs, resulting from the sudden expansion of the army, produced junior leaders whose backgrounds were much the same as that of the men they commanded. Thus, the previous old fashioned discipline was diluted and, without the introduction of enlightened attitudes more suited to the new army, there was a void in command at a crucial level which became obvious when the going got rough. Senior commanders were aware of the problem but, lacking the vigour and ideas to tackle it on any scale, applied only palliatives. In Dhofar, the troops were exceptionally well paid and morale was further enhanced by such measures as unnecessarily lavish logistics and excellent rations, all flown in from Iran to a tarmac strip, called Manston, in the middle of a wilderness where the Iranian brigade headquarters reposed in some comfort.

It was essential that I gained the confidence of the Supreme Commander's Staff in Tehran, for without effective use of the Iranian manpower and logistic support, the war would inevitably drag into a stalemate, the Sultanate having insufficient indigenous resources to achieve a clear-cut result. Together with Erik Bennett and Stuart Green I flew to Tehran. We were accommodated in luxury in the Hilton VIP suite and invited to supper at the house of the Chief of the Supreme Commander's Staff, General Azhari. Prepared for a social evening as a prelude to serious discussion on the morrow, I was surprised to be ushered directly into talks. General Azhari had decided to deal with business first so that we could enjoy supper and spend the following day sight seeing in Tehran. Anne and Jane who had accompanied me were left with the ladies while the conference moved to a side room where I sat faced by my host and a semi-circle of at least half a dozen other senior Iranian officers, including General Ovessi the Army Commander, and Major General Ksrodad the Special Forces Commander. The session quickly became a thinly veiled inquisition to determine whether I was to be trusted with Iranian troops. Ksrodad, a lively young general who had attended the British Staff College, was keen on the theory of counter-revolutionary warfare and, in the face of his pertinent questions, I was very soon driven to pointing out that not only had I taught the subject at the place where he had learned it but that I had infinitely more experience of the business than anyone else in the room. Meanwhile, Anne and Jane struggled for a couple of hours to converse with strangers who, with one exception, spoke almost no English. At the first meeting I thought the Iranian senior command an arrogant lot but I was mistaken, for once they had decided I would do, we became very friendly. I then enjoyed having them as colleagues and they looked after me very well whenever I visited them.

In March, General Sherif Zeid ben Shaker, the Chief of Staff of the Jordanian Armed Forces, came to Oman to discuss a forthcoming Jordanian contribution to the war, a battalion of special forces. We met in John Akehurst's headquarters and went through the arrangements which would need to be made, defining our separate responsibilities, an essential prerequisite to successful co-operation between allies. They were to become part of Dhofar Brigade in similar style to the Jordanian engineer squadron already deployed. General Sherif Zeid, besides being a formidably able soldier, is a most charming man; we got on well and have kept in touch over the years since. On that occasion all was settled in a short while and the battalion arrived a few days later.

Meanwhile Dhofar Brigade, having suffered something of a reverse in operations during January, returned to the offensive in Operation Himmar. The headquarters and elements of an enemy regiment had settled in the Wadi Ashoq, a ravine some 1000 feet deep and about half a mile across in the bare rugged country a few miles west of the Hornbeam Line. Two battalions, directed with panache during the last week in February, routed the enemy and destroyed their headquarters, in the process refurbishing morale which had become a little frayed during the January fighting. The bare rocky slopes above the wadi, where centuries of wind had scoured the limestone into natural weapon emplacements, might have been designed specifically for defence and provided the enemy with every advantage. It was while looking in on this operation I first met Major Kuda Bux, a bearded piratical Baluch company commander in the Frontier Force battalion who had come up through the ranks, certainly never having been to a cadet school and probably to no school at all. I crawled with him to a forward platoon from where he explained his plans. His soldiers had piled rocks as cover behind which they could lie on the otherwise bare and exposed plateau. Further movement forward would entail a well co-ordinated attack involving artillery and air support. The series of subsequent actions demonstrated tactical lessons seldom acknowledged in peacetime exercises: reading the battle, deciding when to withdraw just a little from captured positions to avoid enemy fire and when to reoccupy them to fight off the inevitable counter attack.

For the British officers involved, usually captains promoted to acting majors and the only white faces in their companies, such experience was invaluable. Yet I often found it difficult to persuade the Whitehall warriors who controlled career planning to send out the officers I wanted as they thought the best should go to Germany where, it was said, they would receive essential training and evaluation for promotion. However, one way or another, we acquired the officers we needed and Operation Himmar demonstrated to me their high quality, notwithstanding their irregular dress, beards and other idiosyncrasies (one had his entire accompanying possessions carried in a plastic bucket) which visitors from Whitehall sometimes found disconcerting. But it was a pity that many people who should have known better failed to acknowledge the value of full blown active service compared with soldiering on the North German Plain.

Elsewhere operations were proceeding less satisfactorily. The Iranian brigade commander was difficult and stubborn and devised every possible reason for delay. His brigade was due for replacement within a month and he was doing the minimum before he left, apparently bent on taking no chances. On present progress, the Damavand Line, which needed to be effective before the monsoon shrouded the *jebel* and facilitated enemy infiltration, would be completed neither on time nor to a satisfactory standard. In vain I alternately cajoled and rebuked the brigadier. In desperation I had just sent a message to General Azhari saying I wished to discuss the difficulties when, one evening on my return from a day in Dhofar, I found an Iranian general awaiting me in my house with nothing less than a blueprint of the proposed obstacle. In the course of a working dinner, we spread the paper between us and I verified it was precisely what was required. From the enemy side there was first a triple coil of barbed wire firmly staked every five yards, then there was an anti-personnel minefield some eight yards across and finally a single coil of wire on the home side to keep out humans and stray cattle. In the corner of the paper were initials in green ink, the Shah's. It seemed incredible that he had concerned himself with what for him should have been a minor military detail but there is no doubt that he intervened personally wherever and whenever the reputation of Iran was seriously involved, and the Imperial Iranian Army's reputation was certainly at stake along the Damavand Line.

Although the Damavand Line was now to benefit from scrutiny on high, I was still concerned with the lukewarm response to operational tasks in the Iranian Brigade. I was about to raise this also with General Azhari when, overnight, I detected a change in the attitudes of his staff who had hitherto been turning a blind eye to the difficulties put in my way. They now supported me to the hilt brooking no obstruction which might upset me. My staff and I were delighted but it was some time before we discovered the reason for this abrupt change. It seemed a single incident reported to Tehran did the trick. I was visiting the Damavand Line in company with the Iranian brigadier, some of his staff, Hassan Ehesan my ADC and my two liaison officers, Major Andrew Swindale of the Muscat Regiment, and Lieutenant Mansour from Iran. We drove south from Manston into the *jebel* and after several miles of bumping over the rocks we burst through the bush into an open space where a party of Iranian engineers were making a feeble attempt at wiring and mining. We halted and walked a hundred yards to where the work was in progress. It was a clear bright day but at four thousand feet above sea level reasonably cool and, as I remarked to the brigadier, in an effort to loosen him up, an ideal picnic spot. To the north was the bush and rocky plateau through which we had just driven. West and east were deep spectacular ravines, their sides clothed in trees and scrub with clearings here and there of scorched grass. To the south a cobalt blue sea sparkled in the mid-morning sun. We had no sooner arrived at the working party than there was a familiar crump some distance off and I saw the dark smoke hanging in the air for a moment before dispersing. It was a mortar bomb, but I thought too far away to have been intended for us. I made a further jocular remark whereupon the air was rent about us, filled with smoke and the whine of metal ricocheting from rock. Everyone seemed to be dashing for the safety of a nearly platoon position. 'Don't run', I foolishly shouted to Hassan, 'Generals don't run. Just move briskly!' I felt a stinging sensation on the shoulder and at the same time heard Hassan call, 'I'm hit'. I dropped beside him in the shelter of a large rock to discover the back of his thigh slashed through. I applied field dressings and by the time the bandages had been securely tied, silence had returned as suddenly as it had been broken only a minute before. I seemed to be in one piece, just a nick in my shirt. Andrew and Mansour picked themselves up and we carried Hassan to the platoon position. Mansour counted heads and, on finding some missing, ordered the platoon out to search while he and I, with some trepidation, walked back to our vehicles and drove them in. When all had been sorted out and the casualties evacuated by helicopter, I went in search of the brigadier whom I had last seen some thirty minutes earlier dashing for cover as quickly as his portly frame would allow. I ran him to earth in a dugout refreshing himself from a carton of orange juice. It seems it was my icy rebuke, 'You don't usually move so fast,' which, reported to General Azhain by my Iranian liaison officer, put the staff in Tehran on their mettle.

Shortly after this, the Iranians changed over and a Guards brigade under Brigadier Riyhaie, a forceful commander, began construction of the obstacle in earnest. A ten mile swathe was bulldozed through rocks and bush, half a million iron stakes were hammered in to anchor the barbed wire and the fresh brown earth seeded with thousands of mines. Shortage of wire posed a difficulty as the entire British war reserve, had it even been available for purchase, was said to be insufficient while the Indian sources we usually relied upon could not keep pace with our requirements. Enemy reaction caused me some anxiety when, recognising the threat to their supply lines, they began to attack the engineer working parties. However, Brigadier Riyhaie was not to be denied and his brigade completed a well constructed obstacle on time. It was a notable victory.

The Jordanian battalion had been given the task of protecting the road across the *jebel* from Salalah to Thumrait. They were a fine battalion under a lively commander, Major Tasheen Shurdom, a hulk of a man who was forever on the move. Unfortunately for him I deployed his troops in a relatively quiet area already cleared of aggressive enemy. It would have been impolitic to use him elsewhere as the Iranians had taken the most recent knocks and it was necessary for

Omani units to bear the brunt before again exposing an ally. Tasheen, chaffing at the bit, had it put around in Amman that British commanders were not prosecuting the war with genuine zeal but were keeping it going for undisclosed reasons of vested interest. It is probable that Tasheen, an energetic and able soldier, genuinely believed this because the tempo of operations along the Thumrait road was much slower than in other areas of which he had no first hand knowledge. Tasheen's message caused the British Ambassador in Jordan, Glencairn Balfour-Paul, to be summoned to the Palace where, through lack of detailed information, he was unable to allay the King's unease. I also was very concerned at this misunderstanding and readily agreed to fly to Amman to brief the King properly on what was afoot.

Leaving my wounded ADC behind in favour of a temporary replacement and accompanied by Anne and Jane, I arrived late afternoon on the 15th March, to be met by General Sherif Zeid and his wife together with other senior officers and their wives. I inspected the immaculately turned-out guard of honour which, with their white belts, anklets and rifle slings were obviously trained in the British tradition although their striking head-dress, red and white checked *shemhargs*, branded them unmistakably as Jordanian. We were then comfortably installed in the Intercontinental Hotel and allowed a little time before being collected for an official dinner at the Sporting Club. The dinner was presided over by Field Marshal Habis al Majali, a venerable figure whom the bedu soldiers revered and who had been recalled from retirement during the Palestinian uprising in 1970. At dinner he presented me with a wooden gun case on the lid of which was carved the Hashemite Crown and those sitting around thought no doubt that I was being presented with an expensive pair of shotguns. Fortunately I had been warned beforehand that the case contained an armalite rifle otherwise I fear my face might have betrayed some disappointment. Although I could hardly import this high powered personal weapon into England I made the most of it over the next two years, carrying it with me when I was in the forward areas in Dhofar and at other times winning a number of prizes at various shooting competitions.

The following day, accompanied by the ambassador, I had an audience with King Hussein. To facilitate my explanation I had brought a large map but, in the absence of anywhere to display it, had rolled it and placed it behind a sofa upon which I was primly sitting in my best uniform awaiting the arrival of the King. He entered, dressed in a sweatshirt and jeans, and in true professional style began immediately to talk business. He came across as a man of great charisma, polite but with an air of unmistakable authority. The map was produced and, pushing back the furniture, we spread it on the floor, anchoring the corners with ashtrays and ornaments. With the ambassador peering anxiously above us we crawled over the terrain, our hands thrusting and sweeping in the manner of military manoeuvres. I noticed that King Hussein was wearing a watch exactly like mine, one which Sherif Zeid had given me during his visit to Oman. Military manoeuvres over, to the evident satisfaction of the King, we discussed the process of training Omani officers and, drawing a parallel from his own experience when he was forced to dismiss Glub Pasha, the British Commander of the Arab legion, he urged me to ensure that Omanis were given as much responsibility as soon as possible. My audience ended, the King preceded me to the door where my ADC heard him say to his staff officer, 'He's got one.' (I had obviously been about to receive another watch.) Next day I was awarded the Hashemite Order of Independence First Class, the Jordanian equivalent of a knighthood, while my ADC received a lesser order. It had, I thought, been a most successful visit.

However, Hassan Ehesan who was still recovering from his wounds thought otherwise. On my return from Amman I found him lying in bed in a dark, sparsely furnished room in his little house in Salalah. The Sultan had been to visit him two days previously, a singular honour, and had at the time presented him with a white gold watch which, even in those days, must have been worth several thousand pounds. Hassan was extremely angry that my temporary ADC, with no active service behind him, should have received a Jordanian award and, in an effort to placate him, I referred to the Sultan's visit and the watch. Hassan reached to a shelf behind his bed and as the watch flashed towards me I dived from my chair to catch it in the manner of a cricketer fielding in the slips. Ten years later, Hassan, now a general, entertained me in his magnificent house in Muscat and we laughed in reminiscence.

In April Roy Mason, the British Secretary of State for Defence, and his wife came on a brief visit. It was British policy that the number of loan service officers would be reduced as quickly as possible in order to obviate possible accusations of neo-colonialism, particularly from the Socialist government's own left wing. The Sultan, however, was in no such hurry and recognising the precariousness of the situation, was prepared to pay handsomely for British assistance. Thus, I was put in the unenviable position of being constrained by left wing policies at home while serving a ruler who was well to the right. I skated over these topics with Roy Mason who in the course of his visit seemed to adopt a more accommodating view. We gave a dinner party for the delegation which included two Foreign Office officials whom I had not seen since we were subalterns together in 1947, Ivor Lucas and Martin Ewans. The Masons proved very agreeable guests but perhaps it was the reunion of the three musketeers which turned what threatened to be rather a formal party into a very jovial occasion.

In May it was suggested that I should return to London to be present when King Hussein visited the Ministry of Defence and I flew back for several days, taking the opportunity to visit my parents and sleep in the small room and narrow bed which I had not occupied for some twenty five years. The meeting between the secretary of state and the King was attended on the British side by Field Marshal Sir Michael Carver, who had recently visited me in Oman, and a number of other senior officers and officials. On the Jordanian side were General Sherif Zeid and the Jordanian Prime Minister, Zeid Rafai. I sat on the sofa between these two, thus placing me firmly in the Arab camp. I was regarded rather suspiciously by my British colleagues when I addressed the King as *Seede*, Arabic for 'Sir' and the form of address which all Jordanian officers use in conversation with the King. As the meeting broke up and the Jordanian delegation was escorted away, Sherif Zeid invited me to join him and the Prime Minister for lunch at the Ritz; that was enough in those corridors of power to brand me as a latter-day Lawrence, a soldier of fortune, or even worse!

I sensed, when with the Jordanian battalion, how closely the officers were attached to their King but it was not until he visited the battalion that I realised this deep loyalty extended down to the most junior soldier. The King, accompanied by his chief of staff and Prime Minister, flew into Seeb early one morning where, having been received by the Sultan with the usual courtesies of a guard of honour and a gun salute, they transferred to one of our BAC 1-11s for the flight to Dhofar. On board the aircraft Erik Bennett and I were hosts to the King's entourage, the Sultan, Sayid Faher the Omani minister of defence, and the Omani foreign minister Qais Zawai. It was a precious load and Middle East history would no doubt have been written differently had any misfortune befallen the aircraft. On arrival at Thumrait, John Akehurst joined us and we set off first to visit the Jordanian engineers and then the battalion. I have never before or since in any walk of life seen such a display of affection by subordinates for their leader. The same scene was repeated over and over again as groups of soldiers, varying in number up to a hundred, swept the King into their midst where, arms linked, they performed a vigorous national dance. Then it was a matter of everyone present wishing to kiss and shake hands with the King so that, being short of stature, he vanished into a seething mass of khaki, to reappear with his beret askew, smiling broadly and enjoying every minute. He would not be hurried and it was teatime before we sat down to lunch in the palace at Salalah.

I had no routine in Oman and there were scarcely ever two consecutive days remotely alike. Although Dhofar absorbed most of my energy, I also had to look after the whole of Northern Oman and the Mussandam Peninsular. This inevitably involved a good deal of travelling, most of which I did by AB 205 medium helicopter and the six seater, twin engined, high-wing Defender. I brushed up my flying and Erik arranged a series of lessons to convert me to helicopters and make me familiar with the Defender. I piloted myself a good deal but was always accompanied by an experienced pilot as both Erik and I agreed that senior officers, lacking sufficient everyday practice, might need help should a technical emergency arise. In addition to satisfying myself about security and administration in the north, I needed also to ensure that units were being prepared for their role in Dhofar so that some days were taken up observing training. Inevitably, I needed to spend precious time in my headquarters but this I cut to an absolute minimum, no more than a few hours a week, preferring when in the Muscat area to call on people with whom I needed to keep contact. Whenever the occasion permitted, I would drop in, often unannounced but always made welcome, on Sayid Faher, whose Ministry was in a series of long low bungalows within a few yards of my headquarters. Although on paper I reported to him, in practice I usually dealt direct with the Sultan. I needed, however, to keep the minister informed, and we both agreed that talking over a cup of coffee was as an effective and agreeable means as any. Sayid Faher was the King's uncle who, having remained virtually in exile while his brother was ruling, returned to assist his nephew when the latter came to the throne. A large bearded figure, impressive both in national dress and a city suit, he became a useful colleague and friend.

The Sultan would see me whenever I felt I needed to seek his views or inform him personally of events. We would usually meet in his new palace at Sib, a magnificent spacious building where, from within the central area with its high ceiling and marble columns, one looked across a rectangular ornamental pool and through an expanse of dark glass to the date gardens outside. The Sultan spent a good deal of time in Dhofar so that we sometimes met in one of his two palaces there. Our discussions were wide ranging for the armed forces had at their disposal well over half the nation's gross national product and it was inevitable that I was concerned with much of what went on. I also became involved in policy making as a member of the National Development Council, in effect the cabinet, in which all ministers of the government sat under the chairmanship of the Sultan. However, it was through personal audiences, at which the only other person sometimes present was Brigadier Tim Landon, that I conducted most of my business with the Sultan. Tim had been a junior officer on loan to Oman at the time when Qaboos acceded to the throne. He left the British Army soon after and, having become equerry, gained the Sultan's confidence so that by the time I arrived he had considerable influence. He was somewhat suspicious of British loan service officers, perhaps because many of them failed to understand his true position, and he was one of the Sultan's close advisers who seemed to think that I was under instructions from Whitehall. This was far from the truth and the suggestion would have undermined my position had I not strongly refuted it.

Finance was a subject inevitably well to the fore in the National Defence Council and my private audiences with the Sultan. Oman did not have enough oil or other indigenous resources to finance the war and her neighbours, in acknowledgement of what Oman was doing for them, provided some financial assistance. However, money was tight and soon after my arrival, in an endeavour to make money available for what I thought were higher priorities, I tried to reverse or amend a number of procurement decisions which had already been taken. I should have recognised earlier that government finance and procurement in the Middle East are very different from those in Whitehall. I wasted much energy and may have made a few enemies but it was, on reflection, an essential part of finding my feet.

I also kept in regular contact with the British ambassador, Jim Treadwell, whose office and residence occupied the most desirable spot in Muscat. From his verandah one looked towards the open sea, visible half a mile away between the rocky promontories which made Muscat such a spectacular and natural harbour. On either side, high among the burnished brown rocks, were two Portugese fortresses. On the left was Fort Mirani, more or less derelict but being refurbished as a station for the Royal Guard. On the right was Fort Jalani, then a somewhat notorious prison. It suited both the Sultanate and the British Government that I should keep the ambassador informed of my plans but I did so discreetly in order to avoid giving the impression that I was at the beck and call of the British Government.

I had no public relations staff and dealt personally with all journalists. Public relations plays a significant part in counter-revolutionary operations both in explaining government intentions and in countering enemy propaganda. If government forces are too idle or blinkered to keep the media well informed and too proud to justify their actions, they cannot expect public support at home or political backing abroad. I issued an instruction that any war correspondent coming to Oman would need first to see me in order, as I said only half jokingly, to hear the truth according to Perkins before they heard it from anyone else. There were not many such visitors but I saw them all with no holds barred and nothing off the record. It absorbed time but was a policy which paid off and the Omani cause received a very good international press.

May was a busy month. Perhaps the most exciting event was the arrival of a further subvention from Jordan, this time in the shape of sixteen Hunter aircraft. Sayid Faher, Erik Bennett and I were at Thumrait to meet them on arrival. Running a Hunter squadron from Thumrait would be no easy task in view of the very limited facilities as yet there but both Erik and I appreciated how important it would be to create an effective squadron with these aircraft. They could provide us for the first time with a proper air defence and enable us, should the strategic situation change significantly, to strike across the border in the face of the considerable air defences we knew were assembled there. Erik set about the task with relish.

As the monsoon approached, the positions on the *jebel* were stocked with ammunition, supplies and water to enable them to survive during the long periods when bad weather and the state of the tracks would make both helicopter and land resupply impossible. The Damavand Line was virtually complete and I could but hope that my exhortations would cause the Iranians to patrol it properly so that the enemy to the east of it would wither on the vine. When the monsoon cleared in October, we would need to move into a highly geared assault, based on Dhofar brigade but not just it alone. Success would require the co-ordination of all our resources including the air force with its newly acquired but not yet operational Hunters, the Iranians whom I hoped would be reinforced and the navy who had hitherto played only a very small part.

Chapter 11

Politics and Picnics

THE plans for the operation which was to be launched after the monsoon were well developed even in June when the grey mist and rain swirled across Dhofar from the Indian Ocean, heralding the onset of the close season. A few days after my arrival in February I had announced my intention to carry the offensive into the western areas of Dhofar as soon as possible and, after preliminary consideration, decided this would best be done by expanding the Sarfait position in order to block enemy reinforcement and resupply at source. John Akehurst, who would have the responsibility for carrying out whatever operation I conceived, was concerned at the logistic risks of such a plan for it would depend upon helicopter resupply and this, at the delivery end, might be subjected to artillery fire from across the border. I felt the logistics were a risk worth taking but the more I dwelt on the military advantages of my proposal, the more I became aware of the political perils. There was no doubt that the sudden arrival of considerable Omani forces along the border could precipitate hostilities with regular South Yemeni troops who would then have the advantage of operating close to home while we would be fighting at the end of a tenuous logistic link, also with a guerilla campaign at our back. I had no doubt we could cope militarily with such circumstances but only at the price of escalating the conflict internationally, for we would need to employ artillery and air strikes against targets in South Yemen. The alternative was to establish a new obstacle to enemy resupply just out of artillery range of South Yemen and to clear the country up to this before advancing in a less threatening manner to the border. It was the political factor which persuaded me that this plan, although more pedestrian, was preferable.

Thus, on the 23rd March I had written to the Sultan with proposals for 'Operations Post Monsoon 1975'. The aim of the operations were to be '......forces will thin down.....leaving the major protective tasks in the hands of the Firqa.' A line from an area nicknamed 'Furious' to Dhalqut, a village on the coast, was to be seized and '.....developed as an obstacle, which can be held with minimum force, and which will serve as a base for offensive operations eastwards towards Damavand and westwards towards Sarfait'. This concept formed the basis of my instructions to John Akehurst in which I also said that he should arrange a diversionary sortie from Sarfait just before the main operation and that I would order the Iranians to mount a battalion attack elsewhere to occupy enemy forces which otherwise might intervene at Dhalqut. John then decided that he would utilise the monsoon period to drive a road westwards, north of the monsoon affected area, to create a forward logistic base and that his assault across the Wadi Sayq, a deep precipitous ravine almost a mile wide just north of Dhalqut, his final objective, would be by helicopter.

History recounts the contradictions General Eisenhower had to resolve before selecting D-Day for the Normandy landings. Our problems in selecting our D-Day were in a minor key but no less contradictory. It was important to kick off at the earliest time in order to retain the initiative, but the end of the monsoon would fall within the month of Ramadan when all practising Moslems fast from sunrise to sunset. For men in battle there could be special dispensation but it was doubtful if Omani and Baluch soldiers would have broken their fast, so they would have hardly been at their best. Moreover, Ramadan ends with the festival of Eid and I sensed that morale would have suffered further if this important occasion could not be celebrated in traditional style. I anticipated some contention and, to kill it, I dropped a note to John Akehurst copying it to the Sultan: '..... I foresee an extremely tough battle (a view incidently shared with the Jordanian chief of staff who also knows a bit about fighting) in which morale will play a crucial part. For this reason I feel that the advantages of attacking early are outweighed by the problems of morale and efficiency which will arise if D-Day is during Ramadan. There will be a need to train units and firqa in tree line conditions [operating in wooded country] before D-Day and there are advantages in letting some of the vegetation wither before we plunge in. [During the monsoon the grass grows to a height of several feet, providing good cover for troops on the defensive.] I conclude therefore that D-Day should be Ramadan plus five to seven days. You are to plan this.' John selected the 21st of October and within a few days of this being made known secretly to a chosen few, the battalion nominated for the assault, the Frontier Force, announced it was to hold an officers' dance on the 16th. Ostensibly there was no connection between the two dates but, henceforth, I referred to the forthcoming dance as 'the Duchess of Richmond's Ball' after the well known event in Brussels in 1815 from which the Duke of Wellington had galloped to the Battle of Waterloo.

By early July, with operations in the south much reduced in tempo, I could devote more time to Northern Oman and, incidently, enjoy its rugged grandeur. My most pressing concern was to improve the training organisation. I had some time earlier sacked the British officer in charge of officer training after a near mutiny among the cadets and was now reasonably happy with the quality of young officers being turned out. I now removed the Jordanian colonel who was running the whole training organisation, holding my breath for the diplomatic protest which never came, and insisted that he and some of the more worn out instructors were replaced by officers and NCOs with enthusiasm and drive. Too often, in military life, training organisations provide a soft billet for people who have grown out of the rigours of soldiering while at the same time active units hang on to the very people needed in the instructional machine. I insisted that battalions surrendered good instructors, emphasising that it was in their own long term interests that they did so and arranged that, with the exception of a few specialists, the instructional staff was turned over regularly. Thus, refurbished and refreshed, the organisation could now keep front line battalions up to strength with a supply of fit and well trained young men, properly prepared for the campaign ahead.

My interest in the training battalion caused me to spend a good deal of time on the Jebel Akhdar, the Green Mountain, where, at a place called Saiq, the recruits underwent a final battle camp before posting to their battalions. The latter also used the area for exercises with live ammunition during their periods of retraining in Northern Oman, so here was another excuse for me to spend time in what was my favourite place of all. The Jebel Akhdar was an area of magnificent scenery between the Batinah, the coastal plain studded with date palms, and the sands to the west. The mountains rose spectacularly from the plain, the higher crags reaching 7000 feet, and continued, interspersed with deep ravines, for some fifty miles inland before descending as precipitously as they had risen. Here geology was laid bare, the rock face showing clearly how the earth, under immense pressures, had been pushed skywards with its strata writhing into strange contortions. I was sufficiently enthused and impressed to acquire a geological textbook and sometimes even resisted piloting my own helicopter in favour of a more detailed study of the cliffs we were passing. An Englishman would hardly have called the mountain green unless he had an artist's eye practised at distinguishing subtle hues, but to someone accustomed only to barren rocks and sand there would have been an unmistakable green tinge to the slopes, particularly on the high plateau, at the centre of which was the brown, mud walled village of Saiq with its cultivations of corn, limes and vegetables.

Set apart from the village was a small hutted encampment from which Major Chris Bentall-Warner ran the training area. On the edge of the plateau was the stone bungalow of Major Graham Vivien, a retired Gurkha officer who carried administration to the far flung villages. From his verandah one looked down upon green and yellow terraced cultivations, held in place on the mountainside by dry stone walls, giant's steps into the abyss below. Here and there were glimpses of bright water, flashing in the sun as it flowed through the narrow channels of the *falage* system which, fed by mountain springs, irrigated the small fields and fulfilled domestic needs, as it had for centuries past. Beyond and below were more precipitous slopes with now and then the thread of a footpath twisting its way between the tumbling rocks towards the Niwza road, lost in the haze 6000 feet below. When visitors needed entertaining for a day, I often flew them to Saiq, landing on the rough air strip and being met by Chris Bentall-Warner with a small convoy of open top Land Rovers. Depending on the nature of the party, we would drive to watch troops under training or pick our way through the cultivated terraces, enjoying the sunshine, scenery and the cool mountain air, finishing with lunch in the shade of overhanging rocks.

One morning on landing at Saiq I was told that the famous British explorer, Wilfred Thesiger, was in Graham Vivien's bungalow. A quarter of a century earlier, in company with two Arab boys, he had crossed the Empty Quarter by camel, starting from Salalah and finishing in Northern Oman where he intended to climb up into Saiq. At that time the tribes in the north were hostile and he was denied entry. He had now returned, aged 65, collecting his erstwhile camel boys from Salalah with the promise of completing their unfinished journey. The camel boys, now corpulent businessmen, had protested volubly when faced with the climb; it was now possible to fly. But their pleading was to no avail and they climbed with him to Graham's bungalow where I met them after their night's rest. Wilfred Thesiger was a tall, gaunt and almost mystical figure. One could imagine him enjoying the privations he had encountered, exploits behind enemy lines in the Second World War, explorations and travels in Africa and Iraq and, above all, the

Empty Quarter where he had almost perished. As he had twisted his knee during the climb, I flew him down to the military hospital at Moascar al Muturfa. He sat entranced for he had never before been in a helicopter and had, hitherto, enjoyed only a worm's eye view of the magnificent country over which we now skimmed. His knee attended to, we flew on to lunch at Bait al Falage. I radioed ahead to invite some guests and from the moment we sat down until we broke up two and a half hours later Wilfred held their attention with modest but enthralling accounts of his many travels.

Strategic issues involving northern Oman made it necessary for me to travel occasionally to another area of immense grandeur and natural beauty, the Mussandam, a mountainous peninsular which guards the entrance to the Arabian Gulf. The Mussandam is separated from the rest of Oman by a number of small sheikhdoms each federated within the United Arab Emirates and although at this juncture of the war in Dhofar we could ill afford to strengthen the small garrison there, I felt we should do something to demonstrate our resolve to safeguard this vital area. The Sultan was much preoccupied with Dhofar and to attract his interest I quoted the tonnage of oil shipped daily through the Straits of Hormuz which fuelled western economies. I pointed out that the tanker routes passed through Omani territorial waters at the tip of the Mussandam peninsular and that someone, sooner or later, would wish to see these properly protected. The unspoken someone was the Shah of Iran who, although an ally at that moment, might subtly shift his position if he thought his interests were threatened by another's dereliction of duty. From that early talk with the Sultan a great deal of development, both civil and military, ultimately sprang and although most of it was delayed, for economic reasons, until after my time, I was able to initiate some early measures.

The first step was a personal reconnaissance and I set off early one morning from Seeb airport. It was a two and a half hour flight in a twin engined Defender. As usual, Sean Creak, the pilot, let me start up, taxi out and take off. Sean was an ex-fighter pilot who had settled for the quieter life of ferrying people around. He was a flying instructor and had been only too happy to instruct me on the Defender, often to the alarm of other passengers when they realised it was the general taking them into a difficult dirt strip in turbulent conditions. However, there was no turbulence on this early morning flight to the Mussandam as our direct course took us a mile or two out to sea and away from the thermals. The coastal plain on our left narrowed as we flew north and, after about an hour, gave way to a rocky shore line. Here the bare mountains plunged steeply into the sea save for small inlets of bleached sand which slipped past now and then, each guarded by a fishing village squeezed between the shore and rock.

When it came into sight, the Mussandam reminded me of the Norwegian coast and, remembering how in the Second World War shipping had played hide and seek in the fiords, it struck me immediately that a few small boats equipped with missiles could control the shipping lanes in the Straits. A forward replenishment point was needed to obviate the time wasted on passage from the naval base in Muscat and it would be useful to have a land based radar covering the Straits. The bill began to grow in my mind as I thought of the protection these fixed installations would need and I recognised that, for the present, we lacked the necessary resources. The best we could do was to keep a fast patrol boat on station, at least demonstrating a strategic interest. Not much in life is absolutely new and, as we circled the inlets and small islands at the tip of the Mussandam peninsular, Sean said that the small unused stone jetty and derelict buildings passing beneath us had once belonged to the Royal Navy. Here, with some renovation, was our replenishment point. We flew over Khasab, the centre of population in the Mussandam, and, bumping down on the airstrip just outside the town, were met by the infantry captain on whose shoulders the security of this outpost rested.

Mussandam in 1975 was still a wild and isolated place, much more so than even the remoter regions of the Jebel Akhdar. There were a few tracks but movement in the hills could be only by foot or helicopter. In the five years since the accession of Sultan Qaboos, Oman had faced many difficulties, not least the war in Dhofar, and this area which I was now visiting for the first time was at the bottom of all priorities. It was hardly surprising that the Shihu tribesmen were developing a closer affinity with the bordering wealthy United Arab Emirates than with Oman. Here was another reason for strengthening our presence and during this first visit I gave instructions that helicopter support was always to be on hand, both to increase the mobility of the few troops available and to provide transport for civilian supplies.

In Dhofar, John Akehurst had launched an operation in mid-August to secure the area of his new forward logistic base and the road which was to supply it. The lack of immediate enemy reaction illustrated again that although a guerilla force is tactically very mobile, it is slow to react at strategic level. The operation drove for some miles through areas liberally sprinkled with anti-personnel mines and, whenever the presence of these dreadful devices was suspected, an armoured bulldozer came forward to clear the way. On realising that they were being outflanked, the enemy reacted strongly and road building ground to a halt when the civilian labourers came under fire and downed tools. I asked my Jack-of-all-trades, Ian Sprackling, to give the problem his personal attention and by dint of leadership, reorganisation and persuasion, a difficult task was finished in the nick of time. The enemy was also provoked by these operations into the premature use of his recently acquired SAM 7 anti-aircraft missiles, thus giving the airforce the opportunity to revise their flying tactics before the intensive operations which were to follow.

Along the Damavand Line, the Iranians were doing a thorough job and the enemy in eastern Dhofar, being starved of supplies and reinforcements, began to surrender in significant numbers. However, Iranian efforts were not universally appreciated and their habit of calling upon Dhofar Brigade to assist them with casualty evacuation led to some friction. I had to issue specific instructions that in bad weather or at night, when the inexperienced Iranian helicopter pilots could not cope, help with casualties was not to be questioned. This reluctance to spring to the aid of an ally seemed uncharacteristic of the helicopter pilots with whom I had often flown and, together with the doubts I heard voiced among them over the large operation which was planned for October, led me to discuss the state of their morale with both John Akehurst and Erik Bennett. Undoubtedly they were constantly under pressure and many of them, after several years of operational flying, must have wondered if they were living on borrowed time. A change in leadership was needed and Erik Bennett acquired the services on loan from the Royal Air Force of Squadron Leader Tony Nicholson under whose leadership the unit never again looked back.

While the enemy in the east were withering on the vine, those in the west were showing increasing vigour. Intelligence indicated that three companies of regular troops from South Yemen were operating on Omani territory while 85 and 130 mm guns had, from their sanctuary beyond the border, joined the bombardment of Sarfait. Thus, one of the reasons for my choice of area for the post monsoon operations, the avoidance of hostilities with South Yemen, was being negated by that country itself. I knew that Whitehall would disapprove on political grounds of me hitting back but I thought their objections ill founded. Moreover, they had placed me at the disposal of the Sultan who I knew would not object and as a precautionary move I ordered some five point five inch guns, which had sufficient range to reach across the border, to be moved to Sarfait by Iranian heavy lift helicopters. Our other means of retaliation would be the Hunter squadron which, under the hand of its seconded squadron commander, Robin Renton, had been fused into a first class unit. Their operations entailed a return to less sophisticated methods than are usually associated with modern aviation and it was not unusual to see pilots driving Land Rover trains of bombs along the flight line and assisting in the rearming of their own aircraft between sorties.

On the 14th of October, after last light, the diversionary operation sallied forth from Sarfait. It was led by Ian Gordon of whom I had seen a great deal, for he and my daughter Jane had recently announced their plans for marriage. By first light C Company of the Muscat regiment had filed its way through enemy held country to secure a dominating feature called Capstan which had long since mocked the defenders on Sarfait. There the company dug in to await the considerable enemy action which we were sure would follow. On the morning of the 16th, still with five days to go to the main operation, I arrived at Salalah en route to visit Ian's company, anticipating that I might have to fly in between shot and shell. I was met by John Akehurst who reported that while the enemy were still making life hazardous on Sarfait, they had so far ignored our diversion. He thought we should reinforce success and, in anticipation of my approval, had scratched together an ad hoc force as there would not be time to assemble the intended D-Day battalions which were still deployed in the Salalah area. As we drove the few hundred yards to John Akehurst's headquarters I made the decision to switch the main operation to Sarfait that night and out of the window went months of planning together with that potentially hazardous helicopter operation across the Wadi Sayq.

It was now imperative that we take steps to reduce enemy interference from South Yemen. I therefore ordered the Hunter squadron to attack military targets in the area of Hauf and the five point five inch guns to harass these targets between the air attacks. To help with the logistic problem I told the navy to load up a coaster, the Sultana, with defence stores and operate off Sarfait as a resupply point for helicopters. John Akehurst put Lieutenant Colonel Ian Christie in charge of the thrust to the sea; this would be undertaken that night, by a hastily assembled collection of companies from the Muscat Regiment, the Frontier Force, the Southern Regiment and the Firqa. Thus, was the plan completely changed without, as I remarked in an address later that year to the Staff College at Camberley, the issue of a single piece of paper.

Twenty four hours later I was circling Hauf in a Defender when the

Hunters made their first pass 10,000 feet below. Their targets, the gun positions and military installations, were fortunately well away from civilian habitation but the dust drifted in the slight breeze so that soon the entire town lay under a brown pall. I admired the courage of the South Yemeni anti-aircraft gunners as the muzzle flashes of the Russian 23 mm guns stabbed through the dust when the Hunters returned in pairs to rake the area with cannon fire. Within a few minutes the attack was over; the artillery had at least been disrupted and I could see far beneath me the helicopters shuttling between the deck of the Sultana, stacked with defence stores, and the red-brown earthworks now erupting on the scrub covered slopes which stepped down between Sarfait and the sea. Previous experience elsewhere had taught me that in guerilla warfare the military returns from brute force are seldom proportionate to the effort expended but I was seeking more than tactical results. Half a dozen Hunters had just made a political statement, telling South Yemen that it could no longer, with impunity, support the enemies of Oman.

I flew back to Salalah to report to the Sultan whom I had kept informed of my change of plan. There had been no need to seek authorisation for the attack on Hauf as we had recently discussed such a possibility and I knew he would approve. He awaited me with a present 'through which to survey the damage', a pair of Leitz binoculars with a magnification of 10×50, yet not much larger than opera glasses.

The Sultan was clearly pleased with events, as was the Omani foreign minister, Qais Zawai, who came to my house several evenings later specifically to congratulate me, saying that he could now adopt a better stance in the Arab League where his colleagues had been saying for some time that Oman should strike at South Yemen.

The planned Iranian attack had lost its point as a diversion but I ordered it to proceed as a means of maintaining pressure on the enemy and hastening the end. The Iranians had augmented their brigade by a battalion group and provided three frigates. Preceded by a bombardment from these frigates, air strikes from Omani Strikemasters and an Iranian artillery concentration, a battalion was lifted by helicopter to seize a feature on the coast west of Damavand. It was on the direct line of approach to the enemy forward supply area and they fought so stubbornly that the operation might well have failed had it not been for the courageous action of a British gunner, Captain Gordon Allen, whose party, having been spewed from a helicopter which refused to land, co-ordinated the attack and then consolidated the position. For several days it was not a place to linger above ground and helicopters dumped their cargoes of supplies, men and visiting generals without even touching down. Leaving the position entailed an even more hazardous scramble.

The enemy artillery became adept at using the mountainous terrain for concealment and protection and, having made good his losses, continued to bombard Sarfait. I therefore continued the air attacks. Both Erik and I recognised the need to guard against retaliation from South Yemeni MIG 21s and a pair of Hunters regularly flew a photographic mission over the air strip at Rian which, we calculated, would be used as a refuelling stop by any enemy with hostile intent. Rian was a dirt strip some miles along the Yemeni coast which so far had been free of any activity and we concluded that if military aircraft arrived there it would be only to attack us. I issued contingency orders that in such an event they would be dealt with forthwith. The enemy anticipated my plan and one day when Erik telephoned to say the photographs showed four MIG 23s lined up at the end of the strip, I confirmed my orders without hesitation. Fortunately for international relations and my career, the photographs were re-examined before take off and the photographic interpreter acknowledged that he had been deceived by four canvas and wood mock-ups. Strangely enough I never, subsequently in the Whitehall files, found any mention of this although I came across the exchange of telegrams occasioned when Robin Renton, the squadron commander, was shot down during a photographic mission. Many months before when visiting London I had, in discussion with the British chief of air staff, Air Chief Marshal Sir Andrew Humphrey, suggested that there would be problems of leadership and morale if Robin ordered his contract officers to fly over South Yemen when he, as a serving British officer on loan to Oman, was expressly forbidden to operate beyond its borders. Sir Andrew acknowledged my difficulty but could offer no solution and, when the time came, Robin solved the problem by breaking the rules. His aircraft was hit during a photographic sortie but he managed to coax it back along the coast to Hauf where he ejected and, under a hail of fire from the shore, was winched into a helicopter and safely recovered. To me it was one of many incidents and I took but little notice until Jim Treadwell, at a palace garden party, invited me behind the palm trees to unfold a telegram he had just received from the Chief of Defence Staff in London, Field Marshal Sir Michael Carver. Jim was requested, on behalf of the field marshal to ask me exactly what I was up to and, euphoric because events were going so well, I simply replied that I was finishing off the war. The following morning discretion seemed the better part of valour and I rang Jim with a more reasoned reply, to learn that my message had gone. I received no riposte but the field marshal had made his point and henceforth I ensured that no one broke the rules.

Of the eight or so Hunters which were operational, this was the second we had lost to the air defences in South Yemen within a few days. The other had been flown by Captain Mohammed Fajar, a Jordanian pilot, whose aircraft had been hit during an air strike on Hauf. Being unable to swim, and not trusting his dinghy or life jacket, he rejected the option of parachuting into the sea, and decided to try for home. He nursed his stricken aircraft part way but it would go no further than the short air strip at Manston where he attempted a forced landing. For a fast jet such as a Hunter it would have been an impossible task even with an undamaged aircraft and when the dust subsided, the cockpit, with Mohammed strapped inside, was the only recognisable piece of debris. The helicopter which had been sent to winch him from the water now collected him from the wreckage and within a few minutes he was back at his base. Miraculously he was unhurt and his squadron leader ordered him back in the air the same afternoon. As a confidence rebuilding measure it was an order I applauded. After all, I had once been in somewhat similar, albeit more tragic, circumstances although with the situation reversed, for I had intended to put down on land but inadvertently finished up in the water.

At the end of November the British Foreign Secretary, James Callaghan, came to assess the situation and discuss post war arrangements between Britain and Oman. Accompanied by Jim Treadwell, Foreign Office officials and myself, the Foreign Secretary flew to Salalah where a private discussion took place between him and the Sultan. The officials fretted over their exclusion although I assured them that we would catch up with the conversation during lunch and diverted their attention to the opulence of the palace ante-room in which we were sitting. At lunch the conversation flagged a little and, remembering that the foreign secretary was a farmer and knowing the Sultan had recently introduced a herd of cattle to his farm, I turned the conversation in this direction. Jim Callaghan then gave an expert dissertation on farm management. The Foreign Office party, by their looks, made clear their displeasure with me for depriving them of their political fodder but I countered, in a whispered conversation, that we would get back to politics over coffee. However, as the coffee was about to be poured the Sultan invited his guest to inspect the new herd and the pair drove off, with the Sultan at the wheel, in the royal Mercedes. I doubt if the Foreign Secretary ever did brief his officials because when they were next together, on the return flight to Muscat, he first held a press conference and then spent the remainder of the flight chatting with the ambassador and me. The Foreign Secretary remarked that now the war was virtually over the British could soon come home. I countered by saying if we did so the organisation would fall apart . It was a remark designed to deter British politicians from precipitate flight and not intended for my Omani friends who, although they would not want the British to leave so soon, would have preferred it expressed in less uncompromising terms. My remarks were overheard by a reporter and found their way to Oman via the airmail editions, causing me to move smartly around the capital placating my friends. Some years later the *Comité de Soutien de la Revolution* in Paris translated the Times report into French and used my words, taken out of context, on the back of a record sleeve of revolutionary songs.

On the 1st of December John Akehurst, Jonathan Salusbury-Trelawny, commanding the Frontier Force, and I arrived on the scarp overlooking the village of Dhalqut, the one village in Oman still awaiting liberation. The three of us had somehow got well ahead of the final mopping up operations. It was a brilliant day and, with the monsoon now nearly two months behind us, the grass was withered and the vegetation a burnt ochre. There were some figures in the shadows of the houses but the only sign of danger came from three sharks basking uncommonly close to the surf. I suggested that we should scramble on down but reluctantly curbed my enthusiasm when John disclosed that he had invited the press for the following day. Twenty four hours later, on the 2nd December, Dhalqut was occupied by the Frontier Force and the long Dhofar war officially declared at an end.

There was plenty of space for small parties of men to disappear in the wild country of western Dhofar but it seemed probable that those hard core enemy who had neither been killed nor surrendered, had either fled to South Yemen or simply hidden their weapons and returned to their villages. There was still plenty of space and opportunity for guerilla activity should the enemy choose to continue. For this reason I had been conscious, even before victory came so unexpectedly within our grasp, that, in the closing stages, we would need to achieve some political leverage to ensure that South Yemen withdrew the support which alone could prolong the war. I therefore continued the air strikes for some five weeks, calling them off on the 21st November as a demonstration of our willingness to wind down operations if South Yemen was prepared to reciprocate. It took some time for the guns from across the border to fall silent but there is no doubt that the sustained air attacks were an essential complement to the political activity which, through Saudi Arabia and the Arab League, led to the cessation of hostilities.

During December I was invited by the commandant of the Staff College, Major General Pat Howard Dobson, whose tank I had chased round Germany so many years before, to address the faculty and students. It was at short notice and I approached the task with some trepidation as, with only a day or two in which to prepare my address, I recalled other senior officers who had failed before this professionally well informed, generally ambitious and critical audience. However, I need not have worried for it had been a long time since elements of the British Army had been to war in such favourable political circumstances, and I had a good tale to tell. It is, of course, impossible to separate the political and military elements of a counter-revolutionary campaign and I dwelt on this aspect at some length, pointing out that when the government forces are of an international nature, as mine had been, the commander needs to be alive to the varying national political objectives and to anticipate the reflection of these in the attitudes of the national contingents. I ended, amid considerable applause, by suggesting that in war, politics is too important to be left to the politicians. Although my thoughts went down well with the up and coming military generation, they received less approbation when, several years later, I wrote them up for a professional journal. Senior serving officers are required to submit their written works for approval before publication and I found myself crossing pens with a senior civil servant who sought to remove any political thoughts from what he regarded should have been a straight forward military account. He said that the minister would not approve, but it never got that far and my account was published substantially as drafted. However, I agreed my punchline would be less pungent if watered down to read: senior military commanders and politicians need to be well informed about each others' business.

I was also invited to Iran to lecture a gathering of senior Iranian officers before being treated, together with Anne, to a ten day tour of the country. In opening the proceedings, General Azhari generously announced that I had just concluded an example of the most difficult military operation, a counter-revolutionary war. (I thought, privately, that a withdrawal in face of the enemy would be much more difficult but this was no time to be hiding my light under a bushel.) My audience were responsive and, as always in such circumstances, the question and answer time was the most interesting. They appeared to have assimilated the lessons which their brigades had brought back from Oman and I, in common with many who thought they understood the local scene, was surprised when, not long after, Iran went so badly wrong. Within a few years, as Islamic fundamentalism swept through, many of my audience had been murdered, some whilst still in command, others in the exile to which they had fled. General Ksrodad, with whom I enjoyed a lively exchange on my first visit to Tehran, was among the very first victims. Admiral Shafik, the Shah's nephew who had commanded the Iranian ships off Sarfait, was assassinated in Paris, as was General Ovessi, the army commander. General Azhari, I was glad to hear, escaped to join his daughter in New York.

There was no outward sign of the impending revolution in early 1976 when prosperity seemed on the increase, at least in the cities. An immense amount of money had been devoted to modernising industry but perhaps the rural areas had not benefited in proportion. As a visitor I dutifully acknowledged the new but was more interested in the old. There were the magnificent remains of an earlier Persian regime at Persopolis, their ruin accelerated centuries before by the depredations of Alexander the Great. In Isfahan the mosques around the ancient polo field were summounted by magnificent domes interspersed with slender minarets while, in the side streets, girls and children wove carpets as they had for centuries past. The longest covered market in the world was said to be the one in Sheraz where, under a high vaulted roof, colourful stalls laden with carpets and materials of all kinds vied for attention with wares of copper and brass, spices and mundane necessities. If Sheraz boasted the longest covered souk in the world, that in Tehran was unquestionably the largest. Here one could easily become lost in a maze of alleyways jammed with humanity, tourists slung with cameras seeking bargains and housewives draped in traditional black shopping for food. I went north to the shores of the Caspian where the orange trees were simultaneously bearing fruit and snow, the bright golden fruit with their caps of white appearing like some exotic ice cream.

During these travels I was accompanied by a posse of swarthy bodyguards who took it in turns to ensure that one of their number was never more than a few yards from me. They had obvious links with the intelligence organisation but I saw nothing sinister in this. If I had taken greater notice of their authority and the speedy reaction to it of the local police, minor officials and hotel staff wherever we went, I might have asked myself more searching questions about the stability of the regime. As it was I merely thought them more conscientious than the bodyguards I had met elsewhere, as they demonstrated during an afternoon in Sheraz when, feeling in need of exercise, I decided to scramble up the mountain overlooking my hotel. To avoid taking a bodyguard I slipped down a fire escape but somehow my escorts were alerted to my departure and I soon became aware that one was pursuing me. I paused for him to catch up. Limping over the stones in his city shoes, the jacket of his grey suit flapping open to disclose a tidy paunch, he was obviously ill equipped both sartorially and physically for rock climbing and I suggested he should sit on a boulder and await my return. Drawing his hand across his throat he replied, between gasps of breath, that he dare not leave me unattended. He did his best thereafter but he was no athlete and when he failed to appear the following day I hoped, for his sake, his absence was due to medical rather than disciplinary reasons.

I should also have been more alert to a faint alarm bell which rang when I failed to achieve an audience with the Shah. After much prevarication and false promises it became apparent that his senior officers were not prepared to expose him to my informed view of Iranian military capability for, despite my protestations that our meeting would be no more than a social occasion and that my programme was, for this purpose, infinitely flexible, our daily schedules somehow supervened. While during his father's rule no one dared tell a lie, in the Shah's time it seemed that no one dared tell the truth. And the truth was that a burgeoning modern economy could not survive under feudal management.

On leave and away from the everyday pressures of command, I had plenty of time to consider how the Sultan's armed forces should address the tasks ahead and as I flew back to Muscat across the empty wastes of southern Iran my head was buzzing with plans. There were economies to be effected, for we should no longer expect to absorb such a large proportion, some two thirds, of Oman's gross national product. There would, as yet, be political objections to thinning out in Dhofar but it was imperative that we strengthen our forces in the Mussandam and develop that strategically crucial area. There was an undoubted need to accelerate the process of preparing and training officers for higher command and to reduce the reliance of Oman on people like me. Ian Sprackling had already made some preliminary studies but our ideas, based on a comprehensive knowledge of the circumstances, which we alone had the competence to execute, were stillborn. Awaiting me on my return in late February was a letter from the Sultan asking me to co-operate with a Mr Robert Browning who had replaced Brigadier Fergie Semple as the senior official in the Omani ministry of defence. I met Browning that evening when he said he had been appointed to hold the purse strings and I formed the impression that he saw himself as the senior of the two of us. Unfortunately, I had only his version of his terms of reference to light the future. I felt strongly that it was not acceptable for a senior officer on loan from Britain to be thus subordinated but did my best over the succeeding weeks to avoid a personal clash.

Over the next few months in discussion with the Sultan and his immediate advisers and with support from the British ambassador, I confirmed that my personal responsibilities and position would remain unchanged although it was announced that on my departure each single service commander would report directly to the Sultan, so that command of the armed forces would no longer be vested in one man. It was a measure, it was said, in preparation for the appointment of senior Omani commanders when it would be inadvisable to have power concentrated in a single pair of hands. In vain I protested, pointing out that only the army had the potential to cause difficulties; the air force would be largely expatriate for some years; the navy was too small and would, I said in a misplaced attempt at humour, simply put to sea and return to rejoin the winner. The problem, if it existed, had not been solved by splitting the forces. This measure would simply remove the means of co-ordinating inter-service activities and allocating resources. The whole proposal seemed an ill-judged attempt to increase the influence and power of expatriate civilians in the ministry of defence at the expense of British loan service commanders. It erroneously assumed that loyalty purchased by contract was more reliable than that obtained on loan and ignored the occasions I had put my own career at risk when acting at variance with views I knew were held in London. Five years later my words were vindicated by events when Tim Creasey, by then a full general, returned at the Sultan's request to assume command of the armed forces and re-establish effective central financial control.

Some time towards the end of 1976 I perceived a way out of the administrative tangle in which I had been placed when the opportunity arose for a further military operation. The *Wali* of Dhofar, Sheikh Braik, protested to the Sultan that the war had ended leaving part of Habrut, a border village on a traditional route between South Yemen and Oman, in enemy hands and I had immediately offered to mount a small operation to regain it. In suggesting to the Sultan that the area would be lost forever if we did not secure it now, I had at the back of my mind a need to restore the balance of authority within the military administration. Those who were meddling in areas beyond their competence would be pushed into the back seat. Viewed from the nearest Omani outpost, Habrut seemed no more than a square white fort surrounded by extensive date gardens in a wide wadi between high barren hills. Some years ago South Yemen had captured the fort and gardens so that the opposing sides now watched each other suspiciously from a series of observation posts in the hilltops either side of the valley. Walking between these outposts entailed a series of precipitous climbs each of several hundred feet, a hard day's exercise to go round them all, and it was in the course of one such visit that it had occurred to me how simple it would be to regain the lost territory. This was the plan I now put forward. It would entail a battalion attack at night which, conducted silently, would surely overrun the weak opposition which I thought would surrender with hardly a shot being fired. At dawn a pair of Hunters would be circling above to deter any retaliatory action. The *wali* would be on hand to confer with his counterpart from across the border over the use of tracks, which wound their way along the border, and the distribution of water from the one well which would need to serve both sides. It seemed to me that this small flurry of activity off stage from the main areas of interest would restore the lost territory without threat to the recently established peace. Whitehall, through the British ambassador, were aware of what was afoot and, being somehow left with the impression that I was simply following instructions, were content with the part I was playing. However, after some weeks the Sultan decided against any action and the gardens at Habrut remained in foreign hands.

Politicking apart, life remained interesting and rewarding. John Akehurst had left for home and Dhofar Brigade had been taken over by Brigadier Charles Huxtable, who had commanded the Duke of Wellington's Regiment in 24 Brigade. My chief of staff had also changed and was now Colonel Ken Dodson. Northern Oman Brigade, under a new commander, Brigadier 'Scrubber' Stuart-Richardson, began to mould itself into an effective operational formation now that its main task was orientated towards the Gulf rather than support for Dhofar. Its battalions were all battle experienced and by the end of the year it was conducting large scale exercises with live ammunition which even the British Army would have been hesitant to undertake. On one such occasion while walking forward on the flank of a leading battalion, bullets from a machine gun someway behind began raising the dust a few yards to my left. 'Don't worry,' I said to my ADC, 'everything is under control.'

'That,' replied Khamis calmly, 'is what you said just before your last ADC was wounded!'

We also enjoyed our leisure time, camping in the *jebel* or on the various beaches between Muscat and Sur which were only accessible by launch. Sur was a small port with a barren hinterland giving way to the Whaiba sands. In the days when I visited it, the town was much as it had been for centuries, a cluster of whitewashed flat roofed houses beside a creek which provided the only ready access to the outside world. The dhows that tied up at the quayside brought goods and produce of all sorts for the bustling market into which thronged people from all around, their mobility, foot, camel or Land Rover being the measure of their relative prosperity. Sur was the centre of boat building in Oman and on the shores of the inlet there were invariably several dhows in various stages of construction. The Omani shipwrights plied their craft in the manner of their fathers and grandfathers using a limited range of hand tools. Plans and measurements were in their heads; there were no blueprints or tape measures. Keels were laid with a piece of African timber and the rich brown wood cut by eye. The ribs were shaped and fitted in a similar fashion and planked so perfectly as to obviate the need for caulking. Where a slight imperfection occurred, a thin sliver of wood was tapped into the crevice. When work was slack, builders turned their hands to making models, each of which was some four feet long and a replica in every detail of a full sized craft. I was presented with the only remaining model of a type of dhow long since extinct, an irreplaceable piece of heritage which I left in the care of the navy where it has since decorated the entrance to their head-quarters.

In April 1977 my time in Oman was up, that month being filled with a round of parties. Nicola, who had joined us during most school holidays, came out for a last visit. The navy anchored in a semi circle off one of the small islands and provided a weekend long picnic to which guests who could not stay the entire time were ferried to and fro by helicopter. There was a splendid dinner at the Palace attended by several hundred officers of all ranks at which the Sultan presented me with the Order of Oman. Since arriving two and a bit years earlier I had hardly drawn breath, certainly I had spared no time to review my personal progress and it is only now, as I write some ten years later, that I look critically upon my performance. Given another chance, I would hope to get away with the same risks. I might make life easier by rolling with a few more punches although I doubt if I would alter my stance or make different decisions on important occasions.

After all, a war had been won sooner than expected and a sound foundation laid for the future. I could hardly be as fortunate a second time around.

Chapter 12

Insurgent in Whitehall

ANNE and I returned to England and re-opened our house in Haywards Heath. We had several weeks leave during which time Jane was married to Major Ian Gordon of the Muscat Regiment. I was delighted that this brave officer was becoming my son-in-law. He had been shot in the head in Oman and survived the ordeal—which included temporary blindness and evacuation to England—with undiminished courage, returning to the fray and earning a Bravery Medal for his exploits at Sarfait in late 1975.

I had known for some months that my next job was to be Assistant Chief of Defence Staff (Operations) in the Ministry of Defence, a position which would give me responsibility for co-ordinating all tri-service activities and supervising the defence aspects of crisis management in Whitehall. These were areas with which I had become familiar immediately before going to Oman so that Rear Admiral Cameron Rusby, whom I was succeeding, needed no more than a couple of hours to brief me. This we arranged during my leave, thus priming me to start in earnest on my arrival in mid June.

The Ministry of Defence is a sheer sided, rectangular edifice, grey inside and out, with one corridor of power looking like any other, save for the sixth floor which, accommodating the ministers and service chiefs, is better appointed. There, behind oak doors, are pieces of antique furniture, wider desks and deep leather armchairs for the visitors. Of the rest, my billet on the fifth floor seemed as good as any. From a spacious office I looked over the plane trees which lined the Embankment and across the Thames, in June the water constantly churned by busy pleasure boats. Beneath my windows Gordon of Khartoum and Lord Trenchard stood watch from their stone plinths set in a rectangle of green. However, from Day One I had little time for

159

window gazing; as Cameron Rusby observed ruefully some months later, providence had saved the action for me.

Day One began deceptively, allowing me time to assimilate my new surroundings. It started with the signal pack, a stiff black folder containing about fifty overnight telegrams, which I found sitting ominously in the centre of my desk. My personal staff officer explained that the telegrams came first to me in order that I could add instructions for the staff. I handed the folder back unopened saying that henceforth the messages should go direct to the people concerned, giving them the choice of seeking my direction or getting on with the job and telling me later. Although everyone will agree in principle that delegation is a good thing, many baulk at the implications, often reflecting a lack of confidence in themselves as much as in their subordinates. I was to find over the next two years that a considerable impediment to delegation came from the ministers' offices where too often private secretaries would insist that the ministers required to know all the details. The malaise spread downwards and all around me I saw people side-tracked into writing briefs for decision makers who had no need to know the detailed contents and in the event seldom had time to read them. My attitude in allowing subordinates a loose rein is that they will always do their best, usually out of loyalty but at least from self-interest, and if their best is inadequate they should be replaced.

My early days in office had been planned meticulously for me in advance. There would be briefings by my own staff on military affairs at home, in NATO and abroad. I was to lunch with the intelligence services, while the security people wanted to introduce me to various code words as I was now the military custodian of nuclear weapon procedures. People were to call on me and I on them, all in accordance with the protocol of seniority at the rate of half a dozen a day, and I was faced with the prospect of endless cups of weak instant coffee. Fortunately this bleak programme was put into abeyance when the *junta* in far away Guatemala intervened by threatening invasion of their neighbours, the British dependency of Belize.

Captain George Heyhoe brought the welcome news, having gathered it from the signal pack that I had thrown out peremptorily earlier in the day. The system was evidently working already for he came armed with all the information I would need. George was a bluff, weathered sea dog who headed the section of my staff watching over events abroad. I first met him when he visited me in Oman where the soldiers had been mightily impressed by this large figure in white naval uniform crashing through the bush towards the sound of battle. The Guatemalan claim to

Belize was a situation with which I was familiar from the time I had prepared to turn my Caribbean exercise with 24 Brigade into the real thing. Since the mid-nineteenth century Guatemala had disputed the separate existence of Belize, a small country largely covered in jungle, and in recent years Britain had maintained a garrison there to deter invasion or, should that fail, hold the airfield while reinforcements were flown in. In addition to slick military planning this concept depended upon good political judgement. If reinforcement was ordered every time the Guatemalans rattled their sabres, British forces would spend an inordinate effort shuttling to and fro across the Atlantic, while if political resolve seemed lacking through inaction, invasion would be invited and war would follow. George spelt it all out while, beneath my window, the summer tourists queued for the river boats.

Reinforcements on the necessary scale, a couple of battalions, aircraft and air defence missiles, would be a cabinet decision. Even a warning gesture such as the dispatch of a frigate would need political approval. In either case the situation required a submission to the Secretary of State for Defence recommending what should be done. Such a statement, having to be agreed by the three services and needing a favourable political wind if it was to be sympathetically received, could only emanate from a committee representing all interests. This was the Defence Operations Executive, a gathering chaired by me and consisting of a rear admiral, another major general and an air vice marshal, together with representatives from the intelligence, communications and logistics staffs, senior civil servants, foreign office officials and others who sought a voice on one pretext or another.

We met in the chiefs of staff room with its polished coffin shaped table introduced by Lord Mountbatten so that from his seat at the top he could readily look everyone in the eye. This was the first occasion the committee had met in earnest for several years and the prospect of action prompted a good turn out. In addition to the twenty or so of us around the table there was an equal number on the tiered seating behind my chair. At that initial meeting the consensus was for quiet preparation with no overt action other than the sailing of a frigate, but as the days passed, and Guatemala seemed ever more hostile, we felt that reinforcements should no longer be delayed. However, the Foreign Office invariably takes a cautious line—usually getting away with it in the years between Winston Churchill and Margaret Thatcher—and the military case for sending more troops was consistently rejected. All that had been authorised was the appearance of the frigate off Belize which had occurred concidentally with talks in Washington between Ted

Rowlands, Minister of State at the Foreign Office, and his Guatemalan counterpart. This minor display of force was deplored by the Guatemalans as imperialistic and by our own Foreign Office officials as unsubtle, although why we should indulge only in subtle diplomacy when there were obvious troop movements on the other side, was never explained.

It was now early July and the Chief of Defence Staff, Admiral of the Fleet Sir Edward Ashmore, became concerned lest the garrison should be overrun before help could arrive. I suspect he was also annoyed that the Foreign Office seemed always to win the day in cabinet as, during a discussion after we had been turned down for the third time, he turned to me and said with an edge to his voice, 'I think I'll write to the PM; do me a draft.' Sir Edward was exercising a seldom invoked privilege of his office: direct access to the Prime Minister, in this case, Jim Callaghan. The latter now authorised reinforcement without further ado and the forces which had been standing by began to fly out.

The immediate danger had been averted but the situation continued to absorb a good deal of my time for many months. Even before Belize was reinforced, all three services had been finding it extremely difficult to meet their many commitments and there was a need to arrive at a political settlement which would allow us to reduce the garrison to its normal complement. The Foreign Office even contemplated a plan which would cede land in the Punta Gorda area of Belize in exchange for Guatemalan recognition of an independent Belize. However, people do not willingly surrender British protection and the suggestion was summarily dismissed by the Prime Minister of Belize, George Price. Talks continued but it was many months before tension was significantly reduced. To ease the situation, Britain agreed to freeze the force level in Belize so that the constant arrival of resupply aircraft would not be mistaken for further reinforcement. However, the Specal Air Service, recognising a good training area when it saw one, quietly slipped in extra men and ran a small exercise. Downing Street became aware of this and the wrath of Jim Callaghan again fell upon me. I was required to keep Downing Street informed of the exact garrison strength. It was, I thought, a petty imposition but a warning of how careful the military must be in order to retain political confidence.

I had been fortunate to arrive in my new appointment just a few hours before the Belize crisis broke and to have had my first month largely absorbed by it. I was thus enabled, against a background central to my job, to meet most of the people with whom I would have dealings over the next two years and to make timely changes to our crisis management procedures. While chairing the large meetings we needed to cope with our reaction to the Belize problem, I thought that this was no way to run an operation. Of course, with three autonomous services there had to be discussion to hammer out a joint plan and account had to be taken of our own ministers' views and those of the Foreign Office. There were also other considerations but to take them all at one large sitting was hardly conducive to rapid action. People once summoned to a meeting are unlikely to remain silent. They will feel compelled to speak, often with nothing to say, or will regale the assembly with previously prepared statements already rendered irrelevant by the ebb and flow of discussion. Additionally they may raise difficulties and since there are more cautious individuals than chancers, the obstacles increase exponentially with the numbers around a table. In future, I decided, I would try to get the outlines agreed between the principal players before introducing others. It was also crucial to get any papers to the minister in good time and here another considerable improvement was needed. Written by one of my officers, the submission to the minister was then vetted by the principal members of the defence operations executive to ensure it reflected their views. In the hands of the staff it became a vehicle for hobby horses and used to parade issues which their sponsors wished to highlight at that moment. The exchange might go thus: 'We in the army insist on including a paragraph or two about the possibility of using a parachute battalion, although it is barely relevant in the circumstances, if you in the navy are going to suggest using a commando carrier, which we believe you are doing only to strengthen your hand in the forthcoming wrangling over defence cuts.' To me such horse trading epitomised all I scorned in the bureaucracy, but to others it was a ritual conferring importance and the semblance of power. The whole process, from calling a meeting to delivering a paper to a minister's office, seldom took less than twenty four hours and often a good deal more if any of the chiefs of staff decided personally to weigh in. What was needed was a more simple approach. Thus, in future I was to call only the nub of the defence operations executive to the crisis meetings, about six in all, write the submission myself and personally drop it on the desks of my colleagues. When six hours had become par for the course someone asked me how I had managed to cut so many corners. I replied that Martin Weymess provided a smoke screen, Tim Lloyd the jokes, I the booze and Martin Farndale the brains (Rear Admiral Weymess, Air Vice Marshal Lloyd and Major General Farndale who each headed their single service staffs). It was my shorthand for saying we were a small, thoroughly professional team but there was an element of literal truth.

We met periodically in the evenings to exchange views over a gin and tonic when the air marshal would invariably open the proceedings with a joke and the admiral would always have filled a large ash tray by the end. As for brain power, no one doubted Martin Farndale's.

Although for some time Belize was the most pressing of my responsibilities there were many others clamouring for attention. These often concerned committees and I was chairman of several and a member of half a dozen more. Thus, I found myself very soon sitting on the cabinet office committee which was reviewing nuclear weapon release procedures, an esoteric and complicated process providing for the authentication of messages from the prime minister in Downing Street through various intermediaries to the submarine captains deep in the ocean. Committee work seemed to take up an inordinate amount of time but there was no more effective means of dealing with subjects which involved a number of departments and the cabinet office committees, involving civil servants well versed in this work, dealt with their business expeditiously. I observed with interest the different styles of chairmen; most invited discussion before attempting to steer the proceedings their own way. A few began more positively, leading with their own views and this was the method I preferred. (Later I attended several gatherings chaired by Mrs Thatcher after she had become prime minister and I noted that this was how she worked.) I always felt that the military were at a disadvantage in Whitehall, for the qualities which brought men to the top of the armed forces were not necessarily those required of a successful committee man. Moreover, the serviceman was often unfamiliar wth the background, coming to the ministry only intermittently during his career; the civil servant, a life long campaigner in this terrain, had probably been over it all several times before.

I was the United Kingdom exercise director for the NATO annual government war games, called WINTEX and HILEX in alternate years. WINTEX was played by all government ministries and major military headquarters in NATO and, lasting a fortnight, exercised all measures for mobilising Europe and America, together with the procedural aspects of fighting a nuclear war. HILEX was concerned with the civil defence aspects of war. Being responsible for planning and running these exercises was rather like painting the Forth Bridge; no sooner was one exercise over than it was time to start again.

Soon after I arrived, a series of ideas to enhance the effectiveness of NATO were conceived by the Supreme Allied Commander Europe, General Al Haigh. These ideas were to be developed into practical measures by a number of international committees, dubbed task forces. I became the leader of Task Force Seven charged with improvements in electronic warfare. It was the trickiest of all the subjects under review as it required the transfer of highly classified technical data between countries. While the military were happy to swap secrets, industry was not inclined to part with information which would benefit a competitor. I was also involved, as the United Kingdom's representative, in Task Force Six which had the more prosaic, but I felt more important job, of speeding up the reinforcement of Europe in a crisis.

The co-ordination of anti-terrorist measures was another of my tasks and I renewed my acquaintance with the Special Air Service who maintained a specially trained team at thirty minutes' notice to move to anywhere in the world. I enjoyed my visits to Hereford to see these highly trained men, second to none in any army, at that time commanded by Lieutenant Colonel Mike Wilkes, a horse gunner who had also served in 1st Regiment.

I found no plans to combat any terrorist attack on the North Sea oil industry so, together with the navy department, I set about producing some. My initial, tentative ideas did not survive my visit to a storm lashed oil production platform somewhere between Aberdeen and Norway. This multi storey meccano set, garrisoned by three score weather hardened men and approachable only by helicopter or through the heavy swell several hundred feet below, was an unlikely target. An unmanned gas platform would be easier to occupy but, with no hostages, of little value to terrorists. It was the sprawling installations ashore containing tank farms, refineries and distribution facilities which most needed protection. However, as a hedge against the unlikely, we made some plans and the Royal Marines demonstrated their ability to emerge from the heavy seas and climb the huge perpendicular legs, undetected from the platform above.

The days were long and I returned home to Haywards Heath only at weekends, living during the week in a flat overlooking the river at Barnes. I was usually in my office by eight and often worked through the lunch hour, although for preference I would stretch my legs across Horse Guards Parade and through St James's Park. I seldom left my desk before six in the evening and then, once or twice a week, it was to attend a diplomatic party. These blind dates were sometimes amusing, often boring and occasionally hazardous, such as the reception at the Chinese Embassy. It was a gathering of about one hundred and fifty with many eminent guests and a high noise level. After a while, drifting glass in hand between groups of look-a-likes in grey buttoned up tunics,

I found myself talking, through an interpreter, to half a dozen Chinese generals. It transpired that one of them had served as a young officer in the Korean War and had evidently been facing The Commonwealth Division in which I was serving. Emboldened by a glass or two of gin, I ventured the thought that the next time our two nations went to war we should ensure we were on the same side. The general banged a table and, as the din subsided and the heads turned in our way, announced, 'The British general says the Chinese and British must be allies.' I eased into the folds of some nearby curtains before several ministers present could discover who in the military was making foreign policy.

In August I spent several days in Cyprus where, since independence, Britain had retained two sovereign base areas to accommodate the airfield at Akrotiri and some radio installations at Dhekelia. Britain also provided a contingent in the United Nations force which supervised the partition of Cyprus between the Turks in the northern part and the Greeks in the south; an arrangement resulting from the Turkish invasion in 1974.

Partition had emphasised the very different natures of the two nationalities. It was as if the south had been stippled with green and yellow, the paint brush heavily loaded and carefully following the exact line of partition, providing a sharp contrast with the brown unpainted canvas of the north.

Our Belize garrison was the object of my next overseas trip. The commander there, Colonel John Head, had served under me in Oman and had predictably coped well with the influx of forces. Many of the reinforcements were, on arrival, unaccustomed to their new environment, one battalion having no one, from the commanding officer downwards, with jungle experience. This was not surprising as for many years defence policy and the demands of Northern Ireland had, together, allowed little time for jungle bashing. John Head therefore set up a jungle training camp and, by the time I arrived, the troops were behaving like old campaigners.

It was no reflection on John Head that I thought this force on semi-active duty should qualify as a proper brigade and attract as its commander a brigadier ultimately destined for higher rank. My efforts in this direction became a casualty of inter-service horse trading and it was not until the Chief of Defence Staff went to Belize a year later, and thought much as I did, that a brigadier was appointed. However, the chain of events took so long that by the time the brigadier arrived the political situation had improved and the tension vanished. Nevertheless, the new man had his name to make and the resultant burst of military activity along the border caused considerable alarm, not as one might have thought in Guatemala but in the Foreign Office.

The year 1977 ended with a visit to the British Army of the Rhine where, among other activities, I spent a day with the new electronic warfare regiment which Ian Sprackling had just formed. It was part of my research as the leader of Task Force Seven and gave me an excuse to see how Ian was doing in his new job. He was clearly enjoying life and marked my visit with a splendid ball in the officers' mess.

The relentless pace continued through 1978 with a mixture of long days in Whitehall and travel abroad. The year opened with visits to the headquarters of the Allied forces in central Europe. It had a huge concrete and steel underground bunker from which it intended to direct operations in war and our discussions, which centred on future communications, led to consideration of whether this was a more likely form of survival than remaining mobile and well camouflaged above ground. Long exposure to even the most unlikely propositions often leads to self delusion and so it was, or at least so it seemed to me, on this occasion. A large headquarters could hardly remain undetected whatever its mode of operation and the notion of exercising command through a hierarchy of such organisations once nuclear weapons were in use was surely unreal. However, the alternative is equally unreal, for ultimately it would entail surrender. Planning the conduct of nuclear war is essential if potential enemies are to be denied the use of nuclear blackmail and Armageddon to remain only the remotest possibility. I am glad that my soldiering has mostly been of a more practical and immediate nature.

In May I was in Malta, where the Royal Air Force still based a Canberra squadron at Luqa. Malta had changed dramatically. The genteel old world charm had been brushed aside by tourists and casinos. A conservative government had succumbed to an erratic socialist regime. No one called it Malta GC any more, as if the George Cross so hard won in the early 1940s was to be scorned rather than admired, but the generation who had earned it were unchanged and as steadfast as ever. In July I was in Ankara planning an exercise for the Central Treaty Organisation. I have been to Ankara several times but I remember it best for its invisibility under a grey blanket of smog when viewed in bright sunlight from the surrounding hills. CENTO fell apart soon after and the exercise died with it. I went to Washington in October at the behest of Doctor John Gilbert, the Minister of State for Defence, who hoped to introduce the Pentagon style of war gaming into Whitehall. I knew from previous efforts to engage their attention that it would not find favour with ministers in London, among whom there was a reluctance to discuss some of the tricky political problems which strategic games tend to highlight. However, the autumn is a good time to be in Washington and surely the best time of the year, when the leaves are golden brown, to drive in from Dulles airport or out along the Potomac to George Washington's house. In November I was in Gibraltar to see the governor-general—Sir William Jackson whom I knew from previous service—and consider the military aspects of the Spanish claim to the Rock, and in January 1979 I was back in Belize.

These visits had merely punctuated the routine and not so routine weeks in London. Among the less usual tasks we began considering how we would evacuate British nationals from Rhodesia should the guerilla war make their position untenable. Still in legal terms a colony, Rhodesia had unilaterally declared its independence in 1965 and severed its connections with Britain. In March 1978 an accommodation had been made between the white regime under Ian Smith and those black elements commanded by Bishop Muzorewa. Under this the two leaders would rule through a rigged parliament. The guerilla forces, known as the Patriotic Front, would not be fobbed off with anything less than black majority rule and when it became obvious that they could not be denied, we dusted off our plans for the protection of British passport holders. The Ministry of Defence maintained evacuation plans for all countries where a significant number of British nationals might be at risk from a variety of causes but these were written against the less catastrophic background than was now foreseen in Rhodesia. We therefore considered how we could deploy an intervention force to ensure the safety of those at risk and evacuate them along roads and through airports which themselves would need to be secured. As I was heading the planning, it seemed logical, more so in view of my background, that I should command the forces to be deployed in the event. I was attempting to persuade the Chief of Defence Staff, by then Air Chief Marshal Sir Neil Cameron, of this when a political solution brought about the end of the war and removed the possible need for intervention. Meanwhile, there was plenty of other activity to occupy us.

Iran began to go wrong in October. From his exile in Paris, the religious fanatic Ayatollah Khomeni had verbally harried the Shah's regime and encouraged revolt. In November the British embassy was set on fire and although it was decided not to evacuate the 8000 British nationals in Iran, we reviewed our contingency plans against such an event. The country soon dissolved in rebellion, the Shah was forced to leave in January and evacuation of foreign nationals started. In early February the situation became chaotic and I flew to the American headquarters at Strasbourg to see General 'Dutch' Huyser who was controlling the American evacuation. Dutch Huyser, as the emissary of the American President, Jimmy Carter, had recently been to Tehran to say it was time for the Shah to leave. I heard at first hand an account which suggested that Tehran 1979 and Paris 1789 had much in common. The French Revolution could hardly have been more arbitrary and destructive than the turmoil in Iran and I feared for my friends in the Shah's armed forces. As a result of my visit to the American headquarters we co-ordinated our efforts, America and Britain each taking responsibility for countries which had no evacuation plans. British plans took account of, among others, the French, who for once were forced to confer in English in order to take up our offer.

I had always wanted to sample the experience of parachuting but had never found the time to undergo the necessary training course. Now the chance arose. The Joint Air Transport Establishment, a unit which conducted trials in airborne delivery and which was under my control, was due to make a number of parachute jumps into the sea. As this would permit a soft landing, requiring little preliminary training, I said I should be included. It was an exhilarating experience which I recommend to senior officers who are short of physical excitement. More light relief arose when the army decreed that all officers under fifty would undergo an annual fitness test entailing a five mile run. I was over fifty but said I would participate and told my staff that anyone coming in after me would have to go round again. I did not enforce this but the competition had the effect of sharpening us all up.

The unwillingness of ministers to participate in our war games left them ignorant of what might be entailed and meant that the military were in some doubt over the political reaction to possible events. The ministers' views were simulated by civil servants or foreign office officials who would argue that they could accurately provide the political input, but civil servants and politicians differ in the importance they ascribe to the elements of a crisis. A civil servant will approach a situation with intellectual rigour while a politician, particularly where public opinion is involved, will view it more intuitively. I had noted this during the invasion of Cyprus in 1974, been exposed to it from a distance when in Oman and seen it more recently when reinforcing Belize. To improve matters I managed to entice the secretary of state for defence, Fred Mulley, to a discussion but no minister from any other department showed the slightest interest. These attitudes changed abruptly in May when Mrs Thatcher became prime minister and a blast of fresh air swirled through the Ministry of Defence.

Within a few weeks of assuming office she ordered the preparation of two exercises in order that she could verify her satisfaction with our procedures for meeting a major international crisis involving the threat of nuclear weapons. One was to be based on the well worn scenario for such exercises, a threat to NATO. The usual yawn. The other was a direct confrontation between Britain and Russia which left me, as the exercise director, wondering how I could possibly arrange such a match with the rest of the world sitting comfortably in their ringside seats. Fortunately I was rescued by my opposite number in the Cabinet Office, Brian Watkins, who cleverly contrived a sufficiently credible situation. (The reader may object to a lack of reality but the point of the exercise was the procedures for crisis management, not the hypothetical crisis itself.)

The exercises were held during two evenings in the Cabinet Office. The Foreign, Home and Defence Secretaries, the Chiefs of Staff and the appropriate Permanent Under Secretaries sat around the oblong, brown baize covered table with the Prime Minister presiding in the centre of a long side. She would need to confer with presidents and other prime ministers and for this purpose there was a microphone connected to an adjacent room in which sat an amateur actor, a co-opted civil servant, good at voices and briefed to be difficult during the Britain versus Russia game. Not involved in the crossfire of questions I could enjoy the spectacle, not so the individual who, on volunteering an idea at a difficult point in the exercise, was told by the Prime Minister that she did not think much of it. The voice also had a rough ride. The fact that Helmut Schmidt was called Helmut did little to soften the verbal blows while Jimmy Carter was addressed as Mr Carter and his attitude was described as pious. At the end, after the drinks had been served, the Prime Minister pushed her chair back and suggested that we, and that included her, had not done as well as we should. I thought that as a tyro at this particular business she had done very well indeed.

Mrs Thatcher joined in other exercises. One entailed a simulated hijack involving the Special Air Service playing as terrorists, a Royal Air Force VC10 hijacked at Brize Norton and flown via Gibraltar to Akrotiri, and a Special Air Service team in pursuit aboard a Hercules transport. On this occasion the crisis management team was chaired by a Foreign Office official, Jill Brown—who later became ambassador to Norway—so that when Margaret Thatcher arrived to play herself, we men were at the mercy of two very sharp ladies. An unusual situation in Whitehall.

The Muzorewa-Smith regime in Rhodesia had done nothing towards ending the war and in December a conference was convened at Lancaster House in London in order to achieve a solution acceptable to all concerned. Under the guidance of the Foreign Secretary, Lord Carrington, agreement was reached. The first step was to be a cease fire and an amnesty for the guerillas who would gather at sixteen assembly points and be allowed to retain their organisation and weapons. The cease fire would be supervised by a Commonwealth monitoring force with Britain running six assembly points, Australia five, New Zealand and Fiji two each and Kenya one. Britain would provide transport aircraft, helicopters and logistic support for the entire force which would number some fourteen hundred. Major General John Acland was appointed commander and it fell to me to co-ordinate the deployment and subsequent support from Britain. The Rhodesian security forces agreed to provide food, water and medical supplies to the guerillas once they were in the assembly areas. With peace in the countryside, elections would then be supervised by a Commonwealth observer group.

By 13th December agreement was in sight and Lord Soames arrived in Salisbury as Governor. The monitoring force deployed and on the 22nd a cease fire and amnesty was announced giving the Patriotic Force from midnight on the 28th until the 4th January to surrender. The Rhodesian security forces, however, did not fulfil their obligations, leaving the logistic element of the monitoring force, established to cope with only fourteen hundred, to administer the many thousands who were about to congregate at the widespread assembly points out in the bush. Thus, on Christmas Eve, as I sat down to dinner, the telephone rang and John Acland from Salisbury requested the immediate despatch of more helicopters. I now telephoned my colleagues in the army and air force, Martin Farndale and Tim Lloyd. They were also about to dine and, with our Christmas dinner interrupted by one or two further consultations, we had planned the necessary reinforcements by the time the mince pies arrived at our tables. By Boxing Day the helicopters were aboard Hercules transports and en route to Rhodesia. With the bureaucracy closed down for Christmas it had all been so simple. Later on when the Secretary of State, Francis Pym, asked for the lessons to be learned from the Rhodesian operation, I simply wrote, 'We should save crises for highdays and holidays.' When his office asked me not to be facetious I replied that I was in deadly earnest.

In the New Year I flew to Rhodesia for a brief visit, going out overnight on the inaugural British Airways flight. As we approached our destination the jumbo maintained a safe height, waiting until we were over Salisbury before spiralling down to the runway. Clearly, British Airways had doubts over the cease fire. I was met on the tarmac by an old colleague, Colonel Adam Gurdon, who had escaped from the military operations staff in London where he and I had collaborated during a number of emergencies, to be chief of staff to the monitoring force. He drove me to the Monomatapa Hotel, where I changed into uniform, and thence to the force headquarters behind Government House. I needed to obtain a feel for the monitoring operation in order that, seated at my London desk, I could anticipate requirements and have a mental picture to accompany my almost daily telephone conversations with John Acland. It was a matter of seeing as much as possible and Adam Gurdon, who had done much of the planning in London, was well placed to arrange this.

After a morning in the force headquarters John and I walked across the wide lawn to lunch with the governor and Lady Soames. I was looking forward to sampling the governor's cellar which was already the subject of favourable comment in Salisbury and which, together with a Rolls-Royce, had caused some surprise among the air movement staff at home. The flagstaff and Union Jack, open verandahs and white uniformed house staff conjured a vision of colonial times. We arrived a little early and were pouring our own drinks from a well stocked sideboard when Lady Soames appeared. 'General,' she said, seizing my glass and adding a further liberal measure, 'Generals need much more than that.' This was a most agreeable introduction to Mary Soames with whom I was to become more closely acquainted six years later.—Then, at our next meeting she was a guest and I the host. It was my wedding party and I had just married her niece.—Lunch over I spent some time with the hard pressed logistic unit among their varied wares stacked in the open and being prepared for despatch by helicopter or truck to the assembly area. Here were troops used only to the lavish facilities in Germany, improvising as if they had been bush warriors all along. Later I called on General Peter Walls, the Rhodesian senior commander; his was a difficult and nerve-wracking position, squeezed between the Lancaster House agreement and complaints from his own hard liners. I was to hear from one of these later that evening.

John Acland had acquired a house in a residential area and here we gathered for dinner. Assembled were a cross section of military and civilians including the Rhodesian army commander, Lieutenant

General Sandy McLean, and his wife. I sat next to Pamela McLean, from whom during a wide ranging discussion I gleaned no hint of dissatisfaction over the outcome of events. I was, therefore, considerably surprised when, as the party was breaking up, Sandy McLean attacked me intemperately. The British, he said, should have stayed at home; by their interference they had prevented the Rhodesian Forces from defeating the Patriotic Front. I replied that counter revolutionary wars could not be won by military means alone, and left it at that.

The Patriotic Front reflected an ethnic division of the population. The Zimbabwe African People's Union followed Joshua Nkomo, father of the insurrection, and was based on the Ndebele population. The numerous troops of the Zimbabwe African National Union belonged to Robert Mugabe and came from the Shona majority. It was to a ZAPU assembly area I flew on the second morning of my visit. It contained a battalion under the command of a university graduate in his early twenties. He was keen to make a good impression and had asked one of the British NCOs in the monitoring force to drill a guard of honour in proper style for the visiting general. It was the first time these guerillas had turned out ceremonially and the first time I had inspected a parade equipped, among a variety of Russian weapons, with a loaded rocket launcher. The commander and I inspected every tent and hut in the well laid out encampment until we came to the radio shack; this he seemed unwilling to let me enter. I assumed he had a paranoia about security but when on my insistence we looked inside, I found his reluctance was due to some missing equipment which he now explained was en route to Lusaka for repair. How was it being transported? By varous means, on foot, hitch hiking, perhaps a bus. How far was Lusaka? About two hundred and fifty miles! I congratulated him on his determination and he was visibly relieved. As we walked through the hot dusty bush he talked enthusiastically about a future which he hoped for him would include regular military training. He deserved it, for this was one of the better units; I was to find that not all were as well disciplined.

I returned to London to the annual WINTEX/HILEX exercise; in 1980 it was HILEX. These exercises had already demonstrated, at least to me, our inadequacy at handling the immense amount of detailed information required to mobilise Britain for war. The recording system, as I found it, entailed the posting of information on boards in the operations centre showing the current state of each of the preparatory measures, dozens in number. The information was circulated around Whitehall by telephone so that, inevitably, different departments had varying pictures at any one instant. The representatives of every ministry who attended the transition to war committee not infrequently placed their own interpretation on decisions, leading to confusion over what had been agreed. To overcome these difficulties I proposed the introduction of a computer with terminals in the many offices involved in the process, and attended a short course on automatic data processing in order that I could better understand what was entailed. The financiers were reluctant but the arguments were irresistable and money was found by sacrificing something of less importance. The installation was not completed until after I had left but I went back to see it working and felt it was a major contribution to the process of crisis management.

I made a second and longer visit to Rhodesia in early March. Lord Soames and his political staff under Sir Anthony Duff had done a remarkable job in dispelling suspicion, creating confidence and holding all sides to the Lancaster House agreement. John Acland and his monitoring force had conducted an operation which owed as much to the diplomacy of junior officers and NCOs as to their military skills. International journalists had ensured that the world was well informed about the election and they now crowded the long bar of the Monomatapa while observing the formation of a new government. My main purpose was to make recommendations for British military participation in rebuilding the Rhodesian armed forces.

The election had been a landslide for Robert Mugabe to whom the governor introduced me a day or two later. We sat in the spacious ante room of Government House discussing the integration of ZAPU, ZANU and the present security forces into a new national army. Considerable numbers would need to be resettled in civilian life and I foresaw here a possible source of lawlessness. Mugabe, however, thought this would be averted for they were all tired of fighting. Above all he stressed the need for continued British political support and military assistance.

Mr Nkomo, on whom I called at his Salisbury house, looked a broken man, his huge frame slumped dejectedly on a sofa, his entourage milling about in disarray. I thought it surprising they should take his political defeat so hard. It had seemed inevitable that the Shona majority would prevail but Nkomo was nothing if not a fighter and clearly thought he had been in with a chance. After all it was he who had started it all rolling. Perhaps it was the scale of his defeat which caused his bitterness but, whatever the reason, he had little to say except that he intended to co-operate in forming a government.

I spent several days visiting the various elements which would need to be incorporated into any viable and universally acceptable security force. I also came across those whose participation in the future armed forces would clearly be vetoed by the Patriotic Front. Years of bitter conflict had brutalised the contestants on all sides. 'Culling Africans' was an expression used by some hardline whites reflecting this and I have no doubt that similar sentiments were voiced by the Shona and Ndebele about their enemies, but the Patriotic Front had won and would call the tune. Not that it mattered much once the war had ended for those whose assimilation was vetoed were, in any event, set on leaving, mostly for the South African Forces.

After two months in the assembly areas the Patriotic Front were somewhat restless. During the war the villages had provided support as well as occasional refuge. As one Patriotic Front leader said to me, 'There were girls who would also wash your clothes.' Now there were neither girls nor laundries. It seemed unlikely that many ex-guerillas would turn easily to regular soldiering, a doubt reinforced when I visited a large assembly area containing several thousand of Mugabe's ZANU.

The area, if not the inhabitants, was under the command of Major Tim Purdon, an Irish Guardsman who, having served in Oman, was at home in the bush. We drove in a Land Rover around the many acres of scrub and grassland where the Patriotic Front were living in huts and tents, stopping here and there to talk to groups of men. There were also a number of armed women who seemed to expect no special privileges and when I inadvertently strayed into their accommodation, where some of them were but sparsely clad, it was I who was embarrassed. Indeed, the men were far more touchy and trouble began when I approached a group of about fifty bathing in a natural pool. I was accompanied by an American woman photographic journalist whom I had met at a supper party the night before and her presence provoked a hostile reception. After she had withdrawn to a distance and the tumult abated, the leader of the group addressed me in an arrogant tone, 'I must be respected as I have been a soldier for six years.'

The situation seemed to call for both a carrot and a stick. 'Of course I respect you; you are a successful soldier.' Then after a pause, 'But as you seem to measure respect in years of service let me tell you I have got *thirty* six.' Those who understood laughed and the rest joined in. The tension was released but it was obvious that many of these men were not the right material for the future armed forces which the new government then envisaged.

It would have been a pity to leave Rhodesia without sight of the Victoria Falls and a small aircraft was provided for the trip. There were four of us, a lieutenant colonel and a major from Zambia who had been observers with ZAPU and who were my hosts on this day, Major Tony Ling of the Special Air Service Regiment, who had previously helped me in Oman, and myself. We took off after breakfast, our flight plan taking us over Salisbury where the most striking feature from the air was the abundance of small shimmering blue patches of varying shapes and the red rectangular areas of identical size. Leaving the early morning bathers and tennis players behind, we headed west and with the sun behind us had a clear sharp view to the horizon. Ahead and on the right the ground fell slowly away towards the Victoria Falls and Lake Kariba, an endless landscape of green, the subtly changing hues becoming apparent only as we passed overhead. To the left the eastern slopes of the Mhlaba Hills were lit by the morning sun. After about two hours, the vegetation thinned momentarily as the grey coal mines and railway sidings of Wankie came into view. Then, ahead, in the middle distance, was a white veil of mist hanging several hundred feet in the air, thrown up where the wide Zambesi poured over the edge. Minutes later, the Victoria Falls came into view, half a mile of white water plunging several hundred feet into the narrow gorge below. We circled it for a few minutes, a rainbow in constant attendance beneath us, before landing at an adjacent air strip.

The Victoria Falls creates a perpetual rain storm in the immediate vicinity which, as a result, has a tropical ecology all of its own. We changed into bathing trunks at the local hotels before making our way to the gorge. We slipped and slithered down a muddy track to the cable and plank bridge which spanned the gorge. With rain running off us we carefully edged our way out to the middle, shouting to make ourselves heard above the roar of the water. On our return, the Zambian major said that the river was low and in the wet season was a good deal more turbulent. I thought it spectacular enough as it was. We dried off and lunched in the hotel, still almost deserted after years of war, before crossing into Zambia and visiting the museum in Livingstone. Here, in a quiet little town so obviously a legacy of Empire, the curator, an Englishman, maintained one of the best collections of local history and geography I have seen anywhere.

A few days later, I returned to Britain having less than a month to go before I assumed my next appointment. The tempo continued to the end for during this remaining time I spent a week visiting Abu Dhabi. I handed over in mid April, giving a party in the Defence Council suite to mark the occasion and moved to be Director of Military Assistance in the Old War Office building just across Horse Guards Avenue.

Chapter 13

Itinerant General

THIS was to be my last appointment in the service, a fact I had known for some time. It would take me over the usual retirement age and make me the oldest and most senior serving major general, having been the youngest and most junior when I went to Oman on promotion. Normally I would have been either promoted further or retired after my previous job and it was very unusual to be offered a third appointment in the rank of major general. This was a generous gesture from the army and a consolation which offset the momentary disappointment of learning I was coming to the end of my military career. I had been offered a choice for this third appointment and had instantly rejected the alternative, which was to be the senior army director at the Royal College of Defence Studies, a nine to five academic job, in favour of the exciting prospect of gingering up British military assistance world wide.

Military assistance had a chequered past and for several years the main activity had been to help a number of countries in the Third World whose economies were in difficulty. This had been done by providing military advice and officers on loan, and bringing potential instructors and technicians to the United Kingdom for training. It seemed to me that we needed to broaden these activities to include the richer countries in the emerging world, for military men tend to shop where they are trained and British defence industry needed all the help it could get in the export market. I therefore set out to operate in parallel with the Defence Sales Organisation, under Sir Ronald Ellis, and developed a close working relationship with his senior civil servant, Peter Jeffs. Unfortunately, the meagre funds then available for military assistance did not even cover all that was required in the poorer countries so that the expansion which I was considering would need to be self financing. It proved easier than I had expected. My first trip abroad as Director of Military Assistance was to East Africa and I arranged for my return journey to bring me through the Gulf where I received invitations to advise, at the customer's expense, on a number of projects. As I developed my concept I also found that British industry, recognising the complementary natures of assistance and sales, financed some military assistance.

In the early days, Ghana occupied a good deal of my attention. The country had recently returned to democratic rule after a bunch of young soldiers, led by Flight Lieutenant Gerry Rawlings, had attempted to reform the corrupt and ailing economy by shooting a number of politicians and military leaders. It was now a matter of keeping the army happy while democracy was given a second chance. Jimmy Mellon, the High Commissioner, prescribed financial and economic remedies which would undoubtedly have succeeded had they been followed, and I suggested various military measures which were badly needed. Ghana already possessed what was probably the best staff college in Africa, run by Colonel Robin Duchesne, on loan from Britain, and it would have been relatively easy to occupy the army to good effect. Robin produced imaginative exercises which fired the enthusiasm of the battalions but I failed to persuade the president to allow the troops out of barracks. As a result, indolence and apathy again provided a breeding ground for discontent.

It was gratifying, in Ghana, to find Britain held in high esteem, a situation reflected in other former colonies where governments in need turned naturally to us for assistance. One old farmer, while complaining that prices were so low it was not worth taking his produce to town, went so far as to say that he would like the British to return as rulers. He was not at all interested in the idea that it is preferable to rule oneself badly than to be governed well by others. Of course, it was only an old man's fantasy but the political and military leaders were equally unrealistic in thinking that Britain could still afford the economic and military assistance which might have enabled them to continue their erratic courses.

It seemed to me, after only a week or two in office, that a good deal more could be made of military assistance. There is never enough money behind any government funded activity to meet all expectations but in the case of military assistance, huge dividends would follow only a modest increase in investment. The subject needed airing at ministerial level and the government luncheons for visiting ministers from the third world provided useful opportunities. In the elegant and informal setting of No. 1 Carlton Gardens, the guest needed little prompting and our own minister could not escape the argument that Britain should provide more assistance, if only in self interest. On one such occasion the visitor concluded an impassioned after luncheon speech by handing a present of an African carving to his host, Richard Luce, Minister of State at the Foreign Office. The minister had been unprepared for this but, without hesitation, made a reciprocal gift of the antique gavel which, for many years, had been used to demand silence when the speeches were about to begin. A year later, when another minister complained of having nothing better than a spoon with which to bang the table, I was able to explain what had happened to the gavel.

I also argued that military assistance should be considered as an element of NATO strategy for there was an obvious need to counter Russian influence in the Third World. Writing in the journal of the Royal United Services Institute for Defence Studies, I said, 'Policies which are concerned with maintenance and stability in the emerging world will require to be based in the main on economic and social considerations but will need to consider the military dimension, power growing from the barrel of a gun in much of the Third World. However, few countries with which the West is associated will accept foreign military facilities or troops on any scale, as such activity tends to offend national sensitivities and is sometimes considered inimical to regional stability. But many emerging countries ask for low profile assistance which can be provided at relatively small cost and this is surely where the West should now be making a major effort in countering activities of the Soviet Union and its allies. It is an area where the United Kingdom, with its advantage of previous connections, can show the way.' In some of the book reviews which I wrote from time to time I managed to insert arguments for more military assistance. Reviewing 'The Uncertain Ally' by Michael Chichester and John Wilkinson I took the authors to task: 'Military assistance is as much a part of defence policy as the positioning of garrisons or sailing of frigates but "The Uncertain Ally" virtually ignores it.' 'Imperial Sunset' by Major General James Lunt provided a deep insight into colonial service and, picking up this point in my review, I wrote that this service 'created a lasting bond' which was largely responsible for the continuing demand for military assistance. The latter I described as 'a significant instrument of national policy', concluding that 'it is even more important that we are welcomed and trusted in emerging countries than in days past when our interests were safeguarded by the world wide deployment of forces'. Gradually military assistance came to the fore as a topic for discussion in Whitehall but there was still no more money in sight.

The break through came when General Sir Edwin Bramall, the Chief of the General Staff, was travelling in Africa and I found myself lunching with him at the Muthaiga Club in Nairobi. He had seen at first hand the effects of military assistance and recognised how much more could be achieved by so little additional expenditure. He warmed to the subject and instructed me to pursue it with him on my return. He remained an exponent of military assistance as an important instrument of policy and was instrumental in increasing the funds available. However, it was to be a long process and one which was not concluded until after I had retired and he had become the Chief of Defence Staff.

During my visit to Kenya, I was looked after by the British Defence Attaché, Colonel Adrian Prestige, and his wife Joy. They had a wide circle of friends so that doors opened easily, providing me with access to all levels of the Kenyan armed forces and a privileged view of this magnificent country. On one occasion Adrian and I drove north from Nairobi through the green country and coffee fields to an armoured regiment camped beneath the forest clad slopes of Mount Kenya. We then took several days off and went into the Aberdares, the bush covered hills abounding with game west of Mount Kenya. We were in the care of Sam Weller, an English farmer, and Phil Schneider, an American game warden, whose combined knowledge of the country provided us with an experience denied most visitors. We halted our land cruiser within a few feet of a rhino which glared at us malevolently before trundling into the bush. We found ourselves on foot facing a herd of elephant from which the matriarch advanced, head raised, ears flapping, trumpeting aggressively. Sam picked up a stone, spat on it and bowled it towards the huge animal who, on seizing it with her trunk, was repelled by the human saliva and turned abruptly away, the herd following her. We sat all night above a watering hole, watching the animals come and go. Driving through scrub we saw lions and large numbers of buffalo, and, descending to the plain, we found ourselves amid the dust and noise of a thousand stampeding wildebeest. On another visit we went north west to see an infantry brigade and the military academy at Gilgil, going on into the Rift valley and skirting Lake Nakuru, its shores and shallow waters pink with flamingo.

In my African travels, I thought Kenya the most visually exciting country although Uganda had more potential. Uganda had been ruined by Idi Amin, whose recent overthrow had led to a cry for military assistance from the new head of the army, Major General Okello, and his chief of staff, Brigadier Ojok. The latter had been a student at Camberley during my time as an instructor there and I hastened to renew our acquaintance. I planned to fly from Kenya but relations between the two countries were somewhat strained and on my first attempt Kenya Airways were refused permission to land. I tried again the following day when two aircraft were required to cope with the backlog of passengers. On arrival over Entebbe Airport, only one was allowed to land; fortunately it was the one on which I was a passenger but when I descended the aircraft steps, the welcoming committee, which I assumed would meet me, was nowhere to be seen. Followed by several dozen passengers I walked across the tarmac and out of the evening sunlight into the shadows of a cavernous airport building. During Amin's reign the spacious, modern structure had deteriorated and I picked my way through refuse and sloppy, heavily armed Tanzanian soldiers who, having formed part of the liberating force, seemed now to have taken up residence in Uganda. I went in search of the baggage to find it had been cross loaded; the suitcases which were being heaped in the centre of an otherwise empty hall belonged to the passengers now returning to Nairobi in an aircraft carrying my luggage. In the gathering dusk I looked for a taxi but there was no transport in sight save for a battered Peugeot. When I asked the European driver for a lift into Kampala, explaining who I was, he said that Brigadier Ojok was awaiting me in the VIP lounge. It seemed unlikely that such a dilapidated airport would boast a VIP lounge but I found Ojok's party sitting in a beautifully panelled room, sipping iced drinks and attended by an extraordinarily good looking waitress. Ojok apologised profusely. He had spent most of the day awaiting my arrival, for communications were bad and no one knew when an aircraft was due until it arrived overhead. He assured me his time had not been entirely wasted for he had spent much of it prowling around the mass of crated imports which had piled up during recent years in a fruitless search for a set of communications which he knew had never been unpacked. We drove the twenty or so miles into Kampala, passing innumerable road blocks where Tanzanian soldiers were searching every civilian car and, judging from the pile of loot beside each check point, confiscating much of the contents. The brigadier, sensing my disapproval, said that he had needed Tanzania's help in overthrowing Amin but, now that the need was past, these troops would soon be returning home.

The following day we discussed the details of proposed assistance while in between these serious meetings the farce continued. We called on the prime minister, being stuck for some time in a lift with a number of fully armed, sweaty soldiers, a huge trolley of coffee and cakes and two pretty waitresses—the army seemed to employ only girls who were exceptionally attractive. I counted ten telephones on the prime minister's desk, nine grey and one red. Afterwards I asked Ojok how the PM knew which telephone was ringing. 'That's no problem,' he replied, 'the telephones here don't work.'

Although military power seemed to be in the hands of Brigadier Ojok, General Okello, with his British ribbons from the Second World War, was host on official occasions. We drove in his car to a reception, closely pursued by a jeep mounting a 106 mm recoilless rifle, which he used as a badge of office, the weapon being devoid of any ammunition. As we wound our way between the pot holes in Kampala, the general said, in a humorous aside, that in Uganda it was the sober drivers who weaved all over the road while the drunken ones, on a straighter course, fell into the pot holes. At the reception I was offered a choice of drinks and then given a glass of warm beer with the explanation that it was the only drink they had! After dinner, the general made a short speech in English which was politely clapped and then an oration in Swahili which brought a standing ovation from his own officers. He was obviously more than the figure head he was made out to be and, even as I write, he remains in charge.

I was leaving the following morning and Brigadier Ojok said he would be in the VIP lounge to see me off. I suggested he had more important things to do but he brushed the thought aside and was there well ahead of me, enjoying bacon and eggs and the attention of the beautiful waitress. As we walked to the aircraft we passed a Ugandan Airways 707, its tyres flat and its flaps hanging dejectedly down. I asked what it was doing, sitting there, when it could have been sold against Uganda's desperate shortage of foreign exchange. There were three such aircraft, Ojok told me, Amin took one when he left, one was flying, and this one had been immobilised by an anti-tank rocket from an over-zealous soldier during the liberation of Entebbe Airport. We then came upon a line of Pilatus training aircraft which obviously had not flown for several months. In answer to my question, the Brigadier explained that these were grounded because the instruments had been sent to Switzerland for refurbishment. I said that it was the lack of propellers which had prompted my enquiry but we were now at the steps of my aircraft and no further explanation was forthcoming. It was the last time I saw Brigadier Ojok. He was later killed in a helicopter accident and Uganda lost a soldier who might well have subsequently influenced for the better the unhappy events which were to follow.

Given the political history of Africa in the second half of the twentieth century, the study of revolutionary warfare was an essential part of an African officer's military education. As an experienced guerilla campaigner I found myself in demand as a lecturer. My first appearance was in Nigeria at the invitation of Major General Domkat Bali, the commandant of the Nigerian Staff College. Domkat told me that I had been preceded by an American general who began by saying that he could not take questions on political subjects. It was an unpromising start, for politics and counter-revolutionary warfare are inseparable. However, he need not have worried because, at the end of his lecture and before the questions could begin, he collapsed through heat exhaustion. The air conditioning had broken down and he refused to drink from the carafe of water provided because it had come from the local tap. The air conditioning broke down during my lecture but, forewarned, I drank the carafe and question time went on until lunch could wait no longer.

I much enjoyed my African travels but by the middle of 1981 the Middle East was absorbing most of my attention and I then delegated our African business to my deputy, Brigadier Brian Marciandi, whose early service with the Tanganika Rifles armed him with an appropriate background.

I had already begun to enlarge our Middle Eastern business when, in September 1980, war between Iran and Iraq increased the customers' interest. The Gulf countries were conscious of their extreme vulnerability while the British government was concerned for the stability of that important strategic area. The French, with their heavy reliance on Middle Eastern oil, were even more concerned and, shortly after the outbreak of fighting, their president, M Giscard d'Estaing, hastened around the Gulf pledging support. Prodded by Mrs Thatcher, a flurry of activity in the Ministry of Defence and the Foreign Office resulted in a British two man delegation to the area: John Moberly from the Foreign Office and myself.

We had no idea what cards the French had played but we had the advantage of John Moberly's fluency in Arabic and his personal reputation achieved through long service in the Gulf. The Ruler of Abu Dhabi, Sheikh Zayed, cleared his majlis and the three of us, accompanied by David Roberts, the British Ambassador, sat cross legged, drinking coffee, speaking only Arabic. Zayed spoke of the British support for him many years before during his territorial dispute with Saudi Arabia over Burami. He said it was a tragedy that the British had withdrawn and he took our visit as a sign that we would once again be active in the Gulf. I managed to remind him that we were never far away for it had been British efforts in support of Oman which had secured the Straits of Hormuz several years previously.—Indeed, he had sent me a couple of battalions to help garrison Northern Oman and allow the despatch of additional Omanis to the fighting in the south.— Sheikh Zayed said that while the threat did not require the deployment of the forces we had on offer, he would like us to ensure that his own air defences were working properly. I telephoned London and within a couple of hours was able to announce that a small team of air defence experts, headed by a group captain, would arrive within three days.

John Moberly and I moved on to Qatar where I already had a good working relationship with the British ambassador, Stephen Day, and the Crown Prince, Sheikh Hamad. At first the Qataris declined assistance but when I mentioned what we were doing in Abu Dhabi, Sheikh Hamad turned to his younger brother, Abdullah, and, after a hurried discussion, replied that he would be grateful if I could advise on the reorganisation of his armed forces. I agreed to return in the near future with a small team to undertake this task. We had secured the inside track and were about to overtake the French who, hitherto, had made the running in Qatar.

Back from the Gulf I lost no time in assembling a tri-service team for the Qatar study. It spent a fortnight there and produced a far reaching but practical report on which the Qatari Armed Forces based their subsequent development.

The one part of the Middle East in which I was still a stranger was North Yemen, a situation which was remedied when the British Ambassador there, Julian Walker, persuaded the Yemenis that they should seek my advice. The problems were centred on an insurgent campaign in the south of the country. Here, the population, encouraged in their dissidence from across the border in South Yemen, showed little allegiance to their own government whose writ did not run much beyond Sana, the capital.

Julian Walker lost no time in taking me to the chief of staff, Lieutenant Colonel Abdul Aziz al Barati, to whom I explained that I would need to see the country and visit the operations in progress if I was to offer advice. As a rule, no foreigners were allowed into the troubled areas, even the American and Russian advisers, who were present in considerable numbers, were confined to the vicinity of Sana but the chief of staff readily agreed that I should go. A helicopter was provided and Julian and I set off.

As we flew south I could see there were similarities with Southern

Oman but here the country was on a much larger scale, the hills more massive, the valleys broader and the population considerably more dense. We landed in a forward position occupied by a company of infantry with a couple of Russian tanks and a Russian twin barrelled 20 mm gun. The troops were beleaguered, their only contact with the outside world being by radio and helicopter. The commander explained that resupply by road was impossible because of mines and when I asked him in what strength he patrolled the surrounding country and how often he visited the villages round about, he replied that he left that sort of activity to the enemy. The position was littered with spent cartridge cases, from the tank guns, 20 mm and machine guns. I asked what the troops had been shooting at and was told that everything that moved, particularly at night, was a target. I reflected that in most cases they would have been firing at their own population and thought that if they were to win this war there would need to be a radical change of strategy and tactics. The army would need to get into the villages and win the confidence of the local population who should be encouraged to look after themselves. Tribesmen would need to be recruited into a local defence organisation somewhat similar to the one we had organised in Southern Oman and for this Britain could offer assistance from the Special Air Service. I made arrangements for one of my staff officers to come out and make the necessary plans.

The staff officer, Major Tony Ling, an SAS officer who had served in Oman, spent a fortnight producing a plan which I then returned to present. The Yemenis accepted it in full but it foundered through lack of money. They were prepared to accommodate and provide all that was needed for the dozen SAS men who would organise and administer the beginning of the local defence scheme but they could not afford the £50,000 which the British Treasury insisted would be the cost of such an expedition. For such a small amount of money we missed an opportunity denied even to the Americans and Russians. It was an example I used with telling effect in arguing the case for an increase in military assistance funds.

My constant travel meant that Anne and I saw relatively little of one another. I therefore arranged to base one of my Far Eastern tours on Singapore where we could both stay with our daughter Jane who had moved there when her husband, Ian Gordon, had become second in command of the Ghurka Police contingent in Singapore. I flew out in December 1981 with an itinerary which covered Bangladesh, Thailand, Malaya, Brunei and Singapore, itself.

Although Bangladesh was new to me, I immediately felt at home with the armed forces there whose traditions had been inherited from Pakistan where I had spent a year at staff college. Bangladesh had then been part of Pakistan—it acquired independence in 1971—and the senior officers I was now meeting had studied at Quetta not long after me. Bangladesh's own military history stretched back to the Bengal regiments of the British Raj, as was evident during the Independence Day parade which coincided with my visit. Several hundred spectators watched from tiered seating beneath a huge red and white striped marquee as the troops advanced in review order with style and precision. Earlier that day I had been discussing the future of the Bangladesh Staff College and its British instructors with Lieutenant General Ershad, the head of the army. He was now standing close behind the president, Mr Justice Sattar, who was taking the salute and whom he would shortly depose, Bangladesh having inherited the economic and political problems of Pakistan.

Thailand was disappointing. Its large armed forces seemed heavily reliant on American equipment and training which, coming at a relatively low cost, left little scope for the activities I could promote. Nevertheless, I was well received and entertained but from what I saw of Bangkok, overcrowded and dirty, its reputation as a place of beauty and pleasure seemed wholly unjustified.

I had last been in Brunei some ten years earlier when, as commander of 24 Brigade, my visit had been concerned with contingency plans for reinforcement. Since that time, the existing treaty had been replaced by one of friendship and co-operation, giving a transitional period during which Brunei could prepare herself for full international responsibilities, including defence. As a result the Royal Brunei Malay Regiment had grown to the size of a brigade, including an air wing and a small naval flotilla, and was even more heavily reliant upon British military assistance than it had been ten years previously. It was encountering the same dilemma which countries in the Gulf had already met: the expansion of the armed forces both in size and sophistication had outstripped the development of indigenous manpower.

Some countries, like Brunei and Oman, had always looked exclusively to Britain for their considerable requirements in military assistance, even when the Labour government in London was reducing the number of officers on loan. Our competitors were ever ready to surplant us and in the case of Oman the door had been opened several years earlier, when Britain felt unable to supply the tanks which Oman wished to purchase at short notice in order that they could appear on a national day parade. Provision would have incurred a temporary shortfall in the British army, against which the requirements of a parade seemed frivolous by comparison, at least in the view of those who made the political decision. They had failed completely to understand the strategic importance of military parades in other parts of the world. The Sultan turned to America so that the tanks could rumble past and remind the assembled heads of state that Oman intended to remain a leading military power in the Middle East. With the tanks came American assistance, one more sign of Britain's deliberate abdication of interest and unnecessary surrender of influence. Now, two years later, it seemed set to happen again.

Major General Johnny Watts, on loan to Oman as the commander of that country's land forces, returned to London to discuss, once again, the purchase of British tanks. When I learned that he had been offered the Vickers tank, which was insufficiently powerful to meet Oman's requirements, I telephoned him with the suggestion that Oman should request the lease of a number of Chieftain tanks with a view to their subsequent purchase. Such an arrangement would enable Oman to be equipped with Chieftains in about the same time as the Vickers could be acquired, new, off the shelf. The request caused some consternation in the Ministry of Defence for it was a set back to the sale of Vickers in Arabia while its fulfillment would temporarily deplete the British Army's reserve. However, Oman would again have looked to America in preference to buying the Vickers and the depletion of our reserves for a short while was a small price to pay for remaining the military mentor and main supplier to Oman, so strategically well placed.

As my military career drew to an end, I thought I should seek a civilian appointment with a military flavour in which my knowledge of Whitehall and my overseas background would be of value. I had barely begun to look around when industry came to me and I probably sold myself short by accepting the first offer. However, I took it, with no hesitation, because it came from British Aerospace with whom I had established good relations both as a customer in Oman and as an ally in my present appointment. Their products were exceptionally good but they seemed to need help in areas in which my experience was particularly relevant. I had just attended a disastrous demonstration to King Hussein of the Rapier missile on a tracked chassis. The director, who seemed to think he was in charge, turned up only on the day and gave last minute instructions which did no more than cause confusion. The vehicle was poorly maintained and belched smoke, giving the impression that British Aerospace knew and cared little about elementary concealment on the battle field. When the equipment drove into action the missiles resolutely declined to perform. I thought I could help the company in such matters but, as I was to discover, those who needed help were often unwilling to acknowledge it.

Chapter 14

Old Soldiers Never Die

I LEFT my office, in Whitehall, on a Friday afternoon and turned up at British Aerospace, in Pall Mall, on the following Monday, 1st April 1982. British Aerospace then consisted of two groups, Aircraft and Dynamics, and it was the latter, concerned with missiles, electronics and spacecraft which I had joined. It was run by Admiral Sir Raymond Lygo who had eschewed any written terms of reference for me, saying that he would leave it to me to judge how best I could deploy my experience in pursuit of the company's business. Thus, I attended board meetings, cultivated my contacts at home and abroad, and shuttled between my imposing office in London and a desk in a small room in the group headquarters at Stevenage.

It was agreeable and for a while I managed to occupy myself usefully. I undertook a lecture tour in America and the Middle East extolling the performance of British Aerospace aircraft and missiles in the recent Falklands war. With the job of defence adviser I had inherited one of the three British seats on the NATO Industrial Advisory Group, a body which met quarterly in Brussels with the object of achieving co-operation between the various national defence industries. This did not involve me in much additional work but it led me to perceive the need for promoting British Aerospace interests more widely within the headquarters of NATO where decisions were pending on the acquisition of new air defences. This I did in the first instance by tramping the corridors and later by arranging a presentation of the company's ideas on air defence to a senior audience.

This was the first occasion on which the two separate groups of British Aerospace had combined their efforts and the difficulties I met, both in persuading them of the need for this joint venture and in reconciling their different philosophies, underlined the requirement for a more co-ordinated approach to the market place. There were too many British Aerospace representatives competing with one another. They were often unaware of each other's existence, to the considerable confusion of the customer, and some resented my efforts to co-ordinate their activities. I said that some discipline was needed and that people should be told to co-operate within the established hierarchy of the company. 'We don't want big boots and short haircuts around here,' came the response at a senior level, suggesting attitudes rooted in an unhappy experience during National Service. Such frustrations increased when Ray Lygo moved on to start the much needed reorganisation of British Aerospace, but I suffered them for a while in order to solve more pressing domestic difficulties.

The exigencies of military life put a considerable strain upon marriage but the difficulties are often alleviated by the environment of a service community which provides support for the younger wives and confers responsibility on the more senior. The strains, however, may induce permanent damage leaving flaws which become fatal in a different environment. So, I think it was with Anne and me and our marriage of thirty four years sadly ended in divorce in 1984.

A happier event in the same year was Nicola's graduation from university. In addition to a good degree she acquired a husband, Paul Harris, who having graduated as a chemist the year before, had turned lawyer and joined my eldest son-in-law's firm of solicitors.

Seeing little point in my job as defence adviser, I assumed responsibility for Middle East marketing in April 1985, initially with Dynamics group but subsequently, upon the reorganisation, for all of British Aerospace. I turned aside a more lucrative offer from elsewhere in industry because the wide ranging responsibilities I was now apparently offered would enable me to work among highly placed and influential friends in a part of the world I knew well. Moreover, implicit in the appointment was the challenge to improve the company's poor performance in the Middle East. In an area which absorbed a very high proportion of British defence overseas sales, British Aerospace had achieved only three missile contracts in the previous ten years and for two of those the door had been wide open. In Oman, in 1974, it was inconceivable that Qaboos would have looked to other than the United Kingdom for its air defence. In Qatar, my own report, made as Director of Military Assistance, had paved the way.

With no family hearth to beckon me, I spent little time in the house I had bought in Chiswick but roamed the Middle East seeking business. I was accompanied frequently by one of my senior executives, Lieutenant Colonel Tony Cawston, who had spent much of his service

and subsequent business life in the Middle East and now lived in
Jordan. Between us we had an unrivalled knowledge of the market but
it was apparently more than the company could handle, particularly
when local agents were involved. There was a Machiavellian atmosphere to the way British Aerospace managed these people whose
activities on behalf of the company would range from straight forward
lobbying to more persuasive methods which reflected the business
ethics and practice of the specific market concerned. The arrangements
were the preserve of a committee of three or four people and I found
myself denied information, vital to my credibility, and often not meant
even to know the identity of the agents. Of course, having moved
through the Middle East as commander of the Sultan of Oman's Armed
Forces and subsequently as Director of Military Assistance, I already
knew much of what was ostensibly being denied me; the rest I soon
found out. I also discovered much wheeling and dealing behind my
back which, had I remained unaware of it, would rapidly have undermined my position. I was not so naive as to expect the same standards of
integrity in industry as I had enjoyed in the services but, feeling that our
marketing methods were inimical to the company's interests, I made
clear my views at the highest level. We were, I said, using yesterday's
men and yesterday's methods, wasting large sums of money on agents
who no longer had influence and relying on others who were also
working for our competitors. It was necessary, I argued, to replace
these people with others more in tune with the times. Some heat was
taken from the situation when British Aerospace obtained a large order
for Tornado aircraft from Saudi Arabia but this, again, was the result of
the British government opening the door.

Since nothing appeared to be changing as a result of my lifting the lid,
I declared myself redundant. Much as some people wanted me out of
the way, my precipitate departure would have underlined the defects to
which I had drawn attention and there was a reluctance to face the facts.
However, after a few months the Company was forced to agree and,
although by then some changes were afoot, I settled on terms which
would enable me to pursue more interesting possibilities beckoning
elsewhere.

My foray into industry had not produced unqualified satisfaction but
it brought unqualified joy. When I took over Middle East marketing
British Aerospace was experiencing some difficulty with its business in
Pakistan and the firm which represented it there was summoned to
account for itself. At the meeting and subsequent visit to Pakistan, the
firm's position was resolutely and successfully defended by one of its

directors, Celia Sandys. All I knew before our rather edgy business discussions was that she was the daughter of Lord Duncan Sandys, whom I had flown in my small aeroplane in Malaya in the 1950s and the granddaughter of Sir Winston Churchill. We met in April and were married in July. Our son Alexander was born on the 14th August 1986, one day before my sixtieth birthday.

Three daughters and a preponderance of girls among their children had orientated me towards female progeny; a son will need a different approach. A preliminary reconnaissance in the course of exposure to Celia's two teenage sons, Justin and Dominic, has confirmed the going to be good providing the potential ambushes are spotted well ahead.

Freed from the constraints of a London office we found a Queen Anne vicarage, a village on one side and on the other, glimpsed between tall lime trees, open fields and woods. From here we pursue varied interests, some of which occasionally demand a city suit or a flight to the Middle East. Celia encourages me to write and paint, not that I lack motivation but had it not been for her suggestions this would not have been written and a painting in the Royal Academy's summer exhibition not even submitted. Alexander is always ready for a game. The garden is in constant need of attention. The house will never be finished. It is all enjoyable and there are insufficient hours in each day to accommodate all we wish to do.

I am, indeed, a fortunate soldier.

Index